The Cultural Meaning of Urban Space

THE CULTURAL MEANING OF
URBAN SPACE

Edited by
ROBERT ROTENBERG
and
GARY McDONOGH

CONTEMPORARY URBAN STUDIES
Robert V. Kemper and Estellie Smith, Series Editors

BERGIN & GARVEY
Westport, Connecticut • London

Library of Congress Cataloging-in-Publication Data

The Cultural meaning of urban space / edited by Robert Rotenberg and
  Gary McDonogh.
      p.   cm.—(Contemporary urban studies, ISSN 1065–7002)
    Includes bibliographical references and index.
    ISBN 0–89789–319–0 (hb).—ISBN 0–89789–320–4 (pbk)
    1. Urban geography. 2. Urban anthropology. I. Rotenberg, Robert
Louis. II. McDonogh, Gary W. III. Series.
GF125.C85   1993
307.76—dc20   92–32179

British Library Cataloguing in Publication Data is available.

Library of Congress Catalog Card Number: 92–32179
ISBN: 0–89789–319–0 (hb.)
ISBN: 0–89789–320–4 (pbk.)
ISSN: 1065–7002

First published in 1993

Bergin & Garvey, 88 Post Road West, Westport, Connecticut 06881
An imprint of Greenwood Publishing Group, Inc.

Printed in the United States of America

The paper used in this book complies with the
Permanent Paper Standard issued by the National
Information Standards Organization (Z39.48–1984).

10 9 8 7 6 5 4 3 2

Copyright Acknowledgments

The authors and the publisher are grateful to the following for granting the use of material:

Royal Commission on the Future of the Toronto Waterfront, for permission to adapt and reprint the drawing of Toronto's waterfront (Figure 11.1).

Klein Post Card Service, Alan Klein, and photographer Jonathan Klein for permission to reprint the photograph, "Dawn Over Boston, Massachusetts" (Exhibit 12.1).

The Boston Harbor Hotel and Rick Harmon, Marketing Director, for permission to reprint the advertisement for the Rowes Wharf Restaurant and Cafe, from the *New England Monthly*, Vol. 4, No. 9, September 1987 (Exhibit 12.6).

Dolphin Real Estate Corporation and Sanford Kaplan, for permission to reprint the advertisement for Seal Harbor Three, from *Boston* magazine, April 1987 (Exhibit 12.10).

Awdeh & Co. and Makram L. Awdeh for permission to reprint the advertisement for "Seawatch at Hull," from *The Boston Sunday Globe*, October 17, 1987 (Exhibit 12.11).

EastBay Condominiums and Marc Goldstine, for permission to reprint the advertisement for EastBay Condominiums, from *The Boston Globe*, February 7, 1989 (Exhibit 12.12).

The Boston Harbor Marina Co. and Hassan Haydar, for permission to reprint the advertisement for The Seaport at Marina Bay, from *The Boston Globe*, October 29, 1987 (Exhibit 12.13).

Contents

Illustrations

Introduction

ROBERT ROTENBERG

The chapters presented here are searching for the basis for ascribing social and cultural values to the cityscape and the built urban environment. Within anthropology, the last decade has seen a growing interest in the serious engagement of the issue of spatial meanings (Richardson 1989; Lawrence and Low 1990). What sets the chapters of this volume apart are the efforts each author makes to understand the meaning of urban spaces through the knowledge of the people who live within them. This is sometimes messy and disorganized, but always greatly satisfying, activity that yields a bounty of insights, surprises, and intriguing avenues for further exploration. Added to the mix of ethnographic experiences in these chapters is an openness to analytical models from other disciplines, especially geography, architecture, environmental psychology, landscape design, and urban planning. It is our hope that specialists in these disciplines can benefit from seeing their models tested in cross-cultural contexts.

Most of the chapters herein originated as papers presented at an invited symposium on the cultural meaning of urban space at the 1990 American Anthropological Association meetings. Additional contributions were solicited to round out the geographical coverage of the volume. The organizers felt that it was time to discover what commonalities exist in the process of giving meaning to urban spaces in various cities. Over the last twenty years, the meaning of urban spaces has been addressed by anthropologists (Bourdieu 1971; Fernandez 1977; Richardson 1980; 1982), social psychologists (Altman 1975; Goffman 1971), planners (Perin 1977), and architects (Broadbent, Bunt, and Llorens 1980; Oliver 1969; 1971; Rapoport 1977) interested in issues of the relation between built form and culture. These studies had influenced urban anthropologists as they began to develop interests in place attachment, group-specific maps and pathways, public and private distinctions, and neighborhood boundaries. Many of these had also forged new approaches to the ethnographic description of the metropolis. The point of this volume is to bring as many of these research experiences together as possible. To our knowledge, this is the first effort to bring together this kind of ethnographic data.

This book is about the difference it makes to people and their valuation of space that they live and act in an urban settlement rather than some other kind of community. The scope of meaning explored here is metropolitan-wide. Even when a chapter focuses on a single neighborhood or specialized group, we see the place or people as possessing a widely distributed knowledge. This view of the urban experience will help explain why the writers have chosen the particular places, as well as the assumptions that underlie their analysis of meaning. All would agree that urban agglomeration invites special treatments of space. These chapters help us realize that all urbanites share life experiences through the commonalities or urban conditions and the shared metropolitan knowledge.

Metropolitan knowledge is a subset of the knowledge people gain from their lived experience and value socialization. In many important ways, city dwellers share meanings regardless of the particular city they inhabit or the history that has shaped their particular culture. This knowledge is highly generalized. It does not overshadow that which people acquire locally, or which they share with their suburban and rural neighbors. It takes an expressly urban experience to create a value for privacy, instill the requirement for consciously planning even the simplest of trips through the urban maze, compose different maps of that maze for different categories of people, generate personal identity out of shared historical memory, or engender the spirit of a place through aesthetic or moral criteria, as well as supply and demand. This list is far from complete.

City dwellers, in particular, share this knowledge because they live within the densest and most specialized concentrations of people, information, built form, and economic activity in an urbanized region. The urban region is a network of hierarchically arranged levels of socially powerful institutions that attempt to organize residents' access to these resources. When operating efficiently, the institutions ensure that this access is not shared equally by all people living in a settlement. Fortunately, these urban institutions are not very efficient, and slippage within the system creates a feeling of pandemonium as the urban region grows larger and more populated. This is the aspect of urban life on which ethnographic fieldworkers can make a serious contribution. Absent from these studies is the sanitary functionalism of location theory and ecological models. On the street one finds people in every class who are highly knowledgeable of the institutions around them, and often quite competent to manipulate those institutions to their own advantage.

Metropolitan knowledge contains similar features in all cities because all cities impose similar institutions on their residents. We need not reduce all aspects of urban meaning to the social, the political, or the economic, the most common arenas of human activity that lead to urban institutions and sustain their development through history. Focusing only on the interactions of residents and these institutions limits the possibilities for describing metropolitan life. People do not just act in the world. They also attempt to understand their world. This understanding is socially constituted. That is, it unfolds according to commonly held assumptions about what can and cannot be understood and takes place in language, in which words have conventionally delimited spheres of meaning. In cities, people force the spaces around them to take on meaning. No space is permitted to be neutral—or homogenous (Kuper 1972). People's understandings transform space into place.

Most of the cities in this volume are involved in the capitalist world, and the spaces described here are subject to the conflicts and contradictions common to this system. Chief among these is the contradiction between abstract space that arises from economic and political practices and social space that arises from the use values produced by the residents in their pursuits of everyday life (Lefebvre 1979: 241). Viewing space as an abstraction is the result of the real effects of state intervention in the production of space, sometimes to serve the purposes of private interests in capital accumulation (Harvey 1973) and sometimes to serve its own purposes (Castells 1977). Abstract space presents itself to us as fragmented, homogenous, and hierarchical (Gottdeiner 1985). The uniqueness of personalized and collectivized spaces reasserts itself when we focus on social space, communal sites, places containing specific activities, the experience of place attachment, the *genius loci*, and the increasing concern for global space. This active naming of spaces by residents, or as Lefebvre characterizes it, "the explosion of spaces," results in a chaos of contradictory and multiple linkages:

Neither capitalism nor the state can maintain the chaotic, contradictory space they have produced. We witness, at all levels, this explosion of spaces. At the level of the immediate and the lived, space is exploding on all sides. . . . Everywhere people are realizing that spatial relations are social relations. At the level of cities we see not only the explosion of the historical city but also that of the administrative frameworks in which they had wanted to enclose the urban phenomenon. (1979: 290)

Political competition to control patronage jobs gerrymanders voting districts. Welfare and public housing policies constitute households with only temporary adult male participants and concentrate these households in low-rent districts. Unequal growth in regional employments reduces once stable middle-class neighborhoods to bungalow wastelands. Groups who act within these spaces contest these spatial meanings (Davis 1986). State actions on space and people's understandings of place form a dialectic. That is, each contributes to the other in a constantly changing pattern of influence. At times, it seems as if the institutional actions have the upper hand in people's understanding of place, while at other times, the institutions appear to be reacting to the appropriation of place by specific groups.

An approach common to many of the chapters of this book is the focus on the historical emergence of spatial meanings. History and culture are closely related analytical categories. All meanings are historically situated. That is, they can be fully understood only when they are seen as either changed or unchanged from some earlier understanding. Each generation reinterprets its world based on the inherited understandings of the past and the experiences of the present. Thus, all meaning, and hence culture itself, is in constant flux. To isolate a single moment and privilege it as somehow truer than other moments is misleading. Spatial meanings must be seen in this light. They are historically contingent. That is, they take the form they do because of the exigencies of the present-time conditions in which they form. Understanding the history of meaning requires reconstructing these conditions. This, in turn, directs us to the discourses about space in earlier periods of the cities we study. By *discourse*, we mean those key ideas and the logical relations between them through which defined groups *validate* their understandings of their world. A discourse focuses on a subset of experiences for a group within a large body of social experiences. The idea of discourse enables us to break up the unwieldy idea of culture into smaller, definable units. Each set relates to particular groups of people, such as conquistadores, urban planners, commercial developers, gardeners, or neighborhood residents. As people participate in the discourse, they act on their understandings to disproportionately shape to their purposes the urban places they control. These places then enter the historical development of spatial meaning as artifacts, preserving forever after the moment when a meaning was given concrete form in space. By retrieving these artifacts and written texts, the authors of this book attempt to breathe life into the layers of these discourses.

This intersection between historical discourse and social organization is where the authors begin their work. Each, then, struggles to move beyond these first principles to more complex frameworks, often involving dynamic interactions between urban institutions, individual experience, and shared history. Each of the chapters in the book is simultaneously an evocation of this dialectic for a particular urban experience and a demonstration of the ways in which one can move beyond the analytical limitations of this view to embrace the understandings of real people seeking order in the chaos of urban change. The enthnographic experiences collected here focus on the relation between action and meaning in urban places. In various localities throughout the world, writer after writer situates the meaning of place within institutional action and the residents' efforts at understanding.

The first part of the book, "The Language of Place," directly addresses the relation between language and the meaning of place. Gary McDonogh explores the issue of shielded and unshielded urban space by looking at the peculiar anonymity available in spaces that people label as being empty. They are the ground against which the figure of the city takes place. McDonogh shows that it is possible to reverse figure and ground, revealing that the empty space is charged with meaning. Drawing on field experiences from Barcelona, Spain, and Savannah, Georgia, he sees emptiness as going beyond the designation of open urban lands to denote those spaces that are undefined, or in which the definition is indistinct because of unresolved conflicts over meaning. These are truly no-man's lands in which different social, political, aesthetic, and moral possibilities may occur. He suggests four possible meanings for emptiness: the place of memory of where a landmark once stood; the place of disuse by dogs, drug addicts, and deviants; the boundary between the behaviorally acceptable and the unacceptable; and the intentionally fallow ground of future land speculation and development. Thus, the emptiness of space is filled with these urban meanings, and potentially more.

My essay explores the tendency of urbanities to label some places as more wholesome and healthy than others. By reasserting the classic statements on salubrity and pestilence by the Roman architect Vitruvius in the first century of the common era, I attempt to anchor the Central European understanding of wholesome environments in a two-thousand-year-old discourse. While researching this topic, I was struck by the commonalities between Vitruvius's language of salubrity and contemporary Viennese language. Here is an example of the dialectic turning toward the people's understanding as the institutions scramble to react. The organic foods movement, the green movement in Europe, and the environmental movement in North America are political mobilizations around ideas about the necessity for healthy living in cities that are much older than the industrial revolution. When we listen to the Viennese speak about the salubrity of their gardens, a very different vision of the possibilities of urban life opens up. There is magic in the feelings of wholesomeness and longevity that people attribute to their life in garden. It is a place we all know. Their words permit us to experience it in a wholly different aspect.

Deborah Pellow develops a model of space for Shanghai to explore how metropolitans understand privacy. In the Chinese context, it is appropriate to draw the boundaries around intimate, social, and public space in a manner very different from that of Euro-Americans. The Chinese have traditionally placed curtains of privacy around the affairs of the family and view sexuality, even between spouses, as procreative only. In Shanghai, the residential density is so high that within the family, parents and children share the same room and often the same bed. Housing is difficult to find. A new emphasis on individuality and sexuality has taken hold in the large cities. The resulting demands for increased privacy, especially for sexual activities, are a fundamental shift in both private attitudes and the meaning of the boundary between private, social, and public spaces. For example, young couples often find privacy for physical contact on crowded buses. Marriages are timed to coincide with the availability of new or vacant apartments. Pellow's analysis places the meaning of urban space squarely on the sense of self and the social patterns that spring from the self-consciousness of metropolitan residents.

Theodore C. Bestor uses the phrase *subcultural ethos* to characterize the metropolitan knowledge of Tokyo residents. It designates specific parts of the city as normative examples of exemplary urban experiences. He explores the old merchant districts, *shitamachi*. Here the meaning of place conjoins with the meaning of personhood. Which district you come from links you with other districts and characterizes those linkages. District provenience even colors the interactions between people and institutions through positive and negative stereotyping. This equation of personal and district qualities telescopes downward to characterize smaller units and neighborhoods. Bestor contrasts the old-fashioned image of shitamachi with the modern, white-collar qualities of its opposing district, *yamanote*, the old samurai district of Edo. As rooted as these meanings may be in Tokyo's past, they are not static. He shows how the shitamachi image has improved recently as a point of authenticity in an increasingly ambiguous social world, the image of place merging with the image of a way of life. In this last effort, he focuses on the neighborhood in the district where residents use the shitamachi/yamanote distinction for understanding their local interpersonal relations and social distinctions.

The second part of the book, "Place in the City," looks at the distinction people make between and among places within a city. For John Mock, the distinctive place is a castle. He shows how the people who live beneath it use this place to forge a sense of identity and of common mission. The Japanese *jokomachi*, castle town, of Hikone is one of the few whose castle escaped the iconoclasm of the Meiji Restoration's symbolic dismantling of the shogunate. Sitting on a hill above the town, the castle was a concrete symbol for the changing community below. The change in national organization obscured the clear social lines in the neighborhoods of Hikone as different classes of functionaries mixed their homes. In the last century, the city has grown in size and population. Through school textbooks, community maintenance and restoration projects within the castle district, and tourism campaigns, the residents have converted their community to a *furosato*, a "national hometown"—that is, a town that to the inhabitants reflects the romanticized values for community life within a progressive city that any Japanese would prize. As Mock points out, this meaning is a burden as well as a benefit to the residents. New neighborhoods are developing that contrast with traditional neighborhood patterns. Traditional citywide festivals attract visitors, but not the excitement or sense of release they once had among the residents. Here, again, the meanings of urban places are not static. They are subject to processes of maintenance, loss, and elaboration as the perceptions of the economic and cultural role of the town change in the minds of the residents.

For Setha M. Low, the distinctive place is the plaza in Spanish-American cities. Working historically, she demonstrates that we cannot automatically ascribe the form of the plaza and its placement within a grid matrix to either Iberian or New World roots. The potential to produce such an organization of urban space existed in all the American civilizations, including the Caribbean. She shows that the plaza in any particular Spanish-American town center can be exclusively of pre-Columbian origin, colonial design, or some complex combination of the two. The people who live around it hardly ever know the actual history of their plaza. Thus, the convergence of potential origins enables residents to use the plaza as an exclusive link to the Pre-Columbian past, or to Spain, depending on the dominant cultural taste. The spatial form confirms an already existing era of ideas about historical identity.

In Donald S. Pitkin's chapter the distinctive places are the arena for public displays of family life. His discussion takes us to the Italian towns where he did his fieldwork. This study invokes the outdoors life of southern Europe, on the Mediterranean. Present are many of the elements common to all the countries in the region: the street, the balcony, the courtyard. Pitkin observes the various ways families redefine public space for their domestic purposes. The quintessential space for such purposes is the *salotto*, a room devoted to the family's efforts to make a good impression upon those who see it. Since easy access to the interior of the house is impossible for most of the public, the family appropriates the street by moving chairs directly onto it, or onto the balcony. He views the use of the piazza as a daily ritual of *passegiatta*, in which the entire square becomes an open-air salotto. The key to the meaning Italians attribute to these public spaces relies on the idea of "una bella figura," a good reputation.

For Charles Rutheiser, the distinctive space is the school. He reminds us that different groups within the city construct contrasting sets of meanings for the same spaces. The literature has usually addressed this question through the issues of territoriality (Newman 1972; Suttles 1968). Rutheiser shows that different age groups construct their own maps of the city in which spaces are defined for purposes specific to those age groups. The case in point is Belize high school students. By describing the "environment of schooling" that the students inhabit, he shows that school space is variable in form, with one end of a continuum in the most regimented of systems and the other in the street corner, the alleyways, and house porches. Unlike

Pitkin, who discusses these spaces as potential bridges between the public and the private, these teenagers view the spaces as wholly private, "back-stage" areas that invert the behavioral structures of the school life. Belize is a city of two cultures for these young people: a school culture of deportment rules, of time discipline, and of regimented spaces; and a counterschool culture of the urban gangs of unemployed and underemployed young people.

Part 3, "Planning and Responses," revolves around discourses of urban planning, and especially the responses of people to the growth, marketing, and decay of residential places. Anthropological interest in housing markets as a feature of the construction of meaning of urban spaces began with the work of Constance Perin in the 1970s (Perin 1977). The chapters by Margaret Rodman, Susan D. Greenbaum, Matthew Cooper, and R. Timothy Sieber address this concern as a problem of spatial meaning. Margaret Rodman explores the assumptions that have guided investigations of the relationship between the formation of meaning within human culture and the formation of cities through built form. As she observes, too often people have looked to built form to inform about culture. While built form may indeed be shown to represent knowledge crucial to the identity of people, it is rare that observation of this relationship serves as the discovery of knowledge that was not already in the grasp of the investigator. The built form merely confirms the importance of the core ideas that stand apart from, and behind, the objects. This strategy emphasizes the urban as product of culture, the analysis of which reveals important features about culture itself. It ignores people's ideas about how the urban world works. A strategy that attends to such a worldview looks first to human action in the world, the ultimate source of cultural meaning. Rodman develops this latter perspective in some detail and discusses recent research that she believes moves us closer to a fuller understanding of the relationship between culture and built form.

Susan D. Greenbaum looks at the meanings attributed to vacant housing in U.S. cities. She bases her argument on her study of residential abandonment between the 1940s and the late 1970s in Kansas City, Kansas. She attacks prevalent notions that ethnic factors, notably rural origins and rapid influx, are responsible for the increased number of vacant housing in African-American neighborhoods. She shows that the dual housing market, the legacy of redlining, and differing demographic growth rates between black and white communities are responsible for the current excess number of housing units in black communities and the subsequent abandonment of these buildings. It is the racism of U.S. society that produces an artificial wall between the high demand for housing in white areas and the excess supply in black communities.

Matthew Cooper also looks at waterfront development and the ways in which the edges of urban development acquire meaning. For him, the design of the waterfront represents the response to the open possibilities of this urban frontier zone. The meaning of the urban waterfront is ambiguous because diverse interests compete to claim it for their own purposes. One can easily imagine the same characterization applied to all open spaces in cities. He describes how the historical analysis of the waterfront bears the features of the larger metropolitan development. Beginning in the pre-railroad days before 1850, the dominant social organizations of technological, commercial, and industrial development transformed the waterfront for their own purposes. He uses the issue of access to illustrate how powerful groups change the meaning of places to suit their interests. As the number and variety of interest groups in Toronto's waterfront have grown, the resulting issues of access and meaning have become exceedingly complex.

R. Timothy Sieber takes a contemporary look at the forces shaping waterfront development. He focuses on the importance of view in the evaluation of the meaning of place by examining the way in which waterfront apartments in Boston have been designed so that one *must* look at the water. He confronts the issues of design's focus on some widely held values because of the marketing potential and its ignoring of others. The design of the apartments promotes the visual connection between people and water. Sieber shows that this emphasis reinforces the desire to combine closeness to nature with urban living among metropolitan Bostonians. He shows that the predilection to romanticize nature through the sense of sight is common in Euro-American aesthetics.

This collection demonstrates the contributions that anthropologists can make to the growing interest among environmental specialists for context-sensitive research methods capable of analyzing subtle nuances of meaning and changing symbolic forms. The connection these authors forge between the lived experience of these diverse urbanites and the specialist-reader is an uncanny one. We begin to put ourselves in these cities, taking up residence next to the people and learning about their lives. As urbanities ourselves, we learn about the universal urban dimension in our lives. As design, planning, or research specialists, we learn to appreciate the complexity of local meanings. The cultural meaning of urban spaces, like all languages, has a standard syntax, but also a local accent. The strength of these chapters is that they together analyze the syntax, while training our ears to hear the accent in the urbanite's valuation of space.

ACKNOWLEDGMENTS

The editors would like to thank Sophie Craze, M. Estellie Smith, and Robert Van Kemper for their support in the early stages of this project. Victoria Simek helped in preparing the final manuscript.

Part I

The Language of Place

1

The Geography of Emptiness

GARY McDONOGH

And dead men's cries do fill the emptie aire.
—William Shakespeare, *Henry VI*, V. ii. 4.

EMPTY (émp-ti) . . . A. Adj. t 1. Of persons: At leisure, not occupied or engaged. Also, unmarried. Only in OE. 2. Of a material receptacle: Containing nothing, opposed to *full*. Also *fig.* of anything that may be said to be "filled." b. Void of certain specific contents; *fig.* devoid of certain specific qualities. 3. *transf.* a. Having one's purse, etc. empty; destitute of money (Only contextual) Obs. b. Having an empty stomach, hungry. Now only *colloq.* c. Of the body; Wanting fullness, shrunken, emaciated. Also of the pulse, "weak, slender." 4. Of space, of a person's place, etc.: vacant, unoccupied. Of a house, etc.: Devoid of furniture or inmates. 5. Without anything to carry. 6. Of persons, their projects, etc.: Lacking knowledge and sense, frivolous, foolish. (Oxford English Dictionary 1971)

Emptiness appears to represent a problematic category to pose to the social and cultural analysis of urban space and place, a study which usually focuses on a "fullness" of interactions, structures, and meanings. Indeed, emptiness as I am using it here remains an evocative category, a stimulus to rethinking conceptions of space rather than a classification from any urban culture. In the cities of Barcelona and Savannah, where I have conducted my primary fieldwork since 1976, emptiness may be denoted by epithets of vacancy, abandon, openness, or even failure—the last in cases of urbanist intervention. An empty space may be "underused," "unfashionable," "forbidden," "voided," or it may have been planned to preclude social activities. Neither city uses a single category for all such spaces; yet I will suggest that these and other spaces share common characteristics, evoke shared reactions, and point to widespread patterns of urban life beyond these individual cases.

Thus, I have situated these anomalies within many urban webs, exploring them through both cultural geography and ethnographic interpretation in order to clarify notions of the city itself.

My use of emptiness shares some characteristics with *openness*, a more common design term. As defined by urbanists Kevin Lynch and Gary Hack:

The *openness* of open space is not a matter of how few buildings stand on it but rather whether it permits the freely chosen actions of its users. Openness is a product of physical character but also of access, ownership and management: the rules and expectations that govern activity. . . . Openness is not a characteristic of most urban spaces, whether interior or exterior, nor of farms, playfields, single-purpose reservations, or even carefully tended parks. These are all places where one is constrained to act in a prescribed way. (1984: 325–326)

As in Lynch and Hack's definition, I would categorize empty space by its social structure, use, and constraints as much as by physical characteristics. Yet "emptiness" incorporates a fundamental architectural and cultural paradox in the definition of space that architect Bernard Tschumi has recognized: "Linguistically, 'to define space' means both 'to make space distinct' and 'to state the precise nature of space.' Much of the current confusion about space can be illustrated by this ambiguity" (1990: 12). An "empty" space must be seen in both its limitation and its cultural definition as a place, even if defined by a cultural construction of non-use. However, where open space suggests freedom to Lynch, I argue that most empty spaces suggest conflict.

An equal stimulus to this interpretation derives from Benjamin L. Whorf's on the problem of "emptiness" at the intersection of language and structure:

Thus, around a storage of what are called 'gasoline drums,' behavior will tend to a certain type, that is, great care will be exercised; while around a storage of what are called "empty gasoline drums," it will tend to be different—careless, with little repression of smoking or of tossing cigarette stubs around. Physically, the situation is hazardous, but the linguistic analysis according to regular analogy must employ the word 'empty' which inevitably suggests lack of hazard. (1956:135)

This explosive quality becomes equally dynamic, I would argue, in those zones which either linguistically and/or culturally become defined as "empty," "*vacío*," "vacant," or as places where one believes "no hi va ningú," or "stay away from there at night." In fact, an equally telling analysis might be developed by reference to the work of linguists who have studied the meanings of silence. Emptiness, like silence among the Apache, suggests unease; yet, as Richard Bauman adduced for seventeenth-century Quakers, silence may also be the zone of revolution (Basso 1972; Bauman 1983; Tannen and Saville-Troike 1985). Ultimately, social and cultural response to emptiness may unite empty space with open space, invoking freedom in the place of the constraints that have constituted a "no-man's land" (DeJean 1987).

EVOKING A CATEGORY

I began by evoking four examples that suggest my definition of emptiness as a category of urban spatial consciousness that is, in turn, not an empty category. Each exemplifies a wider range of processes by which space is conceptualized, identified, and produced; an extended analysis of these cases and their ramifications will suggest richer meanings.

In Pilsen, Czechoslovakia, for example, an American journalist portrayed contemporary changes in the state's control of history through reference to a place that embodied the "wrong" data. A pedestal erected in 1945 for a monument to the American liberators of the city later became a focus for dissent from the Communist regime and its historical claims that the Soviet Army had driven the Germans out of the entire Czech state. The *New York Times* noted that "in later years, as anniversary tributes continued, first the base was removed, and when tributes continued in its former site, the traffic island also disappeared. Money that had been donated by citizens to commission the monument was sent by the Communist government to North Korea" (Kamm 1990). To the Western journalist, this absence stands for both an older regime and alternative Western freedoms.

A second example can be drawn from the irony of socially empty spaces within Barcelona's Raval, a densely populated portside underclass and immigrant neighborhood where I have worked since 1986 (see Artigues et al. 1980; McDonogh 1987, 1991). Jardins d'Emili Vendrell, in the northern Raval, takes the form of a preexisting building with one-story arched walls. Inside, concrete benches flank one interior wall while a fountain flows against another; small trees shade the dirt floor. According to local residents, in the early 1980s, the ruined corner building this garden replaced had become a haven for squatters. Nearby merchants proved instrumental in its transformation, asking for a space that could be locked at night (Ajuntament 1983). Yet, within a few months of its inauguration, journalists identified the square as one that "serves for everything except to walk in" (*Noticiero universal*, November 12, 1983). Alcoholics, drug addicts, and children playing hooky were reported to take advantage of its hidden spaces, excluding and alarming neighborhood residents who began to detour around it. In the late 1980s, students from New College and the Universitat de Barcelona observed that the plaça generally remains empty except for dogs during the day; police lock its iron gates at night, emphasizing its jail-like presence.

In 1990 and 1991, I again queried neighbors about the square and its abandonment in the midst of bustling street life. A merchant across the street complained: "People take their dogs in there in the morning—the plaza is too dirty to use. And drug addicts get in at night. They climb the walls." Other residents complained about both pollution and safety, echoing the general concerns of many Barcelona residents in recent decades. All neighbors insisted that they avoid the spot, although some pointed with hope to a nearby larger, formal plaza in front of a new museum. This museum and square replaced a lot that had served as a center for informal activities and a focus for protest against government inaction (McDonogh 1991).

In Orlando, Florida, empty space has been more intentionally created, according to the investigations of student Ansel Webb. In 1984, the Orlando downtown bus station was demolished; in its replacement, planners and architect Keith Reeves employed research results from the Crime Prevention Through Environmental Design (CPTED) program. The new station has been described as a kind of urban sculpture in the service core. While I have subsequently looked at this and other CPTED projects, Webb, as a former client, vividly depicted the terminal:

The new terminal is a gleaming rectangle of chrome-plated steel. Four huge corner columns of the stuff support a flat roof of like material across which spans, on each side, a yellow truss. There are no walls and only a few cast-in-place concrete benches surround the perimeter of the structure. . . . One's first reaction to the sculpture is "what the hell is it?" A small administration building sits to the side and information and tickets can be gained from a large, faintly mirrored glass window that resembles a mall's movie theater box office. Across from the window are the public restrooms which must be "buzzed" in order to gain entry. It is CPTED for sure. Open space is combined with controlled access, leaving no place for the homeless, and no place for diversity. . . . If the wind is blowing, the benches are exposed to rain and one is further discouraged from sitting. All is under the watching tentacles of the *things inside the glass booth* and the police drive through regularly. Perhaps it can be appreciated, like a painting, from the proper distance and if one has a chilled artistic perspective; it is, nevertheless, nearly as safe as it is sterile.

Here, planning has guaranteed vacancy by the elimination of target populations, even at the expense of other clients.

Finally, away from the city, but still within metropolitan influence, Tony Hiss, in his *Experience of Place* (1990), contrasts the working landscape of rural areas with the disruption of these areas through abandonment, speculation, or uncertainty over future development. He cites an eloquent passage from William Whyte's 1960s work on Chester, Pennsylvania:

Much of the open space that remained . . . was being stockpiled by speculators for resale at a later date. They may have leased it in the interim to a farmer, but often they simply left the land idle. Soon it would revert to a dense growth of saplings and weeds and poison ivy. Some inhabitants would be reassured by this resurgence of nature but to the practiced eye it would be a sure tip-off that the area was doomed. Thus does the speculator leave his tracks. (In Hiss 1990: 121)

Speculative emptiness is intrinsically linked to the destruction of buildings and places as well as to the apparent "fallowing" of vacant lots. Indeed, it generally figures as a natural, short-term phase within our models of growth and change in a "healthy" city (Lynch and Hack 1984; Wallace, ed. 1970). Seeing it from this perspective of "second nature" facilitates a grasp of its other implications of appropriation as an aspect of urban growth.

As I have encountered examples that evoke a new facets of emptiness, I have returned to the cities I know in order to reexamine the meanings of space and place that might be related to them. Across variable settings, I have noted recurrent relationships between emptiness and crises in social structures and cultural interpretations. Given the lifeways and values that associate with cities—the very type-specimen civilization—emptiness disturbs. For some, it may be unnerving or "dangerous" to deal with such spots. For others, the emptiness of "no one goes there" represents such a cultural imposition that it eclipses patterns of use therefore marked as deviant and therefore nonexistent. It may simply seem wasteful, uneconomic, or threatening, but empty space begs explanation.

Moreover, I will argue that emptiness as a complex social space is defined by conflict among groups with distinct visions of the city and presences in its society. The underpinnings of emptiness range from the interstices of neighborhoods to representations of control and resistance. While my examples typify different aspects of this social structure and cultural meaning, they also share a conflict between dominating and dominated. They may also become nuclei of response to different appropriations of place.

EXPANDING A CATEGORY

The illustrations that began this chapter also provide the framework for elaboration of the category emptiness. In the case of Pilsen, the elimination of space, as well as population, seems extreme. Yet in an era of glasnost, its very words are echoed in an article on teaching Soviet historiography, "History Does Not Tolerate 'Empty Spaces' " (Petrunko 1990). History for many, not only for the Ilongot and Hawaiians, is crucially encoded by place, which in turn leaves historical vacuums when razed, one way or another (see Rosaldo 1980; Sahlins 1982). While American journalists were quick to point to such lacunae to promote the communal and whole fabric of a narrative democratic history, selective destruction proves equally common in American cities. Here as well it often leaves a vague unease in both urban cognitive mapping and any physical historical record of the city (Lynch 1967). It is striking, in fact, how such problems in urban planning—focused on the value of a lost landmark or node—penetrate popular consciousness of preservation. In Savannah, the destruction of the old market in 1955 spurred the city's successful historical preservation campaign. In 1969, historian Mills B. Lane noted that his pictorial portfolio of the city is punctuated with pictures of historic and beautiful buildings which have been destroyed and replaced with belching factories, parking garages, gas stations and vacant lots, all monuments to twentieth century American life. Four squares were demolished to make a way for a highway that never really materialized, a veritable rape of the old town. Buildings were demolished because their bricks had become more valuable than the structures themselves. Then Historic Savannah, a public voice for preservation, was created in 1955. (1969: 9)

In New York City, the razing of Pennsylvania Station between 1963 and 1965 spurred similar responses: "Until the first blow fell, no one was convinced that Penn Station really would be demolished or that New York would permit this monumental act of vandalism. . . . Within a year and a half, the city, responding to popular pressure, established the New York City Landmarks Preservation Commission as a permanent city agency" (Hiss 1990: 63).

The elimination of such landmarks, whose powerful presence echoes John Mock's observations (Mock, this volume), approaches the social creation of an absolute emptiness. Although the space may be filled, residents often continue to use it as a referent in absentia: "right near where the market used to be." Eventually, of course, these referents must be adjusted either through the adoption of new landmarks or the disappearance with age and migration of those for whom such references remain intelligible.

By contrast, the absences that permeate private histories appear at first glance less political. In Savannah, for example, historic preservation has generally meant the preservation of a white elite and its institutions and houses: evidence of past black, domestic and working-class space has disappeared from the revitalized historic district. As Lane (1969) notes, even the squares that delineate the historic district's plan have been changed in the twentieth century. One of the key events of lower-class life among both whites and blacks, for example, was an annual bonfire in which neighborhood gangs competed to amass fuel (tires, barrels, and the like) and build massive bonfires on Christmas Eve. Such celebrations scarred the landscape and blistered the paint on homes around them. Only after this nexus of working-class competition ended could the squares be converted into the tranquil if often vacant floral landscapes of contemporary Savannah.

The contemporary life of other urban squares suggests a more tangible cultural geographic experience of emptiness is a place that is—or can be—perceived as underused. The Jardins d'Emili Vendrell, for example, are not seen as completely devoid of human life even according to those who say no one uses them. Drug addicts or dog owners have specialized demands that compete with those of other residents. Although they dominate only marginal hours, their images nevertheless determine use for the whole neighborhood. Neither group was an intended user. Drug users are marginal to urban life although their presence (and remains, in the form of syringes) has become a vivid rhetorical motif in Barcelona. In fact, my observations do not indicate that they really use the Jardins at all: yet they have become key signifiers in mass media and general conversation to explain the abandonment of any building, park, or space. Dog owners form a more socialized constituency, although one not incorporated into the needs of the densely populated city.

Still more complications of emptiness arise in so far as Emili Vendrell juxtaposes contradictory demands of urban planning, neighborhood groups, and social psychology of space. This project has imposed the values of a dominant city onto the spatial relations of another realm. For generations, inhabitants of the Raval have taken over public streets and semipublic bars for activities that could not be conducted in crowded, inadequate private housing, paralleling the Mediterranean street life described by Donald Pitkin (Pitkin, this volume). In contrast to Barcelona's planning ethos since the eighteenth century, the narrow Raval street is an intrinsic social place, despite the multiple transit plans of the municipality. Open spaces, however, with little linkage to social networks have been neither part of barrio history nor valued by inhabitants. Such areas, indeed, are more often potential areas of conflict between groups, generations, or uses that have erupted into open gang warfare between gypsies and Africans over drugs, or between residents and police (McDonogh and Maza forthcoming; McDonogh 1991).

Public architecture and local sensibilities also clash in such urban reforms. The arched facade and gates of the garden maintain the formal unity of the street, which architects Lluis Mestres and others emphasized in their plans (Ajuntament 1983: 122). But this plan does not create a socially comfortable interior space: instead, the perspectives of the site, with its barred entrances and multiple blind points, encourage a psychological sense of unease (Herzog and Smith 1988). In other open, "sculptural" squares, excessive sun precludes social use of space for much of the day. Observations in Plaça Salvador Seguí in summer 1988, for example, showed that activities were confined to shadowed edges most of the day. While children played and transients hurriedly crossed the square, adult interaction remained limited until evening; a floating crap game epitomized social and environmental marginality as it followed the shaded perimeter of the plaza. Structurally (architecturally)and functionally (in terms of control), the values of the city as a whole have proved inimical to the needs and values of the barrio.

This social conflict at the origin of emptiness captures an ambivalence present in the definition of the word itself: "void of certain specific contents." This process of definition of correct or incorrect contents can derive from territorial struggles between groups or users or from the imposition of cultural values upon a space. Older middle- and upper-class Barcelonans, for example, have repeated to me many times that "no one goes to the Rambles," the older downtown's central promenade. "No hi va ningú/No va nadie." What these friends and informants imply, more often, is that they do not go there, nor should I, because of those who, in fact, *do* go. Here, a cultural evaluation again is at face value erroneous: the Rambles remain active at almost all hours of the day and night. The statement means, then, that the tourists attracted there are "not like us," or that drug dealers, petty thieves, and immigrants who circulate there have been reported in mass media and discourage (justify) the absence of other groups. As Tony Hiss remarks for the similar case of Times Square in New York, "That Times Square's reputation as a pornography center has lived on despite a quietly effective cleanup effort suggests that in times of rapid change our mental maps of places quickly get obsolete" (1990: 81).

Such cultural perceptions may merely indicate differential emptiness, blankness of mental maps among distinct groups (Lynch 1960 on Jersey City). Nonetheless, the conflicts that take place in these areas immediately evoke other power relations. Gloria Anzaldúa evokes the borderlands and its inhabitants:

A borderland is a vague and undetermined place created by the emotional residue of an unnatural boundary. It is in a constant state of transition. The prohibited and forbidden are its inhabitants. . . . Gringos in the U.S. Southwest consider the inhabitants of the borderlands transgressors, aliens—whether they possess documents or not, whether they're Chicanos, Indians or Blacks. Do not enter, trespassers will be raped, maimed, strangled, gassed, shot. The only legitimate inhabitants are those in power, the whites and those who align themselves with whites. Tension grips the inhabitants of the borderlands like a virus (1987: 3–4).

In this passage, it becomes apparent that another corollary of the perception of conflicts in "emptied" space can be the reactive regulation of space to exclude the "wrong" people. Here, delinquents, the homeless, or other culturally defined marginal groups are frequent candidates for regulation. Yet one must pursue links between these exclusions and others posited on the basis of race, class, gender, or seniority. Control, as Charles Rutheiser and other authors in this volume point out, may be exercised in many other ways while representing a fundamental policy issue of urban space.

The Orlando bus station points to the meaning of planned emptiness with unintended consequences. A decade ago William Whyte labeled "undesirables" as the primary obstacle to construction and use of good urban spaces, yet

they are not themselves much of a problem. It is the measures taken to combat them that is the problem. Many businessmen have an almost obsessive fear that if a place is attractive to people it might be attractive to undesirable people. So it is made unattractive. There is to be no loitering—what a Calvinist sermon is in these words!—no eating, no sitting. So it is that benches are made too short to sleep on, that spikes are put in ledges; most important, many needed spaces are not provided at all, or the plans for them scuttled. (1980: 60)

Similarly, Sarasotans have watched a dialectic of social presence and social removal enacted in a downtown mall that had become a center for the homeless. Redesign in the 1980s altered its configuration to provide less privacy and to control seating by linking it to a commercial concession (Frew 1990). By 1990, nearby benches on which the homeless regrouped were removed and the space "filled" with urban consumers. It returns to emptiness at night.

Emptiness as control rather than elimination of the past or conflict between groups recurs under various circumstances of extreme perceived threat. A *cordon sanitaire* thus establishes the security of a space with no traffic, people, or contagion between the site of an epidemic and some other population. In the cholera epidemic of 1830, for example, Russian military and police were allowed to shoot anyone leaving an infected area, while Spain used triple cordons to establish its ultimately ineffective buffer (Tuan 1979).

The ambiguities of emptiness as a result of contests for power are epitomized in a designation that embodies many of the ramifications of urban emptiness in a more violent setting: the idea of no-man's land. Originally used in reference to an execution site outside the north wall of medieval London, this image suggests a place between life and afterlife, law and disorder (see Tuan 1974; Virilio 1981; DeJean 1987). The term took on more sinister recognition as a space between trenches in World War I. Before the Christmas truce of 1914, this zone encompassed alternate meanings as Allied and German troops exchanged tobacco, sang carols, and even bartered weapons as souvenirs (Eksteins 1989: 112–113). In popular consciousness, the image of a football match between opposing sides evoked the contradiction of war and Christmas (Eksteins 1989: 113; see Fussell 1982). Modris Eksteins evokes a charge into contested land after the halcyon days had disappeared.

The cratered honeycomb of no man's land quickly breaks down any planned order. Men slip and fall. The line becomes straggly. Some get up and continue. Others cannot. In the mud of Passchendaele in 1917 some men drown in the huge, sewerlike craters filled with slime that comes of rain, earth, and decomposition. (1989: 141–142)

He concludes that "the victimized crowd of attackers in no man's land . . . has become one of the supreme images of the war. . . . The whole landscape of the Western front became surrealistic before the term *surrealism* was invented by the soldier-poet Guillaume Apollinaire" (1989: 144–145). DeJean (1987) suggests that this critical space prefigured the appropriation of space outside the literal and metaphoric fortresses of French culture by early female novelists.

The tension between imposed vacancy and social response became equally imposing in Barcelona, where an early modern wall formed a military and political cordon for the city. As a potentially rebellious Catalan center within the centralist state, the city was treated as a military stronghold in which no suburban development might mediate the function of its walls. Until the late nineteenth century, emptiness was ensured within a cannon's shot of the walls, while the burgeoning industrial city reached impossible densities within. Pamphlets decried its morbidity, pleading for destruction of the walls and expansion onto the healthy surrounding plane (Monlau 1841; McDonogh 1990). The intentionality of emptiness clarifies the ambiguous presence of power and conflict in urban place.

Competition pervades the fourth category in a different way. The emptiness of speculation exemplified by Chester County is a familiar theme of urban change and perhaps one that planners regard as healthy in terms of long-term development and market cycles. Before Barcelona burst its medieval walls, for example, epochs of economic decline saw houses and sections of the city abandoned, underused, or devoted to intramural agriculture. This cycle of "fallow" real estates has been as meaningful to Chicago School urbanists as to contemporary investors in gentrification. Yet how well does the concept of emptiness in so far as it refers to developed areas replace "open" in a study of metropolitan Philadelphia?

An examination of the growth in this century of the major metropolitan areas in the United States demonstrates that urbanization develops primarily on open land rather than through redevelopment. The open space interspersed in areas of low-density development within the urban fabric is filled by more intensive uses and open space standards are lowered. Urban growth consumes open space both at the perimeter and within the urban fabric. The result is a scarcity of open space where population and demand are greatest. This phenomenon has aroused wide public concern as the growth of cities, by accretion, has produced unattractive and unrelieved physical environments. Amenity, breathing space, recreational areas and the opportunity for a contact with nature for an expanding population are diminished. (Wallace 1970: 14–15)

Open, here, scarcely conveys Lynch's (1960) liberating sense. Instead, it bespeaks a cultural perception of nonuse and potential—a construction of emptiness.

The potential anomaly of such space often becomes painfully evident to nearby residents. In Manhattan, for example, *New York* magazine highlighted a controversy engendered by a lighted tennis court between two buildings on East 92nd Street, built in 1985 but fenced off to neighbors and unused throughout its existence. Rumors suggested that "real-estate developers must have installed the courts as a 'public plaza' in exchange for a city tax exemption. As the theory went, once the developers had the write-off, they welshed on the public part of the deal." It soon became apparent that the owners were caught between potential uses for the property, actually zoned for the perpetual urban "emptiness" of parking. They finally sold it for a twenty-eight-unit apartment block. While the space was reincorporated into urban use, those who had perceived other possibilities felt deprived and cheated (Ferid 1990: 28).

Richard Wilk and Muriel Schiffer (1979) systematically examined remains of multiple users in this type of empty space in Tucson. They found myriad informal uses by transients, other adults, and children and concluded that

vacant lots occupy a nebulous legal space; as private property, the primary responsibility for protection and enforcement resides with the owner; yet the owner, who does not live there, cannot fully maintain control over use. At the same time, public authorities are unwilling to assume the burden of regulating what is, after all, the use of private property.... The same factors that make vacant lots attractive study areas for archaeology classes are those that make them a distinct kind of urban space. (1979: 534)

Barcelona, on a longer historical scale, presents a related dialectic between the internal plaza areas that characterized Cerdà's nineteenth-century plan for the city and the perception that such spaces were open, empty or "buildable" (Cerdà 1968–1971; Martorell Portas et al. 1970). Hence, year by year, a plan for internal parks was strangled by semilegal development. In recent years, parking garages have eaten away at many of the remaining plazas, producing parks, as it were, with false bottoms instead of public space. Only in the last fifteen years has the city begun to police illegal edification and reopen the spaces of earlier plans (Ajuntament 1985).

In examining each case, then, I have evoked their social and cultural implications through observation, interpretation, and comparison. As such, we have moved beyond emptiness as a metaphor, yet we constantly have circled back to it, dividing as well as reuniting the implications of emptiness as it provides a meaningful urban category. Nonetheless, such examples still represent facets, interrogations, partial readings of a yet larger category and more significant meanings.

EXPLODING A CATEGORY

In this essay, I have argued that we must recognize and explore empty places as culturally created and socially meaningful zones rich in interest for our analysis of the city. As these cases have suggested, such spaces do not define a vacuum, an absence of urbanness, so much as they mark zones of intense competition: the interstices of the city. This intensification may mean points of trace and conflict in history, across social divisions, in planning, although both extremes betray impositions of urban power. My examples have tended to suggest, rather than exhaust, various motifs that cohere in a cross-cultural urban category.

Indeed, the litany of examples could easily be extended. Wolfgang Schiv-elbusch, for example, introduces the emptying of space through rapid travel in his *Railway Journey* (1986: 33–51), suggesting fundamental changes in Western appropriation and use of the environment. Paul Virilio also deals with speed, time, and space: for him, changes in relationships among these terms can suggest a challenge to the concept of the city itself: "The city was a means of mapping out a political space that existed in a given political duration. Now speed—ubiquity, instantaneousness—dissolves the city, or rather displaces it. And displaces it, I would say, in time" (Virilio and Lotringer 1983: 60; see Virilio 1981; 1991).

The transformation of air as space from an unbounded natural feature to an economically meaningful airshed (Wallace 1970) raises other questions about the nature of emptiness. Similarly, the role of toxic or radioactive wastes in permanently precluding habitation at sites also illustrates potential commercial, military, and statist problems in the definition of emptiness and the urban technology of insalubrity.

Spaces that vary in use and meaning between night and day also partake of this same category. Thus, cemeteries, as solitary spaces, evocative of the contemplation of solitude and of fear, can mark the uneasy intersection of different worlds in literature and urban analysis (Tuan 1974; see Cil et al. 1858). And time and technology shape space:

More than any other physical, urban, or architectural barrier, the day marks off differences of regime that affect the consciousness of time passing. . . .

Thus, the region and the city are not organized exclusively through a cadastral system of blocks, neighborhoods, city-centers and peripheries, or clusters of apart-ment complexes. They are also arranged through a calendar system of vacations, leaves-of-absences and holidays off (Virilio 1991: 82).

Such spaces can become critical and revealing, begging interpretation. Hence, methodologically, the category provides new insights for under-standing the city. The political potential for empty space as critique, for example, occurred to Peter Marin in *Harper's*, as he explored his ambivalence about the homeless in terms of the moral construction of society, noting:

We owe them, at least, a place to exist, a way to exist. . . . A society needs its margins as much as it needs art and literature. It needs holes and gaps, *breathing spaces* let us say, in which men and women can escape and live, when necessary in ways otherwise denied them. Margins guarantee a society a flexibility, an elasticity and allow it to accommodate itself to the natures and needs of its members. When margins vanish, society becomes too rigid, too oppressive by far and therefore inimical to life. (1987: 49)

Sara Evans and Harry Boyle attribute different yet nonetheless positive values to an anomalous form of space in which conflict is grappled with rather than avoided. Less rigidly structured or used spaces thus become *free* (returning us to the metaphors of Kevin Lynch): "settings between private lives and large-scale institutions where ordinary citizens can act with dignity, independence and vision." They are "environments in which people are able to learn a new self-respect, a deeper and more assertive group identity, public skills and values of cooperation and civic virtue" (1986: 17). Such spaces, they argue, form the heart of grass-roots citizens' movements.

When an empty space fills, its actors contravert its social construction or planned meaning. Hence it provides a place from which to protest a city and society as a whole, whether by rioters in eighteenth century Paris or by the assembled civil rights marchers on the Washington Mall in the 1960s or by the protesters of Tiananmen Square in 1989. Here emptiness, with its fears and constraints shattered, approaches the experience of "open" that Lynch suggested. Whether vacant, reserved, open, or razed, empty spaces thus play crucial roles in the fabric of the city.

Stephen Kern, in his *Culture of Time and Space*, reviews what may well be the genealogy of a geography for urban emptiness in the transformations of modernity at the turn of the century:

New constituent negativities appeared in a broad range of phenomena: physical fields, architectural spaces, and town squares; Archipenko's voids, Cubist interspaces and Futurist force-lines; theories about the stage, the frontier and national parks; Conrad's darkness, James's nothing and Maeterlink's silence; Proust's lost past, Mallarmé's blanks and Weber's pauses. Although these conceptualizations were as diverse as the many areas of life and thought from which they emerged and upon which they had influence, they shared the common feature of resurrecting the neglected "empty" spaces that formerly had only a supporting role and bringing them to the center of attention on a par with traditional subjects. If figures and ground, print and blanks, bronze and empty spaces are of equal value, or at least equally essential to the creation of meaning, then the traditional hierarchies are open to evaluation. . . .

The old sanctuaries of privilege, power and holiness were assailed, if not entirely destroyed, by the affirmation of positive negative space. (1983: 179–180)

However one might be stimulated to further explore the category of emptiness, for students of urban space, this classification reveals itself as neither negligible, uninteresting, nor unsociable. As a cultural value of urban place, emptiness itself provides a unique vantage point from which to more completely understand the intricacies of the city around it.

2

On the Salubrity of Sites

ROBERT ROTENBERG

Residents of cities cling to the evaluation of wholesomeness and noxiousness in their environment. When people can choose their own places of residence, marked activities, and workplace, they look for clues to a place's healthfulness. Environmental degradation certainly ranks among the more obvious outcomes of the process of urbanization. The information people share with each other for recognizing and evaluating the urban environment is locally constituted. That is, the criteria for what differentiates a healthful site from a dangerous one will vary geographically and historically. The level of acceptable health risk also differs from place to place and from person to person. The salubrity of sites is, therefore, a problem of interpretation for city dwellers. Through it, they define a distinctive feature of the meaning of urban spaces. My aim here is to illustrate how local and specific this interpretation is.

According to the *Oxford English Dictionary*, English speakers' use of the word *salubrity* dates only from the late eighteenth century. It was used to describe the health-promoting properties of food and climate. There are four senses in which the word salubrity (or the adjectival form, salubrious) is used in English. When referring to an everyday practice or a condition of life, the word can mean healthful in the sense of hygienic or salutary. When referring to a person, it can meant fit, well conditioned, or sound. When referring to illness and health, it can mean curative, restorative, or healing conditions. When referring to a place, it can mean safe, healthy, or uninjurious. Its opposites, noxiousness or pestilential, invert these conditions. Noxious conditions, people, health behaviors, or places are not as deadly as pestilential ones.

Outside of universities, one rarely finds the word in common usage today.

People manage to evaluate the wholesomeness of a place without it. Salubrity is a salient, though unnamed, quality of urban spaces. This is not the case in Western Europe. The four senses of the term identified above are all available in the Latin root, *salus* (health). One finds common recourse to cognate qualifiers in all of the Romance languages. For speakers of French, Italian, and Spanish there is no alternative except to speak of wholesomeness as some form of *salu*. German speakers split the meaning of salus between *gesund*, meaning healthy; *erholsam*, meaning restorative, recuperative; and *erspreisslich*, meaning beneficial or pleasant.

The first-century Roman architect Marcus Vitruvius Pollio devoted an entire chapter of *De architectura* to the problem of assessing the salubrity of urban space. In discussing how the architect should choose the site for building a city, he writes:

First, the choice of the most healthy site: Now this will be high and free from clouds and hoar frost, with an aspect neither hot nor cold but temperate. A marshy neighborhood should be avoided. For when the morning breezes come with the rising of the sun to a town, and clouds rising from these shall be conjoined, and with their blast shall sprinkle on the bodies of the inhabitants their poisoned breaths of marsh animals, they will make the site pestilential. Also if the walls are along the coast and shall look south or west they will not be wholesome because through the summer the southern sky is warmed by their rising sun and burns at midday. (1931: 35)

Vitruvius's concern is to minimize the noxious influences of nature on the lives of the people. He identifies these as sites subject to morning fogs, sites that are too exposed to the sun or too shadowed from it, or sites that are near wetlands. In contrast, the best location is on the southern slope of a low hill near the summit. In the following lines he explains how the physical properties of bodies change under different conditions of moisture and temperature:

Therefore by the changes of heat and cold, bodies which are in these places will be infected. We may even perceive this from those bodies which are not animal. . . . We may also consider that this is so from the fact that in summer, not only the pestilential but in salubrious districts, all bodies become weak, and also, through the winter, even the regions which are most pestilential, are rendered salubrious because they are rendered solid by freezing. . . .

Therefore in laying out the walls, we must be aware of those regions which by their heat can diffuse vapors over human bodies. For according as from the elements all bodies are composed, that is from heat and moisture and earth and air, just so by these mixtures, owing to natural temperament, the qualities of all animals are figured in the world according to their kind. (1931: 35–41)

His aim in situating the city is to optimize the strength of the body in spite of the seasonal alternation in temperature and moisture. This provides humans with the best opportunity for maintaining their physical equilibriums, permitting them to live wholesome lives.

Antique humoral science specifies a system of equilibrium among the four elements of heat, cold, dryness, and wetness. This science was widespread throughout Mediterranean civilization. The rediscovery of Vitruvius's encyclopedic work on city planning, Greek orders of architecture, interior decoration, waterworks, military machines, and human proportions in architecture were a major influence on Renaissance and Mannerist architecture, and on the classical revival of the eighteenth and early nineteenth centuries. Even today, moving beyond Vitruvian aesthetics is the principal challenge for architectural criticism. Cultural historians often overlook the continued existence of this substratum of humoral thought. These ideas have never ceased to influence popular ideas about nature in those parts of Europe that continued to support Latin institutions. Central Europe, particularly Vienna (and possibly other parts of Austria) belongs to that group.

The balance between salubrious and noxious places in cities is constantly changing. The issue becomes public and political when residents believe that the wholesome qualities of their home neighborhoods are threatened. In this essay, people who maintain garden plots in the city of Vienna, Austria, appraise the wholesomeness of their environment. The people I interviewed are like canaries in a mine. They are the first to perceive and the first to respond to changes in the qualities of their home environment. Their evaluations of salubrity are the keenest and most vigilant of all residents. I will analyze the language used by contemporary gardeners in assessing salubrity, investigate the revival of the language in the nineteenth century, and offer some ideas about the variation in the positions staked out by the various interview patterns, variations that require us to explore the ways in which urban space can mean different things to different metropolitans within the same civilization.

THE LANGUAGE OF SALUBRITY

In this essay, I concentrate on the private, domestic garden. These include both gardens attached to the house and leased allotment garden plots some distance away. When the Viennese gardeners try to explain what these places mean to them, one feature they find easy to describe is the relaxation and peace they find working, or just sitting, in their gardens. This is a feeling that is hardly unique to the Viennese. What is audible in these voices that one can otherwise miss is the progression of thought from "relaxation" through "exercise" to "healing" and "restoration."

This progression makes up a significant portion of the discourse on urban salubrity. By *discourse*, I mean the historical unfolding of attitudes within an area of knowledge as constructed in speech and modified by unequal relations of community power. The phrases, clichés, and aphorisms people use to allude to an area of knowledge are neither freely chosen nor accidental. They are the stuff of the discourse, the verbal vehicles through which the knowledge is coded, modified, and most importantly, validated. When we pay attention to oft-repeated phrases of gardeners, the discourse reveals its scope. To possess such a garden is to enjoy a highly valued object that was once considered the possession of the most powerful persons in society. How the social production of space changed to generate a greater number of gardens will be discussed in a later section. All of the gardeners I spoke with felt great humility and good fortune in being able to work their small plots. By employing the restricted set of descriptive phrases for salubrity that are currently in vogue, these gardeners justify their responses to their good fortune, confirm its social value, and warrant their continuing stewardship of its salubrity.

The most common expression of the idea that gardens engender relaxation sounds like this: "Yeah, when I get home from work, it's relaxing, restoring, to take two or three hours in the garden in the evening. There is a noticeable recovery."[1] This frequently heard sentiment sets up the dichotomy between the domestic garden and the exhausting and debilitating world of work. The powers of the garden are such that only a few hours are necessary to compensate for the eight or nine hours spent at work. One fellow made the connection between relaxation and garden work as follows: "At work I don't move around much. Sitting mostly. When I think how much of that carries over, it is no exaggeration [to see my garden work] as getting some exercise like others might get in housework. Get right to it and then take the next half hour off, right! And say, yeah, I did that for my needy body. When I mow the lawn, say, I am getting exercise where one doesn't ordinarily find it, and that helps, right!" The contrast here is one of movement versus sitting still.

The exercise is psychic as well as somatic. The following statement explores the restoration of psychic balance: "I come home after a long shift: two days and two nights of work at the hospital on the cancer ward. Even after so many years of service, the shift never grows shorter. Oxygen starvation, and always having to look upon grief, you know, it occurs so often among the critically ill. And then home again, outside in the fresh air and physical activity! And I can only say that after an hour one is a different person . . . And they say 'How do you cope with it?' And I don't know if I would survive if I didn't have this oasis. I don't believe I would." Psychic balance is restored faster than the physical. Here one hour compensates for over forty-eight hours on the job. Notice also that this balance is achieved through breathing in the fresh garden air, symbolized as oxygen, in contrast to the stifling atmosphere of dying and disease in the cancer ward. The condition of the air recurs often in people's evaluation of salubrity, as it did in Vitruvius. It is a taste or a smell that only growing things can produce. It is also a sight, a color, as is evident in this statement: "It is like this. If I am very tired or have just come from the city, especially in summer, with its bad air, heat, and congestion, and I sit down here and just look upon the green. And then it restores me completely. There are still many other possibilities, but that is an example."

The restorative effects of salubrious sites work on chronic illness as well as the workaday stresses of everyday life. This account reveals the power of the garden to mend even the most crushing of post–traumatic stress syndromes: "I was in Spain during the Civil War, then I was with the Partisans in France, so everything, the whole thing, and I worked very hard. When I got back, I suddenly fell apart. I could simply no longer live in the apartment. If we could somehow live outside, then so be it. And I had to, I don't know, I just could not bear to be in a confined space. When we came here [to a garden apartment], my wife naturally went to work. I was no longer able. The children were gone. The garden was like a fountain of health, somehow. Not because the children or my wife had encroached on my life, but because, how should I say it, outside I had everything I had ever wished for as child. And then this area is especially healthy because there is so much water around here. There are many eighty-year-olds in this settlement, and ninety-year-olds, and at least one person has even reached one hundred." Here the garden life returned to the man a sense of peace. The account brings in two more elements that one hears in evaluations of gardens—water and longevity. Like the fresh air, water represents a powerful natural element that even in small doses restores the harmony of the body. In the logic of humoral science, the air lightens the excessive earthiness of the sedentary work life, while the water cools the fires of the psychic stress of modern life.

Every one of my fifty-three interview partners agreed that their gardens were *Erholungsgärten*, literally "gardens that make one whole," filled with health-sustaining qualities of *frische Luft* (fresh air), *Sonne* (sun), *Ausspannung* (suspending of activity), *Entspannung* (relaxation), *Freibewegung* (unrestricted movement), *Erholung* (regeneration), and similar praxis. These concepts constitute the current discourse on salubrity. Almost all offered the view that their gardens made them healthier people. Many could provide concrete examples of recovery from illness that they were convinced was due to their garden life.

In this anecdote, a medical treatment is given a boost by the wholesomeness of place: "When I was a small child (I was born in 1919, after the War), I had tuberculosis. And I was very undernourished. I was very small. I'm still not very big. I have actually always been told over and over again by my parents, my family, and my friends that I was cured by this garden. I was twice in a pulmonary sanitarium, and became cured, but not by the institute alone, but also here in the garden, through the good air, the living here, through the freedom to run about as a child." The cure is begun in the medical world but is only fully realized when the salubrious effects of the garden are added. Another salubrious element plays an active role here, unrestricted movement. The idea that salubrious places are those that permit the breaking of behavioral constraints is also widespread.

In this second example, air and exercise come together as therapeutic, the salient mechanisms of place: "I need quite a bit of fresh air. I once had a lung infection, and scar tissue remains on my lungs, reducing the capacity. So I need a lot of air, and if I go out in the garden, I never get tired. I certainly don't overexert myself. If I have something to do outside, I feel there like I can fill my lungs with air, with oxygen, and then I feel that I did good. If I am tired in the evening after working in the garden, it is a pleasant tiredness, which I believe does me good. I find exercise in the garden quite agreeable, even when it is accompanied sometimes by aches and pains. I think that this is healthy for me. It is for me a therapy." Here the product of the garden work is not unlike the product of ordinary work, a feeling of tiredness. The tiredness of work is harmful. It leads to imbalance, stress, and disease. The tiredness of garden activity is beneficial. It restores the balance, alleviates the stress, and mitigates the disease.

The image of the garden as a wholesome place conflicts with the knowledge that the garden itself is under threat ecologically. Half the partners said they tried to maintain a *Biogarten*, an organic garden. The practice is hardly without controversy. The following remarks are typical of the futility some gardeners feel: "No, [organic gardening] doesn't work. Now first, yesterday the trees were sprayed there. So, if this were an organic garden, I couldn't allow the spraying with poisons. In the spring when they spray, we have to cover the young lettuce plants, if we have them. Besides, I'm not sure I want a garden that is completely sterile. It isn't anyhow." Others said such an attempt is futile since the world itself is polluted: "I guess because I don't think very much of the whole movement. By my calculation organic materials no longer exist. At all. I can do nothing about it. It doesn't matter if from today on, I only use organic fertilizer or something else. If I use pure cow manure, the cow had already grazed in a chemically fertilized field. I think the whole organic gardening movement is just a big business with nothing behind it. By my estimate pure organic potatoes or organic cabbage cannot exist. And there is nothing one can do about it." The fertilizing of the garden and the protection of its plants from parasites was seen as a path for introducing artificial, and therefore, harmful elements into the garden system. "Organic gardening is certainly important, but then there is the problem that if one is not experienced, the insect pests come anyway. And most gardens are so infested that whatever one puts out becomes full of lice. If I don't spray with chemicals, it only gets worse. Then I don't want to eat the produce. But I won't eat insect-infested stuff either." The garden is as harmful to plants as it is salubrious for people. It is a piece of nature that is out of balance because of its necessary isolation in the city.

This contradiction in the central value of the garden, in the very core of the garden experience, fuels the general insecurity people feel toward environmental quality. The metaphorical extension of the garden to its owner is an easy one for most gardeners to make. While the people can seek reintegration with nature through the garden, the garden can only be reintegrated through the destruction of the city. This is precisely where the discourse on salubrity leads us.

THE DISCOURSE ON SALUBRITY

The idea that nature can heal is known in Austria as *Naturheilkunde*. This homeopathic system is a popular way of understanding health in Central Europe. Even school medicine adapts its rhetoric to incorporate the better-established ideas of Naturheilkunde. This includes prescribing rest cures, exercise, even gardening, as part of the therapy for infectious illnesses. These principles belong to the tradition of medical knowledge that stretches back to Galen and Hippocrates. At the same time, they are unmistakably modern. Homeopathy was revived and reinterpreted in the late nineteenth century to incorporate the ideas of Ernst Haeckel's ecology and Charles Darwin's natural selection, as well as the psychophysical principles of Gustav Fechner and Wilhelm Wundt. The folk system originally saw health as the product of the balance of the four elements. Under its academically legitimated guise, the system views the human organism as an entity that is open to and contingent upon a larger environmental system. The original four elements persist. The ecological system puts pressure on the human organism through heat and humidity, but these are now understood as environmental stress factors that can select for, as well as against good health. The human who confronts these stresses affirmatively, through unrestricted movement, Freibewegung, builds up strength and improves the functioning of his or her organism. The person who encounters nature passively loses strength, weakens the organism, sickens, and eventually dies.

This principle was the seminal observation of Dr. Daniel Gottlieb Mortiz Schreber, a mid-nineteenth-century doctor and physical culturist from Leipzig. He related how he came to this realization through an anecdote. A medical school colleague had left school to participate in a scientific expedition to the South Seas. When he returned, he was larger, more muscular, suntanned, and more energetic than his schoolmates, who had seen nothing but laboratories in his absence. Schreber remarked on the differences and concluded that the friend's active movements resisting the forces of nature while on board ship were the primary cause of his good health. Health lay in affirmatively engaging nature's stresses and building the body to meet the challenges.

Schreber, like other leaders of the physical cultural movement in the nineteenth century, was a strong German nationalist. He saw in the program of exercise and physical development the way to strengthen the German people and give them an evolutionary advantage over other industrializing societies. He saw the working class as particularly in need of the salubrious effects of free movement out of doors. He popularized the need for the process of strengthening the body to begin in childhood through discipline, directed play, and exercise. His friend, Dr. Ernest Innocenz Hochschild, director of the fourth Bürgerschule in Leipzig, disparaging of the lack of playground space for children, organized a group of parents to build and supervise a playground on an open meadow near the school. He named the primitive playground Schreberplatz, after his friend. One of the supervising teachers, Heinrich Carl Gesell, laid out a flower bed on the edge of the meadow to encourage children to plant flowers and hedges. The children collected around the garden, and it grew in size until the parents, too, became involved in it. From there it began to incorporate vegetables with the flowers. Families would work on in the garden beds together. By 1870, there were more than 100 such gardens on Schreberplatz. As the number of families grew, so did the organization. Already in 1870, it had a central committee, a chairman, and a general meeting. The purpose of the organization, as stated in its charter, was to nurture the emotional and intellectual development of children in the spirit of Schreber and Hochschild. Later, this mission expanded to include the following phrase: "to support gardening, especially the cultivation of fruit gardens, and to transform the gardener into a practical settler" (Albrecht 1989: 98).

Over the next thirty years, this movement spread to cities throughout Germany and Northern Europe. Wherever it spread, it combined two elements whose association was quite novel for urban dwellers: the opportunity for working-class people to work marginal plots they did not own into salubrious precincts. Known as the *Schrebergärten* movement, these allotment gardens could soon be found tucked along railroad right-of-ways, in empty lots near housing projects, and on the edges of large public parks. The first Schrebergärten in the Viennese region began in 1903 in the Wienerwald between the villages of Purkersdorf and Baunzen. Officially called Deutsch-Wald, it was known to its gardeners as Heim-Garten. Both the reference to the "German Forest" in the official title and the reference to the garden in Heimat in its nickname are not accidental. They reflect the confluence of physical culture, landscape practice, and national ideology that formed the worldview of the young middle-class couples that founded it. In the end, very few garden societies were founded by the children of the bourgeoisie. The first two Schrebergärten that actually lay within the boundaries of the city were established in 1911, "Rosenthal" in the 12th District and the "Lust- und Nutzgarten" on an arm of the Old Danube. These names lacked reference to national ideology because they were founded by working-class families for whom the physical culture and landscape practice were wedded to subsistence and economic security. By the beginning of the First World War, there were over 500 gardens occupying a mere fifteen hectares of land. The popularity of these garden societies grew rapidly, doubling every year between 1914 and 1918. By 1921, there were 30,000 Schrebergärten in Vienna covering 900 hectares, or 3.2 percent of the area of the city (Fischer 1971: 61).

Initially, the desire to have a small garden plot developed from the *Biologismus* or *Lebensreform* movements sweeping Europe at the time. These movements combined Schreber's physical culture with vegetarianism, nudism, natural fibers for clothing, a "back-to-the-land" movement among urban youth, and similar elements. These movements were part of a wider Western romanticism that gave birth to hiking societies, conservation groups, scouting, and the national and municipal park movements (Schmidt 1969). The small garden plot was a miniature version of the grander search for Arcadia that inspired two generations of German-speaking youth. The theorist of Biologismus was Raoul Francé. In his most popular article, "The Law of the Forest," he writes that the goal of the human community should be to create a "harmonious organism" that "always responds to the ever-changing occurrences of the struggle with the environment and is the result of all the adaptations that derived from the struggle for existence (1908: 40)." Published in a hiking magazine with a very large readership, Francé became the most popular scientist of his generation. His interpretation of ecological relationships reinforced older concepts of humoral equilibrium while employing modern formulations, especially systems language. As one early supporter of the philosophy explicitly stated, "humans, animals, plants, and soil build a living unity" (Rust 1924: 165). The roots of the contemporary ecology movement in German-speaking Europe can be found in these pre–World War II writings.

Clearly, the city is pathological according to this model. True balance could only be found in idealized landscapes that had escaped the ravages of industrialism. This anti-modern, anti-urban program was one of the most popular social movements in Europe in this century. Participants included people from all political persuasions and social classes. The movement legitimated the existing language of salubrity, giving it a patina of modern scientific authority. The movement also increased the social value of possessing a garden, sparking the increased demand for more garden space in cities. The garden had a specific role to play in combating the essential pestilence of the city by providing a small piece of the ideal landscape with its ever-changing environment against which individual urbanites can build their living unity.

This romantic naturalism was so popular in the first four decades of the twentieth century that all writers on the garden experience used its phrases. Writing in 1920, after the experience of the war and the rapid expansion of Schrebergärten, the small garden advocates Franz Siller and Camillo Schneider characterize the Viennese small gardeners as follows: "It is practically impossible in our time to lead a humane, healthy life without a garden. We always emphasize the economic value of gardens, but every farsighted person must acknowledge that the educational and health giving values contained in the Schrebergärten are far more meaningful" (1920: 79). In this way, the language of Schreber's and Francé's romantic naturalism came to underlie the language of salubrity in metropolitan Vienna.

THE SOCIAL PRODUCTION OF SALUBRITY

The preceding descriptions of the language of salubrity do not imply that possessing a garden in Vienna is an ordinary occurrence. Gardens did not become widespread until the 1930s. Previously, gardens had been the preoccupation of the nobility and commercial elites who used them as representations of their social power. Salubrious precincts were a by-product of this representational intent. The nineteenth century began with a profusion of house building by the emerging middle classes. These included both detached houses and courtyard townhouses. These residents planted gardens to contain the activities of the closed family circle. The plots were airy, but sunlit for only short periods of time. The truly salubrious areas were found in the public parks. These had first opened in the late 1780s. By mid-nineteenth century, there were copious, airy, sunny, green spaces in the heart of the city. Throughout the second half of the century, as the building boom rebuilt entire sections of the old suburbs, much of this space was lost.

The growth of the middle class sparked a series of building booms that transformed some nearby villages into residential suburbs. These so-called cottage districts featured detached two- and three-story houses set on small plots, often with a small garden on the side and rear. The wealthier classes had larger plots given over to the garden. In both cases, these were pleasure gardens constructed and maintained by professional tradesmen and rarely involving the labor of the owner. The gardens were intended to enhance the value of the house, which in turn was seen as a financial investment. The garden design favored representational purposes. These were gardens to be seen, rather than inhabited.

The nineteenth century also saw the city swell in population from approximately 80,000 in the 1820s to over 2 million in 1900. Two-thirds of these inhabitants had been born elsewhere and moved to the city for industrial jobs. Their housing was limited, poorly constructed, inadequate for their needs, and lacking in running water and sanitation. By the first decade of the twentieth century, the problem had reached crisis proportions. Progressive elements in Vienna favored the building of garden settlements, modeled on Ebenezer Howard's Garden City ideas (Howard 1902). Many garden settlements began as squatter settlements on public land by employed people who could find no housing. When the Social Democratic party took power in the city following World War I, it began a public housing building program that included garden settlements. The party also rehabilitated existing squatter settlements according to the same principles. These are not mere flower beds. They are good-sized yards with areas between 75 and 300 square meters. In the most common landscape form, they are strips of land running outward from the backs of row houses.[2] The strips often have trees of various kinds, flower and vegetable beds, a lawn, and a concrete walk running roughly down the center. Most plots are fenced to separate them from neighboring gardens. This housing was built using the labor of the people who wanted to live in it. These were mostly employed, unionized, skilled workers. Unskilled laborers and the unemployed rarely got the chance to participate in these gardens. By 1935, there were 41 such settlements, with approximately 7,700 housing units (Novy and Förster 1985; Posch 1981).

The two world wars and the economic crisis of the 1930s slowed private construction. When it picked up again in the 1960s, including the garden as part of the house design was a firmly established principle in the minds of both architects and home buyers. Today, private and public housing incorporate garden plots either on the ground floor or in wide terraced setbacks on the upper floors. Roof gardens have proliferated. Empty lots have been landscaped as vest-pocket plots in denser areas. Small garden clubs continue to thrive around the edges of the city. These small garden settlements represent a consistent pursuit of salubrious places throughout the twentieth century. Nevertheless, it takes a lot of money to buy into both the established garden settlements and the new garden housing. Attractive housing in general is scarce in the city, and real estate values are very high. Only the wealthy, the lucky, or those willing to take on considerable debt can enjoy the salubrity of a garden today.

SALUBRITY AND URBAN SPACE: CONCLUSIONS

Up to this point, the discussion has focused on certain ethnomedical ideas of wholesomeness seen through the urban garden plots that people construct to realize these ideas. The history of the development of urban places did not proceed as Vitruvius envisioned. Spaces were chosen and metropolitan areas enlarged without regard for prevailing winds, swampy areas, or the heat of the air in summer. The anarchic growth of the city cannot insure salubrity, but parts of it can. I see a strong connection between the ideas of Vitruvius, the ideas of Schreber and Francé, and the language of the gardeners. Ideas about salubrity are at the core of the evaluation of urban places in Vienna. There are other dimensions of meaning possible, especially the economic, the sociopolitical, and the formal-aesthetic. Before any of these other dimensions are applied, the Viennese must first deal with the fundamental problem of urban life, namely, that at its heart, urban agglomeration is pestilential in character. Only by reserving certain enclosed, protected places can the urbanite insure a salubrious precinct. The garden, in all its multifarious forms, is the guarantee of a salubrious respite. All other spaces are then evaluated in terms of their proximity to the salubrious reserve.

The economic, the sociopolitical and the formal-aesthetic assessments of place can all be related to the salubrious and share in its meaning. Wholesome features of nature, such as a body of water, a view of the mountains, the higher (natural or architectural) elevations of an urban valley gain greater economic value while the clearly pestilential places that lie next to dumps, swamps, sewer rivers, and factories lose value. These health-giving features identify the houses that look out upon them as more desirous and ensures their sale at a premium. One could draw a zoning map around the salubrious districts of cities and predict that these are places that will develop as enclaves of the well-to-do and powerful. The places designated as sacred to socio-political activity situate themselves in public gardens or are otherwise for-mally designed to imitate the salubrious places in the locality. Socially neutral places are lacking green features and slowly devolve into increasingly pestilential zones. Even the formal designs of urban greenspace over the last two hundred years respond to the existing evaluation of salubrity before they respond to the needs of the architecture. Thus, a public garden is more likely to be architectonic in its form if the preexisting area had no previous claim to salubrity. Alternatively, such a preexisting evaluation is more likely to support a parkscape design.

As these ideas suggest, the salubrity of sites can become an axis of meaning for urban spaces as these are looked at from various problem perspectives. We may live in industrial cities, but the idea of the city is much older than industry. Nor was industry able to erase all of the meanings that urban life has sustained from its classical designers. Vienna, after all, started out as a Roman fortress. If what Vitruvius was reporting was common knowledge among the architects of the ancient Mediterranean, he was also describing a spatial meaning that is salient for contemporary cities as well.

NOTES

1. Many of the conversation partners spoke in Viennese dialect, a speech quality that I have tried to capture in translation by rendering their statements in a very informal English diction.

2. This form is associated with the Central European garden city movement. It first developed in Berlin and moved to Vienna in the 1920s (Kampffmeyer 1909). The form was applied to both newly built garden city complexes and to the re-habilitation of established small garden settlements into garden cities. This was intended to be worker housing. The strip form, as well as the long, narrow shape of the row house apartments, came about as an effort to reduce the infrastructure costs of roads, plumbing, and sewerage. All of the comments included here come

from residents of garden city settlements. Other kinds of gardens exist in Vienna, notably those surrounding detached housing. These gardeners' evaluations of salubrity are no different from those of the garden city gardeners. The consensus on salubrity crosses class lines. Compare Rotenberg 1992 for a discussion of the consensus-producing processes in garden city settlements.

3

Chinese Privacy

DEBORAH PELLOW

Changes have occurred in China's sociocultural environment that shift attention from the group to the individual, thus enabling redefinitions of sexuality and the right to privacy. These changes, in concert with changes in the physical environment (that is, multistoried apartment complexes as the preferred residence), have led to disturbances in the psychosocial balance of Shanghai residents.

How might we examine the changes and the disturbances to better understand today's China? In 1971, F.L.K. Hsu's *jen* hypothesis presented a new way to explore the relationship of the individual to society. Hsu viewed the nature of the individual's external behavior in terms of how it fits or fails to fit the interpersonal standards of the society and culture. Hsu chose the Chinese word *jen* because it denotes a bilateral relationship and "puts the emphasis on interpersonal transactions" (1971: 29). Such a focus makes it possible to better understand cultures in general, and in particular cultures like the Chinese, for whom group identification is primary.

Fundamental to his hypothesis is the process of psychosocial homeostasis. This is a human constant, whereby "every human individual tends to maintain a satisfactory level of psychic and interpersonal equilibrium" (1971: 28). Hsu diagrams the human psychosociogram as a series of eight concentric layers. The innermost layer represents the unconscious, while the outermost layer represents the world at large. Hsu suggests that every individual makes his/her existence meaningful through intimate relationships with others. These others in turn are drawn from/compose one's intimate society and culture (layer 3). The individual's expressible conscious (layer 4) is the wellspring for action and communication with others. Layers

7 to 4 concern the individual, layers 3 to 0 the interconnection of the individual and society.

Failing to find an anthropological definition of intimacy, Hsu offered his own as "a relationship in which all parties can afford to let their guards down, can communicate their worst troubles to each other without the fear of rejection, and can count on comfort, sympathy, and help from each other without the onus of charity" (1971: 26).

I accept the underlying concept of Hsu's psychosociogram, but to explore the impact of social change in contemporary urban China, I suggest recasting his diagram to focus upon space and the correlation of different kinds of privacy with different kinds of space. The model I propose also sets out concentric layers, moving from the individual to outer society, in the mode of Hall's distance zones of interaction (1969: 114–125). My model has five basic layers:[1]

1. unexpressible internal space
2. expressible internal space
3. intimate space
    a. sexual partner
    b. living space partners
    c. extended family
4. relational/social space
    a. apartment building
    b. neighborhood
5. public space
    a. city
    b. nation
    c. world

Ethnographies typically have not explicitly dealt with the issue of privacy.[2] I shall do so, emphasizing the sociospatial component. I shall look at attitudes from traditional China ("the old"), which continue today as behavioral patterns that are changing even as they are subtly powerful. Quite basic is the Confucian ethical stance that demands the sacrifice of the individual to social obligations—the definition of the individual by society. I shall also look at two areas ("the new") where patterns are changing: housing and sexuality. These affect and are affected by understandings of the self-other relationship.

CHINESE INDIVIDUAL AND SOCIETY

The Chinese person is a totality of social roles; without a network, one is no one. The " 'individual' is organized and motivated by the 'other' (if not the 'nation' then the 'family'),'' regarding himself "as an instrument of others" (Sun Longji 1989: 31). In Chinese culture, from birth on, each person is enclosed by a network of interpersonal relationships that define and organize existence. One's circle or sodality is essential for mutual assistance, as well as for the definition of the self.

The notion of *ren* (*jen*) forms the basic substratum, the "deep structure" that "has remained unchanged up to the present day" (Sun 1989: 163). That one might live "alone" or be "single" carries the connotation of "pathetic" and "immoral."

For Neo-Confucian philosophers, the self is accorded "an irremovable centrality as the carrier of moral action" (Elvin 1986: 174), but at the same time, the self should not be too distinctive else it be regarded as morally suspect. Even the philosophers of the late-nineteenth and early-twentieth centuries "began with a search for the liberation of the self, but end with the desire for its extinction: for its absorption into a collective consciousness, the homogenization of its individuality, its perpetuation as a fragment of a greater Social Self" (Elvin 1986: 174). The emphasis upon the social whole, the collectivity, was reinforced by the ideology of the Chinese Communist party. Maoism also preached selflessness, but of a revolutionary sort: "the good Maoist is supposed to subordinate all 'natural' obligations to family, associates, and friends to the cause of the Chinese revolution" (Madsen 1981: 154).

Among the Chinese, group orientedness "begins early in life with emphasis on identification with the family and on behaving in a manner that will reflect creditably both on the family as a unit and on other individual family members" (Wilson 1981: 11). While the ideal of the cohabiting extended family is no longer easily fulfilled, there are always one's parents and siblings and close relatives with whom one is engaged.

In the "old" China there was some difference between being at home and being in public, which included some relaxation of etiquette (Moore 1984: 262). But many well-to-do households (for which we have data) and perhaps peasant ones as well, contained so many individuals of differing age, sex, and status that "it is unlikely that the home could serve very well as a private retreat where one could let down one's social guard and relax" (Moore 1984: 262).

In the "new" China, family attachment is reinforced by attention to such phrases as "domestic discipline," "family honor," and "filial respect." Moreover, family members and relatives will usually get together for family celebrations, such as marriages or funerals, or at Spring Festival, the Chinese New Year (Kong 1989).

Identification with larger groups, such as brigades and communes, has been encouraged through school, the media, and associations. In China's cities, hometown associations (*tong xiang hui*) are very popular, among students as among migrants. These can be characterized as intimate society for the "stranger." "The emphasis in training is on shifting identification to these larger secondary groups and on investing them with the same degree of commitment that traditionally was reserved for primary groups such as the family" (Wilson 1981: 11).

PRIVACY (INTIMATE SPACE) AND THE PUBLIC ORDER IN CHINA

In traditional Chinese, there is no character for the word *privacy*. Two characters put together—*yin si*—literally mean something hidden (even the hidden self), something that can be protected from anyone's knowing. The term carries a pejorative connotation.

Just prior to the unification of China in the third century B.C., the philosopher Han Fei Tzu regarded private behavior as potentially subversive, claiming that ancient roots for a strong state lay in the public domain. Confucius also distinguished between private and public life. But he supported the private obligation of the son to the father (to not bear witness to the older man's theft) over the public obligation to obey the law (Moore 1984: 260).

Thus even in ancient China, there was a sense of privacy—in my model, intimate space. But it was privacy for the primary group, as expressed in the concept *jia zhou bu ke wai yang*—that is, domestic shame should not be made public. In this culture where the family is the core group, it is a moral imperative not to reveal shame or ugliness to the outside world. Such can only be shared among the family members, one's intimate society and culture. The jia can be the nuclear family, or it can be the whole country. It refers to the contrast with the outside—for the family, other families; for the country, tourists or other countries.

Even within the household, there are rules (hierarchies, manners, avoidance) that help control interaction. It is believed that the patriarch would (should) know everything that is going on in the household (see Zhang Jing Ai 1990). He also would not want outsiders to know the family's "ugliness." Spatial divisions (transitional spaces marking levels of privacy) reflect rules of social appropriateness that determine distribution of living quarters in the family home.

CHINESE SEXUALITY

In Yunan Province in the 1940s, a married couple was not to express any erotic interest in each other; even newlyweds could sleep in the same bed for only seven days (Hsu 1967: 57). Estrangement between the sexes was necessary to observance of filial piety. Sex was considered unclean, and women were regarded as inferior (Hsu 1967: 209).

In the "old" China and the "new," "immoral" sex behavior is anything which does not fall within the customary bounds and may be attacked by gossip, ridicule, or ostracism. There is no place for romance.

The emphasis on the continuation of the father-son tie means that the behavior and the ideas of new or prospective members of the family must be predictable so as not to sever this tie. Romantic love is, in theory at least, unpredictable, and the emphasis is on individual attachment between the spouses. That is why gestures of intimacy in public, even between man and wife, are socially disapproved. (Hsu 1967: 241–242)

Sex is a taboo subject in the family, as are emotional problems. To promote social harmony, the Chinese believe that "they must 'desexualize' the individual, that is, make him unaware of his own sexuality" (Sun 1989: 227).

Desexualization helps to maintain harmony within the family, and with the family as the basic unit of society, its orderliness is necessary. Desexualization also helps maintain peace between the generations, for it prevents the individual from breaking away and thus becoming an independent being—that is, in line with the theory of the Oedipus complex, he does not mature sexually and thus does not rebel against authority (Sun 1989: 227).[3] And between spouses, sexuality is discouraged, since intercourse is regarded as a means of procreation rather than for personal enjoyment (Sun 1989: 228).

Sexuality is not only repressed by Chinese culture but by the political system of the Chinese Communist party as well: "During the Cultural Revolution, no public word was spoken about sexuality. Even marital sex was a taboo subject, an aspect of private life and therefore a 'bourgeois' concern" (Honig and Hershatter 1988: 51). Even today, spouses are routinely separated in locale when placed by the government in jobs.[4] This corresponds to the theory of desexualization and the fear that sexuality would disrupt the social fabric of the society at large. Sexual estrangement thus serves as a social safety valve, helping to maintain psychosocial balance and prevent the culture from breaking down due to inner conflicts.

URBAN HOUSING AND THE HOUSING PROBLEM (INTIMATE AND RELATIONAL SPACE)

In Shanghai, China's largest city, the residential housing shortage is so acute that even those who speak little English use the English expression "the housing problem." Today's per person, square footage (for comparisons, see Table 3.1) is about the size of a kingsize bed!

In Shanghai, there are two types of housing: the *shikumen*, a characteristically Shanghai-type dwelling, literally translates as stone multiple-storied gate. It derives from the traditional courtyard house, which protected the private nature of the Chinese family, as it was protected by an outside wall

Table 3.1
Residential Space Per Person (in Square Meters)

1949	3.9
1956	3.0
1970	4.4
1989	6.3

and all of the rooms within opened onto an enclosed courtyard. While the courtyard form is absent from Shanghai, all built structures are bounded by a wall.

The second type of housing is the *xing cun*, new apartment "villages." These contain apartments with kitchens and bathrooms. They were first built in Shanghai in 1952 and were two-storied. The more recent versions are either six-floor walk-ups or elevator high-rises of twelve-plus floors. The buildings are uniformly drab.

In the shikumen, the courtyard itself is recognized and retained in its layout. This house style consists of a number of buildings of two or three stories, arranged on a grid of lanes. The entirety is walled in, and it is entered through a formal doorway (gate), which leads out onto the street. The shikumen incorporates four areas of interaction: (1) The private is the individual apartment to which only the occupants have free access. (2) The public is an entryway, just inside the gated entrance. Often there is a kiosk where, among other things, one may make a pay phone call. It is also here that many people, residents and nonresidents, who have business in the area may park their bicycles. (3) There are the semipublic lanes that cut through the shikumen. (4) For want of a better expression, there is the semiprivate lane along which the entrance to one's apartment house (and thus apartment) is located. Between the entryway and the semipublic lane, there may be a front courtyard that serves as a transitional space between the two.[5] Moreover, the stairways and hallways within the buildings may be regarded as extensions of the semiprivate lanes.

Each building contains apartments whose occupants are unrelated to those living in the other apartments. Chinese apartments are not spacious. In my project, the space per person averaged 6.9 square meters, not much larger than the above-cited Shanghai average of 6.3 square meters.

Apartments often consist of one room, even though they may accommodate multiple generations; their residents vary according to the stage in domestic cycle. In the older buildings, the ceiling is high enough to build in a loft, in effect creating a second room. Furniture is used to demarcate functional divisions of space (eating area, sleeping area, sitting room). None of the old shikumen have either toilets or bathing facilities. Most people use chamber pots, although there are also public toilets throughout the city.

As there is no piped-in hot water, children are bathed in the main room in a wooden tub; adults shower weekly during the winter at a public bathing facility or their work unit. There is no kitchen; thus individuals use the semiprivate lane (where there is a water tap) for domestic chores. Hall space is often shared by neighbors, with each family having its corner to cook.

In modern housing, each xing cun apartment consists of one, two, or three rooms, plus a kitchen that may be large enough to use as a sitting room or for family activities. The average size of a room is 158 square feet. As in the shikumen, once there are children or elders resident, families run into problems with the division of space. Bulky furniture is a favorite solution. Because there are functionally specific rooms—bathroom and kitchen—the main room has fewer defined areas than in the shikumen.

Unlike in the shikumen, neighbors in xing cun are not familiar with one another. They share less space and no private facilities. In fact, what most find attractive about the new apartments, despite the often limited space within, is that they have a toilet and kitchen and that residents do not have to deal with the noise or interference of neighbors as one does in the shikumen.

In both the shikumen and the xing cun, the main room serves the functions of sleeping, eating, dressing, reading or studying, playing, and entertaining. The activities are separated temporally and may necessitate the redefinition of the same space.

The Chinese architectural standard is that children will sleep in the same room with their parents through age twelve. After that teenagers of each sex should have separate rooms, though a grandparent may share a room with teenagers of either sex. (Whyte and Parish 1984: 80)

Not only do children sleep in the same room; in the shikumen they sleep in the same bed as their parents until six or eight years of age. Those who do not seem to be the exception to the traditional rule. In some cases, if it is too crowded in the bed for husband, wife, and child, the husband sleeps elsewhere.

Those couples who reject the idea of having the child in the conjugal bed live in the new housing. They may have a tiny bed for the child, but, for lack of a second room, the child remains in the room with them.

For those planning to marry, housing becomes more of an issue. Where will the young couple live? Under the best of circumstances, one either comes from a family with extra space (an extra room) or works for a unit (*danwei*) that has enough housing to accommodate its employees. Until an individual is registered as a married person, the Government will not allocate an individual an apartment. The Catch–22 is that the speed of a marriage is a function of housing; in the danwei, there may be only one available apartment and several couples wishing to marry. If one has access to a house in Shanghai, that becomes a kind of currency in the marriage negotiation.

China's housing industry has been affected by a growing privatization of life. Before 1983, all housing was built, owned, and managed by the state. In 1983, five pilot cities were chosen where apartments-for-sale would be built, and " 'after sale, an apartment is private property' " (Schell 1984: 35). Private house building boomed both in the countryside and in the city.

EMERGENCE OF THE SELF (INEXPRESSIBLE INTERNAL SPACE)

Under Mao, the omnipresent revolutionary songs invaded one's space and made private thought almost impossible (Schell 1988: 103). And in very concrete terms, the Communists broke the "tacit covenant between ruler and ruled" by interfering in individual family affairs (Leys 1990: 10). Even children were encouraged to tattle on their parents, upending the traditional line of authority and the right of the unit to remain invisible to the outside (see Feng and Shapiro 1982).

How different the scene following the upheaval of 1989. The Chinese leadership came up against passive resistance and a refusal of the citizenry to cooperate with the campaign against "counterrevolutionaries," apparently crippling the effectiveness of the policies intended to return China to its Communist path. Most of the million-plus people who had been on the streets demanding the resignation of Prime Minister Li Peng have gone unreported by their colleagues and bosses.

[The Chinese] contrast the present altruism with the persecutions during the Cultural Revolution from 1966 to 1976. At that time, people say, ordinary Chinese did awful things to each other; this time they go out of their way to shelter each other. (Kristof 1990: A8)

The Party had already been suffering "a prolonged erosion of its moral authority—and its ability to intimidate" (Kristof 1989: 29). *Guangxi*, connections, ever present as a means to making one's way through the cumbersome bureaucracy, have more and more come to be used to individual ends.

Privacy and sexual pleasure as options for the individual are part of the new China. Inveterate China-watcher Orville Schell writes of his own incredulity in 1986 when he read the following Xinhua News Agency dispatch: "People should keep their noses out of other people's personal affairs and respect their right to privacy," as well as the commentary in the *Workers' Daily*: " 'the right of privacy' originated in Western countries, but it is about time the concept was applied in China" (1988: 36). It was stunning, because "the Chinese Communist Party had [in the past] made it its business to put its nose into other people's affairs by every means possible: spying, an elaborate system of informants, interrogation, forced self-criticisms and confessions" (1988: 37).

EMERGENCE OF THE SELF (EXPRESSIBLE INTERNAL SPACE)

In the 1980s, the whole notion of a private sector came into vogue, most volubly proclaimed in the economic domain and the proliferation of a new class of entrepreneurs, known as *getihu*. They own repair shops, sell goods, own restaurants, run inns, work as domestics. Deng Xiao Ping in his 1983 *Selected Works* affirmed "To get rich is glorious" and "Get rich by working" as politically correct. "They were arresting slogans for a Communist Party that had formerly threatened anyone who exhibited any privatistic tendencies or interest in personal gain with the ignominy of being labeled a 'capitalist roader' " (Schell 1984: 14).

In 1980, with the opening to the West, Pierre Cardin and then Halston were invited to bring their fashions to China "much in the way that experts in hydro-electric projects" were brought in as advisers on technical matters (Ibid. 158). Fourteen hundred employees from the Chinese textile and garment workers' unions in Shanghai flocked to the Halston showing:

Their reactions varied from polite admiration to outright dismay as the Halstonettes twirled about in an assortment of plunging necklines and other revealing styles. The *pieces de resistance* of the show were a see-through jumpsuit and blouse, both made of dark net, which left the audience aghast and caused one Chinese viewer to suggest that the wearers belonged in a mental hospital rather than in a fashion show. (Schell 1984: 156)

The Chinese leaders did not seem initially to appreciate the subversive role that fashion, as an expression of individualism, could play in such a society. Their ambivalence was notable; on the one hand they felt that the Chinese should be familiar with Western fashion to help modernize the Chinese textile industry, yet they confiscated the shoes and underwear that Cardin bestowed upon his Chinese floor models.

In December 1988, an art exhibit at the National Art Gallery was the first show of female nudes. Yang Yi, writing in the *China Daily*, was struck by the Chinese patrons' reactions. There were those who gaped, "feasting their eyes on female bodies"; others hurried by in horror or refused to look at all, both revealing "their excessive consciousness of sex" (1989).

There was a sense in China that "it was no longer taboo or dangerous to focus on the self" (Schell 1988: 79). At least one consequence was the development of body consciousness and the emergence of bodybuilding as a legitimate sport. The official censors tolerated public nakedness in this form, and female bodybuilders appeared in bikinis. Female bodybuilders represent a blow against the system, because they are scantily clad, and according to Schell, they are symbolic of people redirecting the "focus of their lives from society as a whole to their individual selves" (1988: 79). The Chinese Communist party, therefore, has enabled the "new man" or "new woman." Previously, one was supposed to be one of the collectivity (like the even more previous traditional sodality), that is, a group player. Again, as Schell observers, "To cultivate the distinctiveness of one's own individual consciousness bespoke an entirely different private world of concern: to cultivate the individual human body and put it on public display asserted the primacy, even the glorification, of the self " (1988: 79).

In the past five years, issues relating to different facets of privacy have been appearing in the Chinese press. A newspaper article (Xiu Jun 1990) tells the tale of a 24-year-old post office clerk in a rural area who, in 1988–89, opened and stole more than 800 pieces of other people's mail. Once his actions were revealed, he was sentenced to six years in jail, clear recognition by the legal system of individual rights. Yet, of perhaps greater interest is the fact that although many of the peasants knew what was happening, knew that their mail was being pilfered, they kept it to themselves; they did not dare inquire, not knowing that they had rights.

While people know *about* privacy, they have no consciousness of the individual right *to* privacy. But this is changing: famous people (those in the public eye) are beginning to sue for the invasion of privacy. In Beijing, couples seeking privacy prop their bicycles against one another and crawl in underneath. In Shanghai, couples who want privacy find it in the crowded rush-hour buses.

Middle school children, on the other hand, are quite concerned about such rights. A 14-year-old asks in the newspaper whether teachers should have the right to inspect school bags and desks. In middle school, he writes, students have small secrets; for example, they want to read a novel or a magazine not assigned in class, and they keep such items in their bags. The teachers, however, believe that students should read only assigned texts and to ensure this behavior, they inspect the bags and the individually allotted desk drawers. If they find the "contraband," they dispose of it. The student is quick to compliment the teacher on the latter's intentions, but he also observes that such action is psychologically unsettling to the children and asks if this action is against the law (Bian Lei 1987).

The same issue comes up with respect to students' diaries, commonly assigned in Chinese classes to improve student writing ability. A female pupil observes in hers: "The diary records our innermost thoughts, especially for our girls. We have many many secrets. Naturally I will write some of my secrets in my diary. But when our teachers often inspect our diary—that means we have to close our heart—only write something [not very important] in our diary" (Zhang Wan Hua 1987: 26). One critic points out that the teachers often betray the confidences written and create psychological havoc in so doing, but that it is allright for teachers to read the diaries; only, they should not make the material public (ibid.). Another critic insists that a diary is one's own thing; no one has the right to see it unless the person agrees. And even a lawyer writes that keeping a diary for oneself is endorsed by the law (Hua Shan 1987).

THE NEED TO REBALANCE

Over the years we have been more or less accustomed to thinking and talking about China as a very puritanical society. When speaking of some patterns of deviations in sexual behavior, we tend to say or believe that they are "uncommon" or "virtually unknown." We tend to accept or equate official denials or official disapproval of something with its low incidence or even nonexistence. (Chu 1985–86: 8)

Attitudes toward sex are indisputably changing in the "new" China, although these attitudes are being nurtured cautiously. Sex is officially condoned only in the context of marriage. Couples are warned that premarital sex is considered promiscuous and may endanger a woman's chances for marriage. Homosexual activities are officially disapproved, yet in a village in Fujian Province, a homosexual couple openly celebrated their wedding (*Tianjing Daily*, February 12, 1989). An examination of 77 court cases related to marriage shows 13 dealing with adultery, 11 with cohabitation, and 24 with premarital sex and/or pregnancy (Chu 1985–86)—all officially disapproved behaviors.

Disapproved sexual activities are cited as reflecting the "decadence" of Western society, demonstrating that individual desire is not in keeping with socialist society. American-style sexual liberation "took the 'self' as central, fanatically pursuing selfish desires" (Honig and Hershatter 1988: 115).

Despite all of the official disapprovals, books and articles on sex have blossomed in the usually puritanical press—a clear sign "that traditional policies of sexual repression are undergoing attack" (Leo 1986: 64). Moreover, the reported incidences of premarital sex are increasing.[6] Friends of classmates refuse to report sexual liaisons to the authorities. Public parks in Chinese cities have become make-out zones. In 1989, the president of one of China's premier universities sent his assistant off at night with a flashlight to beat the bushes and break up amorous couples. That same year, a graduate student was expelled when it was revealed to the authorities in his department that he was not only bedding one young woman premaritally but two.

And yet, there is also a pattern in which the boyfriend's family willingly absents the home to give the young couple intimate space, because premarital sex reduces the cost of the wedding to the boy's family (the unchaste girl is less valuable), the marriage is ensured, and the future mother-in-law gains greater control over her future daughter-in-law. In Wuhan they have coined the new term "mother's lock" (*popo shang suo*): the boy's mother locks the couple inside the bedroom to prevent an invasion of their privacy (Zhou Xiao 1989).

In addition to the contradictory signals noted above, there is raging ignorance of "how to do it." This helps to explain government publication of sex manuals. From letters to magazines, it is apparent that some do not know the most basic facts of human anatomy and physiology. One man writes, "My wife is very shy and also I don't know where the vaginal opening is. Several attempts at intercourse have failed. Could you please tell me where the opening is?" (Honig and Hershatter 1988: 182). Some women are terrified by their husbands' sexual expectations, and their fears are sometimes exacerbated by the sight of the enlarged penis (Ibid. 182).

Adolescents also suffer from a lack of sexual knowledge, permarital sexuality notwithstanding. A Shanghainese middle school student was approached by an American teaching nearby. He tried to kiss her and she drew back, fearing that she would become pregnant. He tried to explain the process of sexual intercourse, of the flow of bodies moving together. "That sounds very violent," she said. "My husband would never do that to me." He: "Many find it pleasurable." She: "But my parents have never . . ." (personal communication).

This lack of sexual know-how follows centuries of restrictions (the Communists building upon "old" China's puritanical attitudes), and it has resulted in what Yang Yi refers to as the average Chinese person's "unhealthy psychology concerning sex" (1989)—prurience counterbalanced by embarrassment and fueling the fear of learning the ropes. Married women express dissatisfaction, due at least in part to ignorant and incompetent spouses, and this is causing serious marital problems (Honig and Hershatter 1988: 182–183).

Even with adequate knowledge of sexual arousal and performance (and perhaps aggravated by it), many urban married couples are experiencing disharmonious sex lives. Their problem is "the housing problem." Because of the terrific housing shortage, many couples must delay marriage; or they may opt to live with family. This often means sharing one room with several others of multiple generations. Because living space of any kind is at such a premium, according to one informant, the primary issue is to find a place to live; secondary is the matter of privacy.

However, the combination of increasing sexual knowledge and desire with greater individual rights has led many Chinese to crave intimate space. Within the home, the only means of coping may be to create walls out of bulky pieces of furniture, a partial solution that does not give the couple auditory privacy.

The lack of intimate space may have serious consequences for the marriage. One case at a counseling center in Shanghai concerns a man and woman who have been married for ten years without pregnancy. During the first two years, they had an apparently normal sex life. Then the husband began to suffer from premature ejaculation. The counselor saw that they shared their room with the husband's brother and sister-in-law, with only a curtain to divide the room. Sexual dysfunction had become a way to control being heard. During the first two years of their marriage, when they did not share the room, their sex was successful (Zhou Yen Chang 1985).

PRIVACY MORE BROADLY DEFINED

Having begun to explore concrete elements of privacy in contemporary China, it is useful to step back a bit and take a look at privacy more broadly, as a concept that goes beyond the Chinese scene.[7] For help, I turn to environmental psychologist Irwin Altman. While he has defined privacy as "the selective control of access to the *self*" (1974: 24; my emphasis), he subsequently notes that privacy regulation involves "an individual or a group" (1977: 68)—more in keeping with my perspective. Moreover, he asserts that the "psychological viability" of the individual or group is at stake, dependent upon being able to control interactions with others. Privacy is "a dynamic and dialectic interaction with others... involving a network of behavioral mechanisms that people use to achieve desired levels of social interaction" (1977: 67). I would amend his designation of "interaction" to include a more passive sense; privacy may imply the desire to avoid exposure to the eyes or ears of others, for example the "symbolic shelter" of the veil or an out-of-view section in the house for Muslim women.

Anthropologist Christine Eickelman observes that "anthropologists, especially those concerned with the Arab and Mediterranean worlds, are increasingly recognizing the culture-bound nature of notions of 'public' and 'private' (1984: 90). In Oman, for example, the private sphere relates to the family exclusively and includes information that others are not to know, even if they know it. The family unit (the self) must regulate interaction with or exposure to outsiders (the other). Altman cites cases from the Mehinacu in Brazil, the Javanese, the Mbuti Pygmies, the Chinese in Malaysia, to illustrate his point: that cultures, individuals within cultures, and groups within cultures use verbal, nonverbal, environmental, and cultural mechanisms to make themselves accessible or inaccessible to others for privacy regulation.

Does this make privacy so universal a notion that it loses its significance? Privacy, as understood in the West, refers to the individual. Can one simply say, well, we're talking about the family, or the band, or the community, and redefine privacy to incorporate the distinction of more than one person? Is it the same notion of seclusion or withdrawal from public view, especially as the cultural understanding of public varies? These are issues we must explore as we do cross-cultural comparisons and as we reflect upon processes of culture change.

Hsu's *jen* hypothesis (1971), which presents a model for understanding the relationship between individual and society, emphasizes group identification. Such a focus is particularly applicable to "old" China. The question is whether his hypothesis can explain the impact of social change in "new" China.

Without rejecting Hsu's model, I have amended it. I have shown how one might apply a spatial model to (1) intimacy, (2) psychosocial balance, and (3) the relation of the self and other in the "old" and the "new" China. Overall, these matters help us to better examine and comprehend the relationship between the individual and society.

My ultimate focus has been on privacy in contemporary China. One area where concern with privacy is evident is individual expression, marking an important change from group consciousness. Changes in sexuality and sexual expression evidence the changing relationship of individual and group.

There are a variety of things that one can look at in examining privacy among the Chinese. For example, libido and rank have an interesting correlation for *men*. In both "old" and "new" China, highly ranked men have always had access to sexual relationships, even outside marriage. Concubinage, impossible for the poor and a status symbol for the wealthy, presented an escape for those men trapped in inimical marriages. In the "new" China, high-ranking cadres are said to use their political connections to procure new work positions for nubile women who repay them with sexual favors. These men, in both "old" and "new," have also had access to more space in which they can conduct such relationships. This enables those engaged in illicit unions to circumvent the Chinese norm: if a man and a woman are not permitted complete sexual intimacy, they should be allowed no intimacy whatsoever (Hus 1967).

Do things change for women? According to Zhou Xiao (1989), women in the "new" China continue to be owned by men, as they were in the "old" China. Traditional understandings of male-female relationships persist. To what extent is there room for an individualistically based morality? Chinese today can more easily protect their individual rights because they have a better sense of what they are, and they are coming to see that it is their right to do so. The younger generation is more aware of what is good for them and which relationships they want to protect.

In the West, there may be a place (socially and spatially) for individual privacy and sexual expression. In China, social and spatial understandings of privacy and of private behavior are not synchronous. Chinese space is encoded with generations of culture. Space has been allocated, decorated, divided up, and used, in accordance with group norms. Privacy has been encoded for the sake of the family unit. But social change is redefining the group and the individual, as well as the relationship between the two.

For social-psychological homeostasis, norms of social behavior need to be congruent with the way individuals and groups use space. Behaviors are enacted in space, they are routinized in space. The spatial environment is not simply incidental to the changes; it has been produced by the culture and it in turn reproduced that culture.

NOTES

This chapter is based upon research that I carried out while teaching at Fudan University in Shanghai, PRC, during fall 1985 and spring 1989. I read an earlier version at the session "Studies in Civilization and Culture in Honor of Francis L. K. Hsu" at the American Anthropological Association meeting, New Orleans, 1990. I am greatly indebted to my research assistant, Liu Xin Yong, without whose help none of this work would have been possible. Setha Low, Bob Rotenberg, and Gary McDonogh gave helpful comments on an earlier draft. David Cole's smarts and editorial eye have been indispensable. All errors, of course, remain my responsibility.

1. My perspective is influenced by Edward T. Hall's work on proxemics (1969) and Anthony Giddens (1984) on the incorporation of time and space into an understanding of social life. Layers 1 and 2 bear resemblance to what Giddens (1984: xxiii) refers to as practical consciousness ("All the things which actors know tacitly about how to 'go on' in the contexts of social life without being able to give them direct discursive expression") and discursive or expressible consciousness respectively.

2. In a cross-cultural overview of privacy, anthropologists John M. Roberts and Thomas Gregor (1971) suggest that the neglect of this topic may be due to variation in privacy patterns within traditional societies studied by anthropologists, and between those and modern privacy patterns.

3. See Maxine Hong Kingston (1976: 12–14) for a powerful delineation of the dangers of sex in traditional China.

4. Nicholas D. Kristof (1989) indicates that this had added to the growing disinclination of Chinese to join the Party and/or to follow the Party line.

5. Nelson Li (1988: 17) rather suggests that the front courtyard is transitional between the semipublic lane and the private home. This does not make sense to me, either in terms of location or with regard to the people who are free to use it.

6. Zhou Xiao (1989) observes that for young women, despite changing mores and social contacts, the psychological pressures to resist premarital sex are still great. Men and women fare differently in sex and marriage. Premarital sex is encouraged for men because after sex, they "possess" the woman; a woman, on the other hand, has more power before engaging in sex. As a result, men use various strategies to have their way.

7. There are a variety of common meanings of privacy, which include being alone, not being bothered, controlling access to space (Margulis 1977), and which often implicate intimate activities, such as going to the toilet. Scientific definitions deal with personal psychology, interpersonal interaction, rights of a legal or political sort. See, for example, Barrington Moore (1984) and John Roberts and Thomas Gregor (1971) for extensive discussions in an anthropological vein.

4

Rediscovering Shitamachi: Subculture, Class, and Tokyo's "Traditional" Urbanism

THEODORE C. BESTOR

The contrast between tradition and modernity is frequently and forcefully drawn in studies of Japan, as common a theme in works by Japanese as in those by foreign observers. Tradition and modernity are often seen as mutually exclusive domains of social and cultural process, existing parallel to one another and interacting only to the extent that modernity inevitably and inexorably erodes and replaces elements of a gradually disintegrating tradition. Almost by definition tradition is considered static: the dam that impedes the flow of social and cultural change, or the anvil upon which forces of modernization work. Rarely is tradition thought to be an active living part of society, created—at the same time it is put on the defensive—by the spectrum of social, cultural, political, and economic forces that shape a modern, industrial, urban society.

Yet, as Eric Hobsbawm and Terence Ranger and others have pointed out in *The Invention of Tradition* (1983), traditions are seldom (if ever) simply historical legacies. Rather, they are creations or inventions of a society at one historical moment trying to make sense of that time by drawing out putative similarities or contrasts between the present and the past. What is thought in the present to have been the common stuff of life in some previous historical moment becomes the basis of tradition, but that tradition is a culturally constructed version of the past, rather than the past itself. The creation, maintenance, and elaboration of tradition can therefore only be understood as processes reflecting the social and cultural concerns and processes of the present.

The historical development and elaboration of many of the major institutions of Japanese society offer fertile fields for examining the invention of tradition. Although few scholars of Japan have explicitly adopted the perspective developed by Hobsbawm and Ranger, the works of many scholars nevertheless illustrate the processes they discuss. To mention just a few examples, Robert J. Smith (1983, ch. 1) demonstrates the uses of imperial mythology to lend the Meiji regime in the late-nineteenth century an aura of continuity with the past and the ways in which this mythology, this tradition, was shaped and grafted onto new institutions to imbue an entirely new manner of constitutional monarchy with an ethos of sacred kingship. Wilbur Fridell's research (1973) on Shintō at the turn of the twentieth century shows the revamping of a generally uncodified and loosely organized religion into a highly structured system of beliefs and institutions that centered ideologically on the emperor and was focused organizationally on the administrative subunits of the emperor's new state. Kawamura Nozomu (1983) has argued that the normative model of the traditional Japanese family system was created in the late-nineteenth century from idealized notions about upper-class *samurai* families that were subsequently enshrined in the Meiji Constitution of 1889 and related Civil Codes. Sally Hastings (1980) and Henry D. Smith (1978) have examined the creation of new community movements in urban Japan in the 1930s as a response to urban disorder couched in ideological terms that consciously evoked the solidarity of the preindustrial village. And even the Japanese managerial and employment systems—embodying a highly disciplined labor force, company loyalty, lifetime employment, paternalistic concern for employee welfare, and great attention to quality—now touted as the most quintessential products of enduring traditional Japanese values have been shown by many researchers, including Rodney Clark (1979), Robert Cole (1971), Ronald Dore (1973), Mark Fruin (1983), and Andrew Gordon (1985), to be recent creations, established in the late-nineteenth and early-twentieth centuries as industrialization coincided with the development of modern capitalist institutions.

Microlevel analyses of traditionalism as a contemporary phenomenon—the interpretation, creation, or manipulation of contemporary ideas about the past to bestow an aura of venerability on contemporary social relations—are less common.[1] But I argue that processes of inventing or reinterpreting tradition to serve present-day needs are as important now as they were in prewar Japan, and may be as commonly found operating in the minutiae of urban daily life as in the affairs of industry and of state.

In this chapter I am interested in examining the role of tradition (and the creation or invention of tradition) in providing a sense of meaning and structure for urban life. I propose to examine Tokyo through the lens of a subcultural ethos, an ethos that embodies a model of urbanism which classifies and encapsulates particular forms of urban experience to project normative ideals for urban living. This subcultural ethos—which is derived (in ways I shall explain shortly) from the heritage of *shitamachi*, the old merchant quarters of Tokyo—both identifies and demarcates person and place across

Tokyo's vast social landscape. It provides a means for linking one segment of urban society to other segments and provides a meaning for those links. Equally it defines, structures, and gives specific content to patterns of interaction and social institutions that are found in very minute bits of social space.

This chapter focuses on three facets of the shitamachi ethos. First, I briefly discuss the long-standing division of Tokyo between two major subcultural regions: shitamachi and its opposite, yamanote.[2] Shitamachi is the old mercantile quarter of the city, still thought of as the province of shopkeepers and artisans; yamanote is the region historically defined as the samurai district of Edo (as Tokyo was known before 1868) and today considered home to the quasi-elite "new middle classes" of white-collar businessmen and bureaucrats.[3]

Second, I sketch the recent revival of interest in shitamachi and the transformation of shitamachi's image in recent years. From being a place thought, with slight disparagement, to be dull, conservative, old-fashioned, and declining, shitamachi's image has been elevated. Now it is a place portrayed in the media as exciting, yet quaintly traditional, a place where one may recover or replenish authenticity in one's life, a touchstone of cultural heritage for the modern urbanite.

Third, and finally, I suggest that ideas about shitamachi as a *place* have been conflated with ideas about shitamachi as a *way of life* to create metaphors for classifying, understanding, and responding to social stratification and differentiation throughout Tokyo. Within the context of a single tiny neighborhood—Miyamoto-chō[4]—where I have carried out intensive fieldwork, I examine how a sense of identity based on social and cultural elements nominally drawn from the shitamachi heritage, and bolstered by the current shitamachi revival, is used to create and control community life by members of the mercantile old middle class in ways that reflect the use of the shitamachi/yamanote dichotomy as an idiom for structuring and mediating questions about class.

HISTORICAL SHITAMACHI AND THE SHITAMACHI/ YAMANOTE DICHOTOMY

Tokyo, as Edo before it, is roughly divided into two large spheres: shitamachi and yamanote, the mercantile districts of the low city to the east of central Tokyo and the more elite, more residential foothills to the west. This division is not merely geographic but reflects an enduring subcultural dichotomy that is presumed to rest on profoundly different historical antecedents. During the Tokugawa period (1603–1868), when Edo was the capital of the ruling Tokugawa clan, the low city along the shore of the bay and at the mouth of the Sumida River was the commercial district, the area to which the *chōnin*, or townspeople, were legally restricted.[5] Yamanote, the hilly region to the west of the castle (now the Imperial Palace), was reserved for the lords and retainers of the ruling shogunate and the various subordinate domains.[6]

Within the mercantile low city, the townspeople developed a distinctive subculture, with great literary and artistic achievements (such as the *kabuki* theater, *ukiyo-e* woodblock prints, and *gesaku* literature), popular entertainments (for example, those provided by *geisha* of the pleasure quarters, vaudevillian *rakugo* story tellers, and *sumō* wrestlers), and aesthetic ideals quite at odds with the more austere norms of the warrior class.[7]

Similarly, the merchant quarters were characterized by forms of social organization distinct from those common in the samurai districts. Life in shitamachi was structured around ties of economic patron clientage, fictive kinship, household organization structured by economic coproduction, and close community solidarity. Social values of empathy, reciprocity, and spontaneity were idealized. Even distinctive personality types were assumed to represent shitamachi, epitomized by the *Edokko* (literally, the "child of Edo"), whose temperament stereotypically was marked by a studied nonchalance in the pursuit of hedonism, a devil-may-care bravado in the face of danger, and high disregard for financial prudence (Kata 1972).

The easygoing communalism of shitamachi stood in sharp contrast to the more stoic, restrained, and rigidly defined social style of the samurai in yamanote. The code that governed life in yamanote deemphasized residential community in favor of feudal clan as the relevant framework for social action. It stressed one's set obligations and devotion to one's fixed position within an enduring hierarchical structure of family and clan and encouraged the subordination of individual emotions and the careful regulation of individual behavior to formally maintain the outward signs of one's proper station in life.[8]

With the fall of the Tokugawa regime and the establishment of the new Meiji government in 1868, the demography, social structure, and social geography of Edo—renamed Tokyo by the new government—were radically transformed (H. D. Smith 1986). In the early years of the Meiji period (1868–1912), feudal restrictions on class mobility, occupation, residence, and many other aspects of life were rapidly abolished or undermined; the city suffered a drastic though temporary population decline as the feudal lords and their retinues permanently returned to their home provinces; and the formal systems of regulation that had created shitamachi and yamanote as social categories linked to specific geographical regions ceased to have effect.

As social and cultural categories, however, the distinctions continued, albeit with modification. In popular thinking, shitamachi changed only slightly. Though the boundaries of what was considered shitamachi expanded and its population greatly increased, the region remained the province of small shopkeepers, craftspeople, the artists and entertainers who had created the popular culture and recreation of Edo, day laborers, small factory owners, and other diverse members of a steadfastly plebeian subculture proudly self-assured of their urbane sophistication.

Both as a place and as a social category, yamanote underwent greater transformations than did shitamachi; yamanote retained its image as home to the elite, but the nature of elite status and the content of elite life-styles changed considerably. Whereas samurai attained their status by hereditary ascription, the social heirs of the samurai classes were the government bureaucrats, the political leaders, the businessmen, and the educated professionals whose positions were achieved through education, entrepreneurship, and bureaucratic advancement. Yamanote was gradually transformed into the district of the new upper and middle classes, willing to adopt or adapt Western material culture, whose lives centered around the new economic, political, and social institutions that drove Japan's industrialization and modernization.

Today, both shitamachi and yamanote have spread far beyond their classical geographic boundaries. Most of the low-lying land along Tokyo Bay and on the deltas of the Sumida and Edogawa rivers is now generally considered to be shitamachi or at least to resemble it. The entire western fringe of Tokyo and the new suburbs stretching miles beyond are all encompassed within the contemporary meaning of yamanote. In popular thinking, yamanote is home to the white-collar organization men who are so often thought to epitomize contemporary Japan, the new middle-class elite (if that is not a contradiction in terms). Shitamachi is home to the old middle class: small-scale shopkeepers and wholesalers, industrial subcontractors, artisans, and owners of small factories. Shitamachi is a crowded, old-fashioned place, noted for the intimacy and informality of community life, a life centered around numerous local voluntary organizations, such as chōkai (or neighborhood associations), and punctuated by boisterous, enthusiastic local events such as festivals (matsuri) for shintō tutelary deities. The emphasis on traditional norms of social reciprocity and the open, emotional informality of the old middle-class residents of shitamachi are in direct contrast to the formal reserve thought to characterize the more "modern," "rational," apparently more affluent, and less community-oriented lifestyles of the sarariiman ("salaryman") households who make yamanote their home.

But historically and even in the present, the division was not simply one of class, nor degree of Westernization along a simple bipolar continuum. Shitamachi and yamanote embodied different cultural orientations, and throughout the late nineteenth century and well into the present century shitamachi and yamanote offered equally viable but quite distinct subcultures of urbanism (R. J. Smith, 1960; Dore 1958: 11–14). These separate cultural and social configurations offered alternative modes of urban living both for those born and bred in Tokyo and for migrants. In particular, the more conservative and overtly traditional shitamachi variant of urbanism provided a model for living, a guide to the nature of urban life, that served as a major path of assimilation to urban life for rural migrants (R. J. Smith 1960; J. W. White 1982).

From the perspective of the present, nineteenth- and early-twentieth-century shitamachi possesses an aura of historical continuity with the feudal past, but recent research (e.g., Ogi 1980; H. D. Smith 1986) has shown that much of what is now considered to be "traditional" about shitamachi customs, attitudes and values, styles of consumption, and social relations was in fact created during the Meiji period, shaped in response to shifting balances of social, cultural, economic, and political power in late-nineteenth-century Tokyo. Increasingly, the cultural center of gravity of urbanism was shifting away from the *chōnin*, the townspeople, into the hands of a new Westernizing elite. This group, without ties to the old city of Edo, began to shape and define new norms of urban life, and from the beginning of this century shitamachi increasingly came to be thought of as a distinctive mode of life, a variant of urbanism set apart from the mainstreams of contemporary life rather than as the norm.

As the twentieth century progressed, the continued existence of shitamachi as a distinctive, coherent, cohesive, integrated way of life—as an ongoing subculture—was undermined on two fronts. On the one hand, society's modernization increasingly elevated the yamanote version of urbanism at the expense of shitamachi's as the formal bureaucratic institutions of the nation-state and the developing corporate forms of economic organization increasingly became dominant forces in society, shaping education, the employment system, family institutions, and consumption patterns accordingly. Physically, the classic shitamachi region was almost totally destroyed and its population dispersed in the two great disasters of Tokyo's twentieth-century history: the 1923 Kanto earthquake and the American incendiary air raids of 1945, both of which took their heaviest tolls in the old, densely populated shitamachi districts (Seidensticker 1983; Saotome 1971).

Research on shitamachi life-styles in the decades immediately after World War II clearly suggested that the cultural and social norms of the low city were part of an older order passing away in the face of unyielding pressure from the modernizing present (Dore 1958; R. J. Smith 1960). Robert J. Smith argued that in feudal and early modern times multiple traditions of urban life coexisted, but that this multiplicity could not last much longer (1960: 54). The heterogeneity of urban life-styles was inexorably diminishing, with the shitamachi version losing ground to the yamanote version exemplified by Japan's "new middle class" (Vogel 1971). To borrow terms from linguistics and computer science, in the twentieth century shitamachi shifted from being the unmarked or default value of urbanism to being the marked or optional value. Yet even as shitamachi became increasingly marked as something special—something out of the ordinary—nevertheless, the distinction between shitamachi and its opposite remained among the most fundamental social, subcultural, and geographic demarcations in contemporary Tokyo.

THE SHITAMACHI REVIVAL

Predictions of the demise of shitamachi seemed to be borne out during much of the 1960s and 1970s. As a whole—in city and countryside alike—Japanese society increasingly adopted or emulated the social and cultural norms of the new middle class.[9] Many Japanese social scientists and commentators argued that traditional bases of social stratification were disappearing. Murakami Yasusuke, an economist and well-known social critic, has argued that there has been a homogenization of values, attitudes, and behavior, and a diminishment of social-structural criteria for differentiation within Japanese society, which cross-cut and mitigate against the formation or perception of class stratification (1982). In his view, worker and capitalist, farmer and shopkeeper, old middle class and new, have merged into what he terms the "new middle mass."

But reports of shitamachi's death were paradoxically premature. Just as the "new middle mass" society, created in part by the role of the mass media and mass consumption in shaping both material demands and social values, was becoming predominant, the mass media and mass marketers discovered "tradition." In recent years, as the markedness of shitamachi life—its separateness from the daily experiences of most urban Japanese—increased, so too did its appeal. Its specialness, its "traditionality" in itself became a selling point. Attention to the shitamachi way of life has increased—dare I say it?—markedly.

Throughout the shitamachi wards of Tokyo today there is a renaissance of shitamachi consciousness, and the media of Tokyo actively promote this shitamachi boom. In the past several years, the shelves of bookstores have been freighted with newly published volumes on shitamachi (e.g., Kata 1980). Guidebooks to old shops, old neighborhoods, and "traditional" events are hot items.[10] One shitamachi ward—Taitō-ku, where Dore carried out his research on "Shitayama-chō" (1958)—has opened an elaborate shitamachi museum complete with reconstructed shop fronts and house interiors from the early twentieth century. In another shitamachi ward, Sumida-ku, the local government promotes mini-museums—some no larger than a couple of rooms—to display and preserve the traditions of shitamachi life. One I visited in the home of a construction contractor was devoted entirely to his massive collection of the tiny paper stickers, called *senjafuda*, which devotees glue on the gateways and pillars of shrines and temples to announce their visits and display their piety or advertise their names.[11] Festivals in the shitamachi districts are now thronged not only by camera-wielding spectators from outside, but by eager participants who travel across Tokyo dressed in brand-new "traditional" shitamachi garb,[12] anxious to join in a real shitamachi festival.

On the border of Bunkyō-ku and Taitō-ku, not far from Shitayama-chō where Ronald Dore carried out research for his classic work, *City Life in Japan* (1958), a similar neighborhood of old wooden houses dating from the early decades of the twentieth century—one of the very few remaining clusters of pre-war wooden architecture to survive in Tokyo today—has gained fame for itself (and has drawn steady streams of nostalgic visitors) by publishing a "little magazine" devoted to recording local history and lore, celebrating the virtues of traditional domestic architecture and the forms of community life that presumably characterized the old shitamachi of low, densely packed wooden homes lining narrow alleyways.

And, not surprisingly, shitamachi has become an advertising motif, as have other symbols of traditions linked to local or regional identity throughout Japan. During the summer of 1986, when I returned to Tokyo after an absence of several years, advertising posters throughout the subway and train systems, and on street corners all over the city, promoted shitamachi pure and simple. Sponsored by the ward governments of shitamachi areas like Taitō-ku, the messages sold no products; they simply sold the notion that for fun, for excitement, for a good time in the simple yet sophisticated ways of the old demimonde, one should come home to shitamachi. The appeal seems incongruous in the midst of the postmodernist glitz of Tokyo,[13] but it seemingly strikes a chord as much with the synthetic nostalgia of the young (perhaps generated by the mass media[14]) as with the more heartfelt reminiscences of those who may actually remember life—both good and bad—in the "real" shitamachi before the end of the Second World War.[15]

Commercial products are also imbued with overtones of the shitamachi ethos. One television advertisement broadcast throughout the fall of 1988 is illustrative; it is an ad for a large chain of stores that specializes in *bentō*, the inexpensive box lunches that many commuters purchase daily from shops clustered around railway stations. This ad sells two varieties of lunches: one lunch consists of boiled rice, pickled vegetables, seafood, and meats prepared with heavy soy sauces; the other contains a hard roll, a small green salad, fried chicken, and a pasta salad. The commercial's spokesperson for the first lunch is a young woman dressed in "traditional" festival garb, standing in front of a *mikoshi* (a festival palanquin), speaking in the staccato dialect of old Tokyo. The spokesperson for the second is a young woman dressed in woolen sweater and pearl necklace, standing in a book-lined study, speaking in the elegant formality of Tokyo's upper-class dialect. Of course, the first lunch is called the Shitamachi Bentō, whereas the second is the Yamanote Bentō, priced at about one hundred yen more, as if issues of social and economic status needed further underlining. On one level, this shitamachi renaissance is simply a phenomenon of "new-middle-mass" society. In promoting the low city as a place to go, a place to have fun, a place to shop, a place to get in touch with one's "roots," shitamachi has been fetishized. It has become yet another commodity to be consumed; its consumption enables one to embellish one's social identity through self-conscious, vicarious participation in a "life-style," in this instance one replete with overtones of a rich and evocative history.[16]

But, in other ways, the reemergence of shitamachi as an eponym for an idealized way of urban life has consequences beyond simply creating a setting against which to try on an identity, a transitory emulation of a life-style.

SHITAMACHI AS AN ORDERING PRINCIPLE FOR COMMUNITY AND CLASS

Over the past decade I have carried out research on community life in a Tokyo neighborhood that I call Miyamoto-chō. It is a neighborhood far from the historical shitamachi districts, but thought by many of its residents to resemble shitamachi in its social character. By this I think they mean to attribute to themselves the qualities of friendly, open, informal interactions within the context of a rich community social life. This communal activity centers around local institutions such as the chōkai (the neighborhood association), the volunteer fire brigade, and the local Shintō shrine. It is sustained by such things as a pervasive sense of reciprocity within local relationships, feelings of obligations to serve communal interests that motivate many local activists, and the sheer excitement generated by the neighborhood's annual *matsuri*, or festival. All these are stereotypical hallmarks of life in the low city, and it is with these that I think Miyamoto-chō's residents wish to identify their community (and of course themselves). Those who proclaim most strongly the shitamachi character of Miyamoto-chō are members of the local old middle class, the many shopkeepers, self-employed artisans, and operators of tiny industrial workshops for whom the neighborhood is both home and workplace.

There are many white-collar families in Miyamoto-chō, and relations between them and the households of the members of the old middle class are almost unfailingly cordial and even close at times. But nevertheless, Miyamoto-chō as it is constituted through local institutions and as it is conceived of in the thinking of most residents is a neighborhood of, by, and for the established local merchants and manufacturers. It is they who hold the leadership positions. It is they who define the goals and set the agendas for local activities and organizations. It is they who can manipulate their community standing to further their own economic and political ends—both public *and* private—within and outside the neighborhood. And in the final analysis it is they who implicitly determine who is to be considered a full-fledged participant in local life.

In setting the local agenda and in deciding who is to be included, leaders of Miyamoto-chō routinely make use of the shitamachi/yamanote dichotomy as an ordering principle, both to classify themselves and others but also to legitimate their own positions, their own dominance of local affairs. Even within the cramped confines of Miyamoto-chō's borders (which encircle an area of less than one-tenth of a square kilometer) the shitamachi/yamanote distinction is applied. Contrasting the dense commercial and industrial section of Miyamoto-chō on the valley floor with the neat domesticity of the more exclusively residential blocks on the hillside where more of the white-collar households live, local residents often refer to the neighborhood as being divided between shitamachi and yamanote. Residents regularly link these differences in outward appearance and residents' stereotypical occupations to the greater subcultural dichotomy of Tokyo. In suggesting that this distinction holds even within the tiny neighborhood, residents underscore the notions that the households of white-collar salaried workers are less concerned with neighborly ties and are less involved in neighborhood organizations and that the self-employed entrepreneurs of the neighborhood's flatlands interact more intimately with their neighbors and are more likely to be active participants in sustaining neighborhood life.

Of course these characterizations may be nothing more than a self-fulfilling prophecy, but that is beside the point. The insistence on categorizing residents of the neighborhood and basing access to particpation and influence on this categorical classification, must be understood, I argue, in terms of many of the same social and cultural dynamics that have shaped the changing fortunes and images of shitamachi and yamanote throughout Tokyo. As shitamachi lost out in the shifting balance of cultural power throughout much of the twentieth century, so too did the old middle class come to be seen as outmoded and irrelevant to the economic, political, and social life of Japan as a whole. As the mainsprings of the domestic Japanese economy shifted away from small-scale enterprises and individual entrepreneurship toward large-scale corporations and bureaucratic management, so too did the new middle-class life-style of the organization man and his family come to be seen as the norm, if not as a statistical norm at least as a normative ideal toward which most Japanese were presumed to be orienting themselves.

Paradoxically, in the face of this process—this homogenization of urban life-styles into the "new middle mass"—the increasing perception of the specialness, the markedness, of the shitamachi variant of urbanism enables shitamachi to be represented as the "authentic" version of urban life. This permits, within Miyamoto-chō and elsewhere, those who can lay some claim to the shitamachi version to assert—with a muted, but almost moral sense of superiority—that they and the social and cultural patterns and institutions they represent constitute an "authentic" and distinctly "traditional" way of life, which has slipped away from most urban Japanese. That is, they are culturally legitimate, even if thought to be economically marginal.

Even in a neighborhood like Miyamoto-chō, which has *no* historical links to the classic shitamachi (Bestor 1985; 1989, ch. 2), the ability to appropriate and manipulate the cultural symbolism of the shitamachi ethos constitutes an important social resource. It enables leaders and partisans of Miyamoto-chō's institutions and communal ideology to legitimate both the present form of community life and their own authority to lead and represent the neighborhood.[17]

The claim to "authenticity" based on "tradition" is in a sense unassailable in its own terms, and therefore those neighborhood leaders—the small shopkeepers—who can control that "tradition" in its local manifestations are equally unassailable in their claims to leadership. That is, the legitimacy of the community and its institutions can only be challenged by those who deny the authenticity, the cultural legacy, of the shitamachi ethos—for example, by members of the Communist party, whose views on class dynamics suggest a less flattering history of shitamachi than its usual portrayal, or by members of religious groups opposed to the mingling of Shintō ritual into community activities. Few are willing to take this radical stand against the weight of tradition, especially as the shitamachi/yamanote dichotomy remains such a pervasive cultural ordering principle within Tokyo. The recent shitamachi renaissance, promoted in part by the mass media, has only added extra weight to assertions of shitamachi's privileged position as the authentic font of urban life.

In this brief chapter I have been unable to present much of the complex texture of social life in Miyamoto-chō around which assertions of "authenticity" revolve, nor have I been able to do more than allude to the historically rich and culturally sophisticated life of shitamachi during the past several centuries. Nevertheless I have tried to suggest ways in the invention of tradition, in this instance a subcultural tradition shaped by and shaping the broader historical changes that affect the city, breathes life into organizing principles that structure social life both at the macrolevel of the metropolis and at the level of the tiniest corner of the city, serving as a metaphor for—and imposing a cultural order on—social differentiation.

NOTES

This chapter is based on both informal observations and formal fieldwork in Tokyo over a number of years: during 1974–76 as a language student supported by a National Defense Foreign Language Fellowship; during 1979–81 when I was conducting doctoral fieldwork generously supported by the Japan Foundation, the National Science Foundation (grant number BNS 7910179), the National Institute of Mental Health (fellowship number MH 08059), and the Joint Committee on

Japanese Studies of the Social Science Research Council (U.S.) and the American Council of Learned Societies. Additional information was collected during three subsequent shorter visits: in September 1983, with support from Sigma Xi; during the summer of 1984, made possible by the Japan Foundation and the Wenner-Gren Foundation for Anthropological Research; and during the summer of 1986, with support from Columbia University and the Northeast Asia Council of the Association for Asian Studies. I am grateful to each of these organizations for their support. Eyal Ben-Ari, Brian Moeran, James Valentine, and especially Victoria Lyon-Bestor made innumerable valuable suggestions, a few of which I accepted. Of course, I am solely responsible for the conclusions reported here.

1. Brian Moeran's study (1984) of a Japanese pottery village caught up by the folk craft boom is one example of research that links the dynamics of social structure at a very microlevel to present-day constructions of tradition and authenticity. William Kelly (1986) examines idealizations of the past as they are created in and shape the dynamics of family and community life in a Japanese agricultural community.

2. Literally, *shitamachi* means "lower town," with the historical implication of the town beneath the castle walls." Edward Seidensticker (1983) calls shitamachi the "low city." *Yamanote* literally means foothills.

3. In popular imagery, both among Japanese and among foreign journalists, today's new middle class *sarariiman* ("salaryman") is the cultural successor of the samurai, "a samurai with a briefcase." This image was used in the 1960s as a slogan by a major Japanese industrial group to epitomize the spirit of their employees. The metaphor has been used repeatedly by foreign journalists writing about Japan's vigorous foreign trade.

4. Miyamoto-chō is a pseudonym for a community in which I conducted research in 1979–81 and during the summers of 1983, 1984, and 1986. For additional information on Miyamoto-chō, see Theodore Bestor (1985, 1989).

5. Extremely detailed sumptuary regulations governed virtually all aspects of life during the Tokugawa period. Strict residential segregation by class and by occupation was imposed, as were proscriptions regarding appropriate styles of architecture, clothing, coiffures for both men and women, pastimes, entertainments, and the like (see for example, Coaldrake 1981). The basis for class distinction was the neo-Confucian division of society among four estates, ranked according to merit and productive contributions to society. As rulers, samurai were accorded the highest ranks; because they produced rice, the true source of all wealth and welfare, peasants were nominally ranked second; artisans, also productive members of society, were third; merchants—mere parasites existing on the labor of others—were last. Artisans and merchants were generally lumped together as *chōnin*, or townspeople. Not counted among the townspeople, and existing outside the four-tiered ranking system, were priests and outcasts, but both groups were nonetheless well represented in the urban population.

6. This type of social and spatial segregation was a typical feature of *jōkamachi* (literally, "town beneath the castle") during the Tokugawa period. Castle towns were the most important type of city throughout the late feudal period. John W. Hall (1955) provides an overview of structure and functions of castle towns in the political and economic systems of Tokugawa Japan. James McClain's works (1980,

1982) give a detailed picture of class distinctions and social life in Kanazawa, one of the largest and most prosperous provincial castle towns.

7. Andrew Markus (1985) provides a vivid account of plebeian entertainments in Edo.

8. It is important, however, to recognize that even though the social norms and the organization of domestic units differed greatly between shitamachi and yamanote, the two subcultures constantly interpenetrated each other during the preindustrial era. For example, Edwin McClellan's fascinating account (1985) of the life of the samurai avant garde of Edo demonstrates that the culture of shitamachi's demimonde was central to their aesthetic and intellectual pursuits and that at least some samurai comported themselves with less than proper feudal dignity.

9. For example, see Kelly (1986) for a discussion of the dynamics of new middle-class values in a rural setting in northern Japan.

10. English examples of this genre include Enbutsu Sumiko (1984) and Paul Waley (1984).

11. Nishiyama Matsunosuke et al. (1984: 357) describe the origins, history, and use of these votive stickers in Edo during the Tokugawa period. Their recent return to popularity has now led some shrines to post signs asking that people refrain from putting up these stickers.

12. The now de rigueur costume for festival participants is a knee-length cotton overcoat (happi), a headband (hachimaki) twisted from a cotton hand towel (tenugui), a set of black, tight-fitting leggings and vest (donburi), and straw sandals (zōri) worn with or without white cloven-toed stockings (tabi). Much of this costume is based on the characteristic garb of Edo period carpenters and firemen. Local residents participating in the festival of their own community normally wear garments emblazoned with the name of the shrine or neighborhood whose festival it is. Festival aficionados—of whom there are many—often belong to clubs that travel the city inviting themselves into local festivals, wearing their clubs' designated costumes. The presence of outsiders is often a source of tension, as in the neighborhood where I have conducted research. The solutions in this case were to restrict participation in the festival to those wearing the neighborhood's costume and to restrict access to the costume (which is sold or rented by the local neighborhood association, but only available if one places an order with a local official several weeks ahead of time).

13. The postmodernist vision of Tokyo, combining high-tech internationalism with a playful appreciation of vernacular tradition, can be seen in the exhibition catalogue for *Tokyo: Form and Spirit* (Freedman 1986).

14. See Jennifer Robertson (1986) for a discussion of nostalgia and the concept of *furusato* ("hometown") as an advertising and political catchphrase. Also see Kelly (1986).

15. Several years ago the Shitamachi Museum—the Taitōkuritsu Shitamachi Fū-zoku Shiryōkan—held an exhibition featuring life in shitamachi during the Second World War, a potentially horrific subject, given that shitamachi was the target of the firebombing of March 10, 1945, in which an estimated 150,000 to 200,000 people were immolated (Saotome 1971; Daniels 1975). Among the displays was a life-sized recreation of a tiny hut built of twisted sheet metal and other debris, typical of the housing that sprung up in the aftermath of the raids. As I examined the exhibit, an elderly woman with a small child in tow rushed up and excitedly told the child she

had lived in just such a place and explained how she had hulled black-market rice in an ungainly-looking device just like that shown in the display: a large sake bottle fitted with a wooden plunger, which served as a crude mortar and pestle. As she turned away, she exclaimed, "*Ara! Natsukashii!*" No translation quite catches the flavor, but perhaps "Ah! What memories . . ."

16. The Japanese critic Yamazaki Masakazu (1984) has coined the term "soft individualism" (*yawarakai kojinshugi*) to describe the sense of self and identity that comes from consumption of goods and the process of creating a social identity through the kinds (and brands) of goods one consumes.

17. As Aoyagi Kiyotaka has pointed out (1983), the strengthening of neighbor-hood associations and the increasing emphasis on traditional forms of community life, such as festivals, are widespread phenomena, not simply something restricted to Miyamoto-chō.

Part II

Place in the City

5

We Have Always Lived Under the Castle: Historical Symbols and the Maintenance of Meaning

JOHN MOCK

As Japan has moved from a feudal state to a modern, industrialized society, the structure and meaning of urban public space has also shifted. A very large number of approaches has been used to describe and analyze these changes in structure and meaning. Denise Lawrence and Setha Low (1990) list 395 references in their excellent bibliographic essay on spatial form. The approach taken in this chapter closely follows the earlier work of Robert Smith (1960, 1973), seeking to trace the multiple strands of popular images that combine to form the meaning of public space. The objects of this chapter are simply to examine how some urban spaces can serve to symbolize the populace's identity and goals and, second, to identify some of the conditions leading to the maintenance, loss, or development of public meaning of urban spaces.

While modern Hikone provides a large number of public places that could be utilized to outline the changes in cultural meaning of urban places, only a few can be discussed here. First, the town will be described in its historical context and then in modern terms, with comparisons made between the two. Then follows a discussion of the maintenance of cultural meaning as it pertains to these different urban spaces and Hikone as a whole.

In the not so distant past, one could first see the castle on stepping out of the train station in Hikone. Castle Hill rose above the surrounding town and rice fields, dominating the scene. The stone and white clay castle perched on the hill was built in the beginning of the seventeenth century. At that time, the whole hill was covered by a network of walls and other structures comprising the middle layers of the castle defense system. The great stone walls and two of the three moats remain, along with the central donjon that so dominates the city. While not so graceful as the famous White Heron castle of Himeji, Hikone castle does have a wonderful three-part curved roof, and the entire building has been designated a national treasure.

At the foot of the castle is an Edo-period strolling and scenery garden, one of the more famous gardens in a prefecture noted for its gardens and a museum built as an exact replica of the original manor and administrative building directly at the base of the main approach to the castle. The great, gray-tiled roofs of this complex are visible from a considerable distance as is the castle donjon itself, up on top of the hill. The castle has been the primary symbol of the city since its completion in 1622.

The city of Hikone was an important castle town in the Tokugawa period (1600–1868), a period when the castle towns, *jōkamachi*, were the focal point of nonagrarian activity (Kornhauser 1976: 143). It was the administrative and judicial seat of the fief ruled by the Ii family, one of the closest supporters of the Tokugawa shogunate. When the Ii family was given the Hikone fief, the castle was built on the central hill, and the population that lived at the foot of the hill was moved away to make room for the samurai and their families that made up the military, judicial, and administrative apparatus of the fief. The personal disruption of this movement was, of course, enormous, with whole families and farming systems being relocated. Even more of a disruption was the diversion of the entire course of the Seri River to allow for the creation of the three rings of moats around the castle and to prevent the tow area from flooding. This was a common practice in the building of Edo-period castle towns (Fujioka 1980, 147–148). The river itself became, in effect, a fourth moat.

This ability to move heaven and earth for their purposes was indicative of the fact that the power of the feudal lord, the Daimyo, was enormous— very close to absolute within the fief. The fief of Hikone, rated at 350,000 *koku* of rice, was the eleventh largest fief in Japan (a koku of rice was the amount of rice considered necessary to support a human for a year, 4.9629 bushels). Moreover, the town and lands ruled by the Ii family controlled the northern end of Lake Biwa, the largest lake in Japan, and one of the primary routes between Kyoto and the Tokugawa capital of Edo.

During the Edo period, the castle represented the authority of the Ii family, who dominated the town and the whole end of the lake, both administratively and militarily. With its massive physical structure and prominent position, the castle symbolized that power in a very graphic way. The very stones of the walls attested to the power of the lord who could order such boulders moved and formed an unyielding maze, impenetrable and unforgiving. The musket and arrow ports, interspersed with barred and shuttered widows, frowned down upon the belittled citizenry from the commanding height of the mountain. Even the architecture of the castle, rigid stone topped by fireproof clay walls and the massive tile roof, could be seen as being rigid and inflexible. These characteristics of rigidity and inflexibility are in direct contrast with all of the other buildings in the town, wooden structures built by the post-and-beam technique that is noted for its grace, flexibility, and fluidity of space (Kawashima 1986: Blaser 1958: Sadler 1962: Drexler 1966).

During the Edo period, the boundaries of the different neighborhoods were defined, in part, by the moats surrounding the castle. The area between the inner moat and the middle moat had housed barracklike structures for the middle-ranking samurai who maintained their permanent homes, with their families, outside the outer moat and even beyond the Seri River. The area between the middle and outer moats housed the thousand top-ranking samurai and some of the townsmen, *chōnin*. Outside the outer moat were the footsoldiers and more townsmen. There were even some townsmen and very low-ranking soldiery beyond the Seri River (Hikone Castle Museum 1989). Farmers were spread out in tiny hamlets. The small commoner hamlets by the lake combined fishing and farming.

With the advent of the Meiji Restoration, the character of the neighborhoods rapidly shifted as the samurai were deprived of their privileges and stipends and the merchant class asserted its economic strength (Ross 1973). The narrow streets lined with buildings in solid rows bustled with economic and social activity. In the old part of town, many of the buildings had small enterprises in the front, at street level, with living quarters occupying the rear and second floors. These living areas were quite small, and everyday life—from raising children to chatting with the neighbors—spilled out onto the street. The open areas provided by temples and shrines in the neighborhood were also included in the social bustle of day-to-day life. Beyond the outer moat, to the south was farmland. The new railway station was built in the early Meiji period to the east of the castle, several hundred meters beyond the outer moat.

As the functional fourth moat, the Seri River marked the edge of town. An openly accessible public space, it would have been the scene of both work and recreation. It was important as a source of water for farming as well as other work. The changing of the course of the river and the building of levees would have improved the lives of city residents, and they might have felt beholden to the lord for that. Even so, the river was still a sizable natural threat, and even as late as Showa 36 (1961) storms and flooding tore away bridges, reminding residents of how the river, despite its benefits, hampered movement in the town and posed a threat to their lives. Even so, the river was one of the few public spaces truly "belonging" to the people, in that they were the ones that used it and occupied it.

One other public area needs to be mentioned in this context, Lake Biwa itself. The lake was seen as a place of considerable danger because of its storms, but it also had economic benefits—fishing, ease of transport, and the limitless amount of fresh water available for all sorts of purposes. Much of the old castle defense network was tied into the lake itself with the network of formal moats strongly reinforced by the morass of impenetrable swamps and wetlands lying to the north of the castle.

Historically, then, the castle, with its associated garden and buildings, clearly was the most prominent symbol of the city. It represented the power of the Ii family as Lords of Hikone. In contrast, the river, the lake, the streets of neighborhoods, the open areas of the temples and shrines and, later, the yards of the new public school system, were all spaces that combined functional importance with symbolic for the populace, providing them with a sense of identity.

Like most cities in Japan, Hikone has undergone a rapid urbanization and expansion in its journey to the present day. During this time of rapid change and shifting of cultural symbols, Hikone has managed not only to maintain older symbols, although their meaning has changed, but it has created new symbols with meaning to complement the new cultural forms. It is this maintenance and development of meaning that have probably made Hikone a city with a strong identity and making it likely to survive the loss of identity that accompanies the sprawling effect of larger urban centers.

Since the Meiji period, the city has grown to a population of 100,000. The core of the city is being modernized in efforts to joint the modern image of Japan, while still being heavily interlaced with historic buildings and now, historic reconstructions. Surrounding suburban areas, the "new towns," as they are called, are made up of neighborhoods founded on a whole different way of life than that of the old neighborhoods. In each of these settings, the public spaces have either lost, retained, or gained new cultural meaning.

The modern castle has lost much of its authority and grim domination of the skyline; still prominent, it has lost its threatening and overbearing aspects. Most of the buildings on top of Castle Hill have decayed, collapsed, or been taken down; the effect of those retaining walls which remain is softened by the large trees that grow near them, and the castle donjon perches quite alone on the top. The symbolism is different because of these changes. As one informant put it, when she first learned she was going to move to Hikone, she was quite apprehensive. However, when she arrived in Hikone and saw the castle, familiar from school textbooks, perched on the castle hill, she felt welcomed, almost as if she had just come home.

Without the oppressive overtones of the military dictatorship that ruled Japan for more than two and a half centuries, the castle now has far more of a whimsical feel to it, with several residents expressing sentiments such as the following: "The castle is really the mark of Hikone. It sits up on the top of the hill like something out of a story or a movie. It makes Hikone seem to be a much more friendly town. My son says that it is really a Chinese dragon, sleeping."

Japanese culture also includes a strong reverence for history. The fact that every Japanese schoolchild learns about Hikone and the Ii family makes the symbolic power of the castle even more pervasive; it makes it a national symbol. Even the English-language version of the *Kodansha Encyclopedia of Japan* uses the city of Hikone and Hikone Castle as classic examples of a castle town, jōkamachi, and castle. Several residents said that they felt at home immediately in Hikone because they had studied about the role Hikone and the Ii family played in Japan's history when they were back in junior high school. This, in a way, makes Hikone a national hometown, or *furosato*, a very romanticized and poignant symbol in a newly mobilizing society.

The castle represents a continuity with the past and is a strong reminder to the citizens of Hikone of the day-to-day connection between Hikone's past and present. Indeed, the schoolchildren of Hikone are reminded of this every day, even if passively, as the castle is visible from almost every schoolyard. This continuity is a sign of a foundation of healthy roots that must have been a source of a certain amount of comfort to the residents during the last few decades of accelerated change in Japan.

Unlike the castle, with its hordes of visitors, the garden is visited only by a relatively small group of residents on a regular basis. While it is far less popular in terms of attendance, the garden appears to be just as representative as the castle of Hikone, and it appears on virtually all of the informational materials about Hikone. The city of Hikone further promotes the popularity of the castle and the garden by giving away, on a regular basis, tickets through the local newspaper. This is an important policy, as it ensures that the castle, museum, and garden do not become merely an attraction for people from outside the city, that the citizens of Hikone continue to see them as their own, part of their heritage.

While the castle clearly represents Hikone, particularly its historical past, the plaza in front of the station with its modernistic fountains and stonework, clearly represents the town's present and its image of the future. The plaza is surrounded by buildings with modern storefronts, partly roofed for pedestrian convenience, and has the latest in shiny plastic, tile, and glass. These replace the old wooden-fronted buildings that faced onto a narrow street. The old buildings had poor light and were cluttered; they were described as "dirty" and "dark." In direct contrast, the new plaza, all built since 1975, is described as *kirei*, a word that means both "clean" and "pretty." The station plaza represents the new, progressive Hikone. To some of the residents, this is a great idea, and they are very proud of the new symbolism. Others are not so happy about it: they see the newly designed and constructed areas as being too slick, too modernistic, not bucolic enough. For this latter group, the new design symbolizes the fast-paced Japan of the great cities, an idea not necessarily positive for people who have chosen to live in a city of 100,000 people.

The streets and the neighborhoods have also changed both their function and their symbolic importance. The old neighborhoods have maintained some of their original architecture and design, but the open drains have been mostly covered and the old buildings are rapidly being replaced. The outer moat of the castle has also been converted to a storm drain to the east of the castle and a small open canal to the south, thereby removing a barrier between neighborhoods. Further, many of the merchants have moved out of the residential neighborhoods to crowd the commercial roads with establishments that are not connected to their residences. Thus, the older houses no longer have so many of the commercial functions, and the spaces previously devoted to that purpose now are used for social purposes or other functions such as places to put one's automobile at night. In the older neighborhoods, however, many of the social patterns have still been maintained. This is particularly notable in the continuance of neighborhood festivals. The houses are still quite small and the street is used as an extension of the households for day-to-day living (Mock 1989).

The streets themselves are the site of the festivals and have a cultural meaning of identity for the residents. In the old neighborhoods, the streets are still used for a great deal of everyday life: child rearing, socializing, working. The streets are extensions of and the interconnection between households. On the roads that can accommodate car traffic, some of the activities are not possible, but one of the symbolic functions of the festivals is to reestablish the streets as belonging to the neighborhood, and for that period the cars do not have priority on the streets. This cultural meaning ascribed to the neighborhood streets is something not fully shared in the new neighborhoods (Mock 1988).

Each neighborhood has a neighborhood association, which, while not carrying the political clout it once had (Mock 1980: Bestor 1989), is responsible for a lot of the grass-roots organization and care for the city that in other places would be done by municipal authority (Brown 1976). For example, the neighborhood association is a means of disseminating information, through the monthly watches, maintaining public spaces, running matsuri and other activities, and running the Children's Association, which in turn is in charge of such things as raising funds through recycling and activities for the children, for example, field trips and gatherings (Bestor 1985).

A great deal of social activity in Japan is centered around the workplace and is divided along gender lines. The neighborhood association provides a time for these boundaries to be broken down, at least within certain limits, because people of very different social class or background may not choose to participate, women tend to spend most of their time with the children at the big gatherings, and men gather into drinking circles. Despite this, or maybe because of this, the neighborhood association is thought of by many as a very large family. One resident said that although the neighborhood association building in her area is rather small, beaten-up, and bare, rather than having an impersonal feeling because it belongs to everyone and no one, it somehow gives her a feeling of coming home when she enters it. She always feels a great deal of relief and is very happy and comfortable when she goes there.

The neighborhood association buildings and their spaces represent the cohesive, familylike nature of the neighborhood, the social norms, and the wealth of the community in the space and range of activities available. These elements are shared by both old neighborhoods and new, although they are probably stronger in the more established, older neighborhoods. It is conceivable that one of the reasons that people choose to live in the new towns is to avoid the obligations and social control of the strong neighborhood associations (Tanabe 1978).

During the past century, the school grounds have come to function both as playgrounds and as neighborhood social centers because of the lack of other open areas for children, and adults for that matter, to play. The school and neighborhood *undokai*, sports meets, are held on the school grounds. These meets draw cross-generational participation and are attended by many of the neighborhood people. If one were to go to any town in Japan on National Sports Day, the undokai would look exactly the same. There is a very strong element of reaffirmation of national identity and neighborhood solidarity as well as a cementing of the connections between generations and smaller groups.

Because of the population increase that has accompanied industrialization (a growth of 15 percent between 1975 and 1991), Hikone now has a belt of new neighborhoods surrounding the older districts. These new housing areas have a markedly different structure to their public spaces, streets and small parks, than do the older neighborhoods. Unlike the older areas of the city, the houses and attached yards in the new areas are fairly large, allowing more play space within the private area. The larger houses and yards also disperse the population, and the wider streets effectively serve as barriers, as isolating forces among the families rather than as an extension of the houses, so family life does not so readily spill out onto the street. Finally, as the private automobile has become increasingly common, the streets of the newer areas have been designated primarily for automobile traffic, not for pedestrians, bicycles, or play. The "auto-centered" design and the associated parking areas that replace at least part of the garden in the new houses have changed the importance of the streets from extensions of private space to a purely utilitarian public space. These streets are still quite narrow by some standards, but they are wide by Japanese standards.

The wide streets represent a kind of freedom from the old traditions, but they also represent a certain loss as well. The newer areas are noted for the increase in light and ventilation in the houses and the greatly increased privacy. Gossip, long a tradition in Japan, as in all societies, is considerably more limited in the areas simply because of the decrease in sources of information and the means of dissemination. The populations of the newer areas also tend to be far more mobile, less likely to have lived in Hikone for a long time, and probably less interested in neighborhood affairs than are the people in the older neighborhoods.

Finally, there is a third kind of neighborhood just emerging, Old New Town (it has been named in English, an immediate indication of a type of cosmopolitan thinking that is very fashionable right now. It is also ironically symbolic that the English is incorrect.) Specifically seeking to draw on Hikone's Edo-period roots, the Old New Town is a reconstruction of Edo-style buildings, almost a living museum. The impetus for this project is largely commercial and tourist industry related. While the interiors of the buildings are modern, and many of the external details, for example, electric lighting and a massive widening of the road to accommodate automobiles, stretch the definition of historic reconstruction, the Old New Town does consciously recreate many features of an Edo-period neighborhood. Interestingly enough, at the same time, in Hikone's old neighborhoods, the old houses are being torn down and replaced with very modern prefabricated houses.

The courtyards of the many Shinto shrines and Buddhist temples also need to be mentioned in this context. Like the schoolyards, the shrine and temple grounds function as a combination of playground, socializing space, and quiet, green space in the middle of the city for a variety of nonreligious functions. Access to these areas is usually open, and neighborhood residents make frequent use of them in an informal manner for reading, for watching children, and just for sitting quietly. Thus, the cultural meaning of these spaces is slightly different than that of the ideologically neutral playgrounds. As holy places, often including dominating buildings, the shrines and temples maintain a strong ideological component and at the same time strongly reinforce neighborhood and regional identity. Temples and shrines, along with schools, are often used as landmarks, a terribly important function in an urban area where street names are very rare and sequential street numbers do not exist. Finally, the cultural meaning of these spaces are of the "old" Hikone because of the considerable age of many of the structures and, it might be argued, the relative timelessness of the architectural design (Blaser 1955).

Cross-cutting the neighborhoods are two kinds of public parks and/or playgrounds. One kind is the very small playgrounds with little equipment. These can include a set of swings and a slide. Sometimes there is no equipment at all, only open space. The little parks found in the new neighborhoods are slightly larger and somewhat better equipped but the differences are minimal. These areas are usually associated with the neighborhood association and have much of the same symbolism. All of these parks serve, as do the school yards, for all ages within the neighborhood and thus function to cement the social relations in the neighborhood (Mock 1980,

1988). The cultural meaning of these public spaces is that of group solidarity and neighborhood identity, parallel to the meaning of the streets in the old neighborhoods.

The second kind of public park or playground is the large civic sports complex just north of the castle complex. The sports complex is made up of baseball fields, tennis courts, a track and field area, a rugby pitch, a children's sports center, swimming pools, and a measured 1.5-kilometer running course around a little children's play area. All of the sports complex was built in 1975 for a large national sports event, on fields and reclaimed marsh. The cultural meaning of the sports complex, like the reconstructed area in front of the train station, is that of civic identity as a whole—the "new" Hikone. This is the image that Hikone's citizens wish to present to the world. This also represents an empowerment because the sports complex was built by the citizens of modern Hikone. They are expressing their own identity and their own idea of progress, an important change from the authoritarian past. Where in the past, the physical representations of the town's identity would have been dictated either by the Tokugawa shogunate or by the ruling Ii family, the modern elements of space are controlled by the city itself.

Like the older neighborhoods, the banks of the Seri River have also withstood the winds of change. The levees have been reinforced with concrete since the course of the Seri was first changed in the seventeenth century, and a beautification project has made clean walkways and plantings a part of the scenery, but it is still basically an open space that is accessible to the public. In fact, it has probably become more accessible, since the flow of the Seri has been greatly diminished by damming far upstream. The obon rituals on the banks of the river retain their meaning, and the annual community gathering to cut the grasses is a time to "give back to the city" and have a good time. The everyday use of the river has given over to more recreational activities such as fishing, wading, and cherry-blossom viewing. The river's position in the minds of the citizens is still one of an important public area that is open to all and offers contact with nature.

The lake is also a public area that has always been openly accessible. It is strongly tied not only to Hikone's identity but also that of the entire prefecture of Shiga and, because of its central location, is often thought of as the heart of Japan. For the local residents the modern concept of the lake is quite different from the historic one. With the construction of a seawall along its entire shore, the lake no longer poses a serious threat even in the most severe storm. Further, the size of the lake, both literally and in the minds of the residents, has been reduced by reclamation of marshlands. This puts the people into a very strong position of power over their environment. In addition, the fishing industry, while still thriving, is not as crucial to the survival of the area, so the role of the lake as determining the lives of the people has been altered.

Economically, the lake is most important as a tourist attraction. However, even with the economic benefits of tourism and the romanticized view of the lake that prompts people to sing the "Lake Biwa Song," it is not always seen in a positive light. Many of the residents see the lake as dirty and polluted. Each time there is a storm, the shoreline is clogged with trash and garbage washed down from the city drains and wave tossed and wind-blown in from other parts of the lake—all of which must be cleaned up. What is more, the city is only just now putting in an updated sewer system that will improve the quality of water being put back in the lake. Thus, the lake is considered to be a bit of a nuisance, while at the same time giving the people a feeling of being in control of their environment. Above all, the lake's image is highly romanticized, both within Hikone and around the nation.

All of the public spaces discussed thus far are either original elements of the town (the castle complex, the old parks, the schools, the river and lake, and the old streets), or they are adaptations derived from the older forms (the plaza in front of the train station, the new streets, and the new sports complex). The Japan Center for Michigan Universities is an example of a completely new space that has been developed. Among other functions, this space was specifically designed, by Shiga Prefecture, to represent the "new" Hikone (and Shiga Prefecture) in the domain of internationalization. Specific planned functions aside, the cultural meaning of the Center for Hikone is clear, it is the figurehead, in effect, for the internationalization effort for Shiga Prefecture. The permanent accessibility of non-Japanese residents and the formal program of the Center serve as a window to other cultures, primarily the United States. The physical structure of the public space itself, the Center buildings with huge green roofs right on the lake shore, serve as an extremely visible symbol of the "new" Hikone with its interest in internationalization.

Through the great many changes since the Edo period, Hikone's historic places—castle, neighborhoods, and garden—have retained cultural meaning. The new areas—plaza, sports complex, and Old New Town—have been able to develop meaning only where the symbolism is based on Hikone's history.

THE MAINTENANCE OF CULTURAL MEANING

At the beginning of this chapter, two goals were set. The first, the delineation of the cultural meaning of urban public spaces and the changes in some of these meanings through time, has been accomplished in the above discussion. The second goal, the examination of conditions leading to the maintenance, loss, or development of cultural meaning, has been touched on obliquely but remains to be specifically addressed.

The first of the three elements to be addressed is the loss of cultural meaning. In a rapidly changing arena such as modern urban Japan, public places that lose cultural meaning tend to be destroyed in one of the successive waves of urban development. In Hikone, the old area in front of the train station, wooden-fronted buildings, narrow streets, and other "old-fashioned" and "dirty" elements were simply bulldozed. The cultural meaning had been lost in the perceptions of the populace, in effect, shifting out from under them. It lost whatever cultural meaning it might have had as Hikone shifted its image from that of a historical relic to a "progressive" city. Since this shift in perception has been happening steadily since the Meiji Restoration in 1868, the actual demolition of the old station area (much of which considerably predated the actual train station) in the 1970s and 1980s really was quite late, long after the shift in cultural meaning had occurred, at least in the minds of a majority of the citizens.

Areas that have maintained significant cultural meaning, even when the meaning has shifted, include the castle complex, Lake Biwa, the Seri River bank, neighborhood streets and playgrounds, and the open areas of neighborhood temples and shrines. In the older areas of the city, the shift in economic emphasis has changed the function and some of the cultural meaning of the streets. The castle complex has moved from being a dark, brooding authoritarian symbol to being a rather whimsical but equally dominant symbol of modern Hikone. The reconstruction of the manor house as a very popular—and extremely high-quality—museum and the opening of the associated strolling garden has served to, in effect, reinstitute cultural meaning. The meaning may be said to have been reinstituted because of the period during the late Meiji through early Showa (about 1900 to 1950), when much of the cultural meaning was lost as the castle and its grounds were allowed to deteriorate almost to the point of extinction.

However, the lesson here is that urban public spaces maintain their cultural significance either because their original meaning still retained effective strength or because new symbols, important to modern Hikone, could be attached. Thus, the symbolism of Lake Biwa moves from its being a feared but economically necessary space to its being a much romanticized and a not-quite-as-necessary space. The castle's symbolism moves from that of absolute authority to that of a unique element representing Hikone's purported ability to maintain a bridge from the past to the present.

The last category, those areas that have developed meaning, is more complex. The new plaza in front of the station was clearly designed as a symbol of the new Hikone, but it invokes the past. The reconstruction of the castle grounds fits into the same category, but with the important difference that the new is clearly tied to the old in the latter case. The newest example, the construction of the Japan Center for Michigan Universities, while being both Shiga Prefecture's and Hikone City's major thrust into the most modern areas of Japan, still maintains a crucially important tie to the past.

The public places discussed can also be reorganized into categories based on the degree of their connection to the past. The public areas unconnected with the past include the sports complex and the new housing efforts, including the new neighborhoods. These areas specifically focus on improving the quality of life, particularly housing-related amenities. The public areas tightly interconnected with the past, including the refurbished castle complex and the Old New Town, are those which focus specifically on re-creating the positive symbols of the past while explicitly rejecting the more negative aspects of those same entities. Most of the public areas fall in between these two poles. The plaza in front of the train station and the Japan Center for Michigan Universities specifically use historically based symbols to establish legitimacy but also seek to connect, to bridge, in effect, the space between the past and the present.

Thus, it would seem that the bridging of time is crucial to the ability to develop cultural meanings for public places that are effective and capture the public imagination. For Hikone, the release from highly restrictive authoritarian regimes has meant more popular and populist moves toward establishing public places with cultural meaning that is essentially different from that of the past. The old symbols, the castle and the old neighborhoods, were shaped by authoritarian forces. The new symbols, the station plaza and the sports complex, are both highly popular developments. Even the "new face on old symbols" such as the castle has strong public support as a result of the release of authoritarian weight.

This has resulted in a strong popular sense of empowerment, specifically focused on cultural symbols. The citizens of Hikone feel that they can set the tone and the cultural base for their own city. They can choose what they will lose, what they maintain, and what they develop. The people of Hikone are now the ones to be moving heaven and earth to change their environment to suit their image of themselves and their future.

6

Cultural Meaning of the Plaza: The History of the Spanish-American Gridplan-Plaza Urban Design

SETHA M. LOW

Explaining built form in its relation to culture provides us with clues to meaning encoded in historically generated spatial forms. The built environment not only reflects sociocultural concerns but also shapes behavior and social action; thus, embedded in these design forms is a living history of cultural meanings and intentions. Built form also structures the world and naturalizes our experience of it in a way that seems not open to challenge (Bourdieu 1977); it retains ideas through a mnemonic process of environmental memory (Quantrill 1987; Rapoport 1982). Thus, the built environment is a repository of historical meanings that reproduce social relations (Giddens 1979; Castells 1978).

Any special form, contemporary monument, or town plan is a product generated by conflicting sociopolitical forces (Harvey 1985). Yet, the seemingly unchallengeable interpretation of the architectural or urban design often obscures the latent or politically unsuccessful subtexts of meanings. There are political implications at the root of all aesthetic sensibilities and certainly the division of land and allotment of house plots that occur with the design of an urban space reflect the political agency of the state. In this sense, architecture and urban planning contribute to the dominance of one group over another and function as mechanisms for coding their reciprocal relationships at a level that includes not only the surveillance of the body but even the movements themselves (Foucault 1975; Rabinow 1989). Thus, the understanding of the origin and derivation of these meanings and spatial forms provides insight into the discourse of power relations expressed in cultural influence and sociopolitical control.

This study began as a contemporary ethnography of two plazas in San José, Costa Rica, and their symbolic meaning for the residents of that city (Low, in press). In order to understand contemporary meanings, extensive research on the history of Parque Central—the *plaza mayor* of the colonial city—was undertaken which produced a series of contradictory and in some cases misleading explanations of the origin of this urban design form in the New World. The inconsistencies and discrepancies in the literature made it necessary to begin a second project on the ethnohistory of the origin, evolution, and ultimately the cultural meaning of the gridplan town and central plaza complex in Spanish America, that is, what is reported upon here.

The gridplan town with a central plaza built under the direction of the Spanish throughout their colonial domain has been interpreted to be an architectural representation of colonial control and oppression. This urban form is thought to be based on Renaissance rules of rationality and order and is not a traditional cultural expression in the donor country (Foster 1960). Valerie Fraser even suggests that "it is as if the Spanish colonists were drawing on some sort of cultural memory, an inherited, almost instinctive knowledge. Under the special circumstances of America the sense of what was right and proper in architecture and town planning comes to the surface to be transformed into physical reality" (1990: 7). According to Dora P. Crouch, Daniel J. Garr, and Axel I. Mundigo, authors of the definitive book on Spanish-American planning, the central square of space, ringed by the cathedral, administration buildings, arsenal and customs house, and later the residences of the social elite, represented the double hierarchy of church and state "conceived and executed as propaganda vehicles, symbolizing and incarnating civilization" (1982: xx). The plaza "was and in many places still is, a manifestation of the local social order, [of] the relationship between citizens and citizens and the authority of the state" (Jackson 1984: 18). In the colonial city, this relationship was one of social and racial domination reflected in the structure of the built environment (King 1980; Gutierrez 1983; Mumford 1961).

These interpretations of the meaning of Spanish-American urban planning are based on a tacit agreement that the gridplan-plaza urban design was of solely European derivation. Yet there continues to be considerable controversy concerning the possible European, Spanish or pre-Columbian origins of the gridplan and plaza form. The interpretation of the evidence is contradictory, with some researchers arguing for a solely European derivation of the gridplan-plaza complex while at the same time presenting evidence that a large number of towns, including Mexico City, Cholula, and Cuzco, were built isomorphic to the indigenous ruins. And, more tenuously, other researchers suggest that the 1573 "Laws of the Indies" or the writings of the Italian Renaissance were the main sources of New World planning even though they were published many years after the establishment of the first Spanish-American towns.

George Kubler comments in 1978 that "during the twenty-five years of sporadic discussion, the main questions have remained the same. Was the great Mexican urban campaign patterned on pre-Conquest native traditions? Were its solutions transferred to America from Spain and Spain alone? Or was the pattern derived from a variety of European sources?" (1978: 328). The hegemonic discourse that privileges the European sources of architectural influence over the pre-Columbian has gone unrecognized; thus, the results remain basically the same (Benevolo 1969; Morse 1987; Palm 1955, 1968; Crouch, Garr, and Mundigo 1982; Hardoy 1973; Hardoy and Hardoy 1978; Kubler 1976; Stanislawski 1947; Ricard 1947; Borah 1972; Zawiska 1972; Foster 1960; Schaedel, Hardoy, and Kinzer 1978; Borah, Hardoy, and Stelter 1980; Morse 1987). Yet cities such as Tenochtitlán (Mexico City) and Cuzco at the time of the Conquest were large urban centers designed with a gridplan pattern centered on ceremonial plazas surrounded by major temples and residences of the ruling elite. The Spaniards upon their arrival admired these exceptional models of urban planning and wrote about the grandeur, order, and urbanity of these newly discovered cities. The correspondence between the indigenous forms and the Spanish reconstruction is so clear that the denial of its significance is startling.

Even Fraser (1990) in her recent work, *The Architecture of Conquest*, is unclear about the role of the indigenous planning influences while at the same time providing archaeological and ethnohistorical evidence that many, if not most, Spanish-American towns were built directly on top of or utilized the existing indigenous settlement pattern and buildings. She also agrees that the indigenous towns and architecture were greeted with admiration and an appreciation of the skill and knowledge that it took to design and build such magnificent urban centers:

Many early travellers in South America were impressed by indigenous towns and indigenous architecture, but this seems not to have weakened their confidence in the superiority of their own culture. . . . As the Spanish colonies are consolidated, so this cultural confidence is in fact strengthened rather than weakened. Once the Indian towns have been appropriated and recognizably Europeanized then there is less evidence of a non-European urban society to upset this confidence. The unsettling possibility that a completely different, non-European people might also have developed a form of town based on straight streets, square blocks and a central plaza surrounded by important political religious buildings could be set aside, to be dealt with by later historians. (Fraser 1990: 80)

But later historians have *not* dealt with this problem. Fraser (1990), even though she provides a plausible psychological interpretation of why the Spanish did not acknowledge the contribution of indigenous planning, still argues that the new town forms were basically European, coming from an almost subconscious impulse to create order. Thus, the literature on the origin of the gridplan town and plaza continues to be Eurocentric, attributing the origins of these forms to predominantly European sources.

The question of the origin of the gridplan-plaza urban design has implications for the cultural interpretation of the meaning of the gridplan-plaza complex. The case of Tenochtitlán (Mexico City) provides a provocative example. Davíd Carrasco (1990) states that for the Aztecs, the ideal city type was a sacred space oriented around a quintessentially sacred center and that the design of the city is a replica of cosmological space. Eduardo Matos Moctezuma (1990) reinforces this position by arguing that "the Mexica's first act upon settling in this place was to build a small shrine to Huitzilopochtli. They thus established their 'center,' the navel of the world, the sacred space from which would emerge the four fundamental divisions of the city. Within this supremely sacred space they attempted to reproduce architecturally the entire cosmic order . . . " (1990: 56). If the central plaza and Great Temple of Tenochtitlán were the sacred spaces of the Aztec world, then what is the meaning of the cultural preservation that occurs when Cortés decides to build Mexico City on the ruins of this space, thus perpetuating the ceremonial plaza and Great Temple in its new Spanish-American plaza and cathedral form? Can it be argued that each time an indigenous plaza is reconstituted while maintaining its spatial integrity, the new syncretic form retains and conserves the original cultural influence of the space? Further, how "Spanish" is the gridplan-plaza complex if it is heavily influenced by what remained of the indigenous pre-Columbian cities and towns, and what would it mean if the derivation of the Spanish-American gridplan-plaza urban form was in many cases as much an Aztec or Inca as a European form? It seems that the gridplan-plaza design form would become a syncretic representation of indigenous and colonial ideas, much like the Virgin of Guadalupe in Mexico, and express the emergent identity of Mexico as separate from its purely indigenous or Spanish roots (Bakewell, personal communication).

This chapter therefore addresses the reinterpretation of the history of the Spanish-American gridplan and plaza through a reexamination of the archaeological, historical, architectural, and ethnographic evidence. In the same sense that Susan Gillespie (1989) suggests that she is searching for historical "truth" so that she can present a more accurate picture of both the events and their cultural interpretation, this chapter attempts to present a more accurate view of the evidence, suggesting that the Spanish-American gridplan-plaza urban plaza had its roots in a multiplicity of architectural and cultural traditions.

The reanalysis suggests, first, that the gridplan-plaza town is not unique and therefore difficult to explain and that there has been a continuity of the gridplan-plaza forms across time and cultures. Most ancient towns in China, Japan, Korea, peninsular India, and the ancient Middle East, as well as in pre-Columbian America, were planned according to a gridiron pattern

(Braudel 1949; Stanislawski 1946). Only two civilizations produced large, irregular towns—Islam and medieval Europe—and even in Europe gridplan towns were being produced as new towns (*bastides*) throughout the Middle Ages. From this perspective the question of the origin of the gridplan disappears, and its continuous existence from many cultural sources emerges. The more relevant questions are what is the meaning of the gridplan, and why is it so pervasive?

Second, there are multiple cultural sources and architectural and planning models for the gridplan-plaza urban design of the Spanish New World. Ethnohistorical research during the past ten years has reinforced the perspective that the origins of any cultural artifact are based on a complex set of influences. Further, studies in the social production of built form suggest that many of these forces are latent rather than manifest and must be teased out of the data, or may be found in other, tangential data sources. Issues such as what the role was of indigenous laborers who were building these new towns, what models the Spanish had in their new environment, and the influence of these models on form and style have not been adequately researched and must be to illuminate other dimensions of the research question (Matos Moctezuma 1990).

Third, the evidence suggests that there were differing forces affecting the planning and building of each city and town, because of differences in available information, individuals involved, chronology, local materials, geographical site, and history and environmental context. By examining three early cities, one sees the interplay of forces and can begin to answer the "origins" question based on the history of a particular place.

This chapter is divided into three sections. The first is an overview of the existing architectural, historical, and cultural evidence pertaining to the origin of the gridplan-plaza urban design form. In order to limit the scope of this overview, only the evidence that pertains to Mesoamerica and the Caribbean basin is explored, although many of the same patterns can be discerned in the South American material. The second section focuses on three case studies of early Spanish American cities—Santo Domingo, Mexico City, and Mérida—as a way to explore the specific influences that may have been at play in their urban plans. One important point that these three cases make is that the details of sequence of dates and events that are often collapsed in general historical discussions are critical to determining influences and possible derivation. The third and final section is a brief discussion of the implications of these findings for reinterpretation of the meaning of this urban planning form.

REVIEW OF ETHNOHISTORICAL EVIDENCE

The Old World evidence for the derivation of the Spanish-American gridplan town and central plaza design is well documented and revolves around questions as to the importance of the contributions of Italian piazza forms and the writings of the Italian Renaissance, and whether the bastides of France that extended into Spain and England during the Middle Ages were a significant link to the gridplan town, or whether it could be explained solely from Spanish origins. There are almost no references to what the early designers might have seen or read or to their level of knowledge of architectural sources outside Spain. The explorers provide some clues of the cities with which they are familiar in their references to Salamanca, Rome, and Seville.

Old World Influences

Italian. Italian planning traditions influenced the design of Spanish-American gridplan towns indirectly through Roman-Greek planning and directly in the post–1550 period of town development through Renaissance planning ideals. Hippodamus, credited by Aristotle with being the planner of the grid-pattern harbor of Athens, was an early planning theorist who rationalized and codified ideas of the period (Stanislawski 1946). The gridplan used by the Romans was an adjustment of this plan as used by Greek traders with influences derived from Etruscan practices (Stanislawski 1946). Roman town planning and design were maintained in the colonies and extended throughout Europe (Ward-Perkins 1974: 15–16, Stanislawski 1946) and were recorded in the architectural works of Vitruvius.

From 1299 to 1350 a series of new towns were founded by Florence for defense, protection of roads, development of new markets, and increased communication with outlying territories. The records show that there were architects who designed these new towns with an orthogonal street system, transverse piazza and back-to-back block system (Friedman 1988: 158). By 1346 in Siena the famous piazza was designed as a public open space for purely aesthetic and prestige-related motives, although in a very different form from later gridplan plazas (Cosgrove 1982).

In 1492, the same year that Columbus departed for the New World, the piazza of Vigevano was redesigned based on Renaissance principles of urban planning (Lotz 1981). The facades were made uniform and the space regularized to conform to new ideas of proportion and perspective. Leon Battista Alberti's (1986) interpretation of Vitruvius's writings in the context of emergent Renaissance advances in mathematics, engineering, and aesthetic theory, combined with practical notions of auspicious astrology and weather, was published in 1485 and further expanded the influence of Renaissance urban design ideals. In fact, a copy of Vitruvius was found in a library of Mexico City by 1550 (Kubler 1948; Torre Villar 1978). Yet Renaissance planning ideals and utopian writings did not have a significant impact on the design of Spanish-American towns until the second half of the sixteenth century with the "Laws of the Indies" of 1573.

French. The French contribution to New World planning derives mainly from the influence of bastide planning and the design of Valbonne on Mendicant order Mexican towns. The European population increase between 1220 and 1250, reorganization of governmental and agricultural institutions, and supplying of the crusades necessitated the building of bastides, population centers established for trade, defense, and administration (Calmettes et al. 1986: 10), particularly in southwestern France, but also in Spain and England. *Bastide* actually means rural landholding (Kubler 1978: 328); the bastides were agricultural communities based on land grants built by "royal authority, either to impose itself over dissident parts of its territory, or to extend its domain" (Morris 1974: 82–83). The bastide form was a transitional stage between the feudal castle and massive formal styles of the seventeenth century; it was characteristically an open town with narrow streets, a fortified church or walled perimeter (Kubler 1948), gridiron plan of rectangular shape depending on the terrain, and limited size (Marshall 1973). The plans of these bastides, similar to the new towns of Italy, Germany, and Holland, are evidence of a continuous history of European town planning from the Roman colonies through the Middle Ages to the Spanish garrison town of Santa Fe, Granada, described below. The importance of this European medieval planning tradition has been generally overlooked as a model for new town planning in the New World. Researchers have been too concerned about establishing a direct link to Spain that actually has always been there in the bastides of Navarre and the sequence of Spanish town planning identified by Foster (1960).

A later French influence has been discussed by Kubler (1978) in terms of the model of new, unwalled gridiron towns built on the initiative of the Benedictine abbey of St. Honorat of Lerins-Valbonne (1519), Mouans-Sartoux (1504), and Vallauris (1501). These high Renaissance towns resemble the bastide but are argued to have influenced the development of the Mendicant towns of sixteenth-century Mexico through links to the Spanish Court.

Other European influences. The Dutch market town of Haarlem was expanded in 1426 in an ordered and planned manner with a rectangular market center and straight streets alternating with canals (Hardoy 1978: 329). The Dutch, as well as the Germans, built an extensive network of new towns along their expanding frontiers.

Other theoretical sources said to have inspired Renaissance town planning include the writing of utopian philosopher Thomas More, whose *Utopia*, published in 1516, describes cities of uniform row houses. Eiximenis, the Catalan Franciscan who published in 1381–86, describes a square, fortified city with a large central open space and four smaller plazas in the four quarters of the town (Reps 1965: 6; Foster 1960: 44). The direct effect of these writings is unclear although Morse (1987) argues that it is considerable. Arciniegas (1975), a Latin American historian, presents an interesting argument that it was information and travel accounts from Amerigo Vespucci that stimulated Thomas More to write his account of an ideal country as a protest against what existed in Europe. Often colonial planning is more of a protest against what exists in the imperial country than a reflection of the needs of the colonial situation (Rabinow 1989). The colonial situation allows for the expression of both social and architectural utopian ideas that are generated by dissent about the traditional European order, but that are not acted upon because of the existence of well-accepted norms of building and behavior.

Spanish. The primary Spanish influence on New World town planning is usually considered to be the garrison town of Santa Fe, Granada, but other influences include the design of Islamic palace gardens, and the codification of Spanish-American planning practice in the directives from Philip II and the 1573 "Laws of the Indies."

Spain, like most of Europe, retained vestiges of early Roman settlement. The gridlike plans of early Roman towns were subsequently built over by the series of invasions culminating with the Moorish conquest and nearly 700 years of Islamic settlement. However, the Spanish knew of the Roman foundations from a number of ancient cities, including Barcelona, where the urban core is designed as a grid such as is found in the Plaça Real.

Most of the cities of medieval Spain are characterized by their irregular plan and lack of open spaces. Built on the Islamic model, they resemble Muslim cities that have winding streets ending in cul-de-sacs, blocks of houses irregular in shape and length, and an absence of defined squares, all features of the walled-in central nucleus—the *medina*—of any Muslim city.

The private gardens, however, of the palaces such as the Alhambra in Granada were organized in gridlike patterns with designs that were drawn upon by the Spanish for the gardenlike plazas (*parques*) of the New World. The sideyard, such as the Patio des Naranjas, an original feature of the Mezquita Mosque/Cathedral in Córdoba, has design features that are retained by the cathedral plaza in Santo Domingo, where the plaza is similarly located. The influence of the Islamic garden is often overlooked by architectural historians who are searching for the origins of the gridiron plan because the Islamic city is renowned for its lack of planning and maze of streets. Nonetheless, Moslem water gardens have a strong influence on the decoration and form of plazas, considered from the point of view of landscape architecture.

The medieval cities of Spain, therefore, were not the models of the plaza-centered gridplan town. The plaza is a normal form in very old Spanish cities, but even in the sixteenth century it remains small and irregular (Kubler 1948: 99). In fact, the plazas of Andalusian cities were added as part of the redesign of urban centers in response to the New World planning, rather than vice versa. And even today, the streets of Spain, such as Sierpes in Seville (Crouch et al. 1982), are the centers of social life rather than the plazas. Ramón Gutierrez (1983) argues that the design of the Plaza Mayor in Madrid, completed in 1619, was a response to the beauty of the designed plazas of the Spanish-American New World.

The strongest argument in favor of a Spanish origin for the gridplan town with a central plaza has been proposed by George Foster (1960). He traces the bastides of southwest France and Navarre, Spain, to the design of the garrison town of Santa Fe, Granada, built by the Catholic kings during the final phase of the reconquest of Andalusia in 1491 (Zucker 1959; Reps 1965; Foster 1960). Christopher Columbus signed the *capitulaciones* for his first voyage in Santa Fe in April 1492, and the physical design form is generally agreed to be the basis for the design of Santo Domingo in 1502 (Bronner 1986; Crouch et al. 1982: 43; Elliot 1987). Spain was basically a country of unplanned, medieval cities that could not have been the models for New World planning. However, there is some evidence of Spanish influence in the design of new towns during the Conquest proceeding from the bastides of the later-thirteenth and early-fourteenth centuries, the Islamic gardens, and the garrison town of Santa Fe, Granada.

The most commonly cited evidence for the role of the Spanish derivation of the grid-plaza town has been the "Laws of the Indies," a set of planning decrees published in 1573, that collected previously executed directives from 1509 and 1523 into a codified form. These so-called laws were written by Philip II of Spain, who was heavily influenced by the new writings of the Roman Vitruvius as translated by practicing architect Leon Battista Alberti in 1485. But as has been pointed out by many scholars, by 1573 the majority of the important cities in the New World had been built, and the laws only reflected what was already established practice. Further, the "Laws of the Indies" state that the cathedral was not to be placed on the plaza, while common practice was to have the cathedral facing the plaza as a central symbol of the city or town (Crouch et al. 1982: xx).

New World Influences

Many researchers have argued that "the design of colonial capital cities has nothing to do with local traditions, or with persistence of pre-Columbian town planning concepts" (Gasparini 1978: 274), yet the evidence from the major cities of Tenochtitlán (Mexico City) and Cuzco clearly refutes this position. These statements were made by researchers with a Eurocentric bias in terms of architecture and town planning. But the influences on New World planning are much more complex. Many of the indigenous cultures were already employing domestic and/or ceremonial gridplan designs that the Spanish would have seen either in Conquest period towns and cities or in the ruins of previous civilizations uncovered in their explorations. This section briefly reviews three of the New World indigenous building traditions, the Aztec, Maya, and Taino, as examples of possible sources of influence for the gridplan-plaza complex.

Aztec. Tenochtitlán, established in 1325, is probably the clearest source of evidence for indigenous influence on planning based on the fact that Hernán Cortés rebuilt the capital of Mexico City isomorphic with the gridplan and plaza foundations of the Aztec city. Tenochtitlán was a monumental gridplan urban center of 150,000 to 300,000 inhabitants with straight causeways that ran directly into the main ceremonial plaza.

Firsthand accounts suggest that the Spanish were impressed by the plan and design of the city: "and they said that they had never seen a square which was so well balanced and of such good layout and size" (Díaz del Castillo 1963: 235). Cortés's Mexico City retained this rectangular plan with the central plaza design. Other Indian towns were also planned with a gridplan-plaza system and had at their center a fortified temple enclosure that stood upon the intersection of a social thoroughfare. According to Motolinia, "In the whole land we find that the Indians had a large square court in the best part of the town; about a crossbowshot from corner to corner, in the large cities and provincial capitals; and in the smaller towns, about a bowshot" (Kubler 1948: 101).

One of the explanations for the gridplan of the Aztec ceremonial sites is the use of the four cardinal points in much of Aztec cosmology (Touissant et al. 1938). The Aztecs were developing principles of general city planning in order to achieve an efficient urban organization (Hardoy 1973: 178). The plan of Aztec towns was roughly rectangular and evolved from the division of land among the clans. The central plaza was destined for communal gatherings and as a marketplace and simultaneously represented the courtyard of the central temple. Both Zucker (1959) and Calnek (1978) suggest that social status was reflected in the architectural markers and the distance of houses from the plaza in the pre-Conquest city, with the highest status locations being those on the perimeter and surrounding blocks of the central plaza. A correspondence can be seen not only in the economic and social structure of Aztec and Spanish culture but also in the planning and design of the gridplan towns and plazas. William Schell (1986) argues that with the exception of the Mayan Yucatán, Mesoamerican culture and economic structure resembled that of Iberia in a number of ways including landholding systems, governance by city-states, and market laws.

Mayan.

Topographic surveys of large Maya sites like Tikal and Seibal in Peten . . . reveal a very amorphous pattern of structures ranging from great temple pyramids . . . down to individual house mounds arranged around tiny plazas. This pattern is a far cry from the neat gridiron layout of Teotihuacan in Central Mexico which conforms to our idea of what a city should be. (Coe 1987: 89)

Preclassic and Classic Maya sites are less rectangular in their plan and in the placement of their ceremonial plazas than Aztec or Toltec (Teotihuacán) plans. However, even though the ceremonial sites were not in a grid, lowland Maya house sites were organized around plazas (Ashmore 1981), and social status is attributed to plaza design (Becker 1982). Some of the Maya Classic and early Postclassic ceremonial sites, however, did exhibit a gridlike structure such as in the Puuc city of Uxmal.

In the Yucatán, late Classic and Postclassic Maya sites show evidence of foreign Toltec influence, which may account for the gridplan design of the main plazas such as is seen at the site of Chichén Itzá. The Maya Yucatán town of Izamal also illustrates how in the Mayan region the Spanish, in this case Diego de Landa, built the Spanish church and monastery next to the massive Maya ceremonial platform topped with a pyramid. Mitla also was one of the few sites that the Spanish friars found significant enough to destroy, though not completely, and build a church on top (Mullen 1975: 3).

Descriptions from firsthand accounts throughout the Maya region suggest that the Spanish were aware of the design and grandeur of the abandoned indigenous sites. In a geographical description of Guatemala on March 8, 1576, Diego García de Palacio described the plaza in the ruins of Copán:

Near here, on the road to the city of San Pedro, in the first town within the province of Honduras called Copan, are certain ruins and vestiges of a great population and of superb edifices, of such skill, that it appears they could never have been built by a people as rude as the native of that province. . . . Near this, is a well built plaza or square, with steps or grades, which from the descriptions, resemble those of the Coliseum at Rome. In some places it has eighty steps, paved, and made in part at least of fine stones, well-worked. In this square are six great statues. (Parry and Keith 1984: vol. III: 546).

Although the Maya evidence is not so clear as that of the Aztec/Toltec tradition, it is still adequate to suggest some indigenous influence in the Maya area, and this evidence will be returned to in the discussion of the development of the city of Mérida.

Taino. From the writings of Bartolomé de Las Casas (1951) and Gonzalo Fernández de Oviedo Valdés (1959) and from archaeological evidence of the West Indies it can be concluded that plazas were situated in front of the hut of the *cacique* (headman) where ball playing, and in some cases ancestor worship, took place. The majority of these excavated plazas are reported for Puerto Rico as quadrilateral or rectangular, and enclosed by flat stones standing on end (Loven 1935). Some of these plazas were very large, about 258 yards long by 96 yards wide; however, the relationship to settlement is not always clear (Wilson 1990).

In his description of the villages of the Tainan islands Las Casas (1951) states that the house of the king or gentleman of the town is in the best location, and in front of the royal house is a large plaza, very level and well-swept for ball playing. There are also houses near this plaza, and if it is a very large town, there will be other plazas for smaller ball games (Loven 1935: 94).

From these firsthand accounts it appears that there were plazas and minimal planning even in the Taino villages of the West Indies. Therefore, not only the urban Aztec, Maya, and Incan cultures had this design form, but plazas were also widespread in the domestic sites of villages and towns on the islands of the earliest discovery.

Other arguments. One other line of argument concerning the design of gridplan-plaza towns is that this plan was of practical use during the period of Conquest and settlement. There are primary sources that outline the negotiations of such practical concerns, such as the "Minutes of a Debate on the Choice of a Site for the (First) City of Guatemala" in July 1524" (Parry and Keith vol III: 1984), during which the conquistadores argued about the siting and design of the town. Such evidence does suggest that practical and "ready at hand" issues of designing and planning a town were important and may well have been relevant to planning decisions.

CASE STUDIES: SANTO DOMINGO, MEXICO CITY, AND MÉRIDA

Three cities have been selected as examples of how different combinations of cultural models and influences were important at different sites. The first two cases, Santo Domingo and Mexico City, are the earliest well-documented cities in the Caribbean and Mesoamerican region, and the third case, Mérida, although it is poorly documented, is reported to have been built on indigenous ruins of Tihoo in the Mayan Yucatán. The cases illustrate that each plaza and gridplan evolved on the basis of its own unique historical moment and within a distinct sociopolitical and cultural context, also unique.

Santo Domingo. In December of 1492, Christopher Columbus built a crude fortress known as La Navidad from the timbers of the wrecked *Santa María* on the northern coast of the island of Hispaniola (Columbus 1493). La Navidad, the first primitive military outpost of Europeans in the New World, did not survive, and it was not until 1496 that Bartolomé Colón founded Santo Domingo on the southern side of the island (Reps 1969).

Columbus and his crew found a number of indigenous Taino towns on the island, and it appears from the already-mentioned account of Las Casas that the towns on the island attained a size that can only be explained by the enormous wealth of good land suitable for cultivation. The streets were generally straight, with plazas for ceremonial use. In the same narration, Las Casas (1951) finds a definite plan for building where after felling the trees to clear a place for the plaza, four "streets" were hewn out in the form of a cross. However, not all of the towns were large enough to have real plazas laid out, and many houses aside from those of the cacique (headman) were built in an irregular pattern and without streets (Loven 1935). Many early chroniclers, including Las Casas, Columbus, Fernández de Oviedo y Valdés, and Peter Martyr, (1511) recorded seeing these plazas and house sites (Wilson 1990; Parry and Keith 1984; Wagner 1942; Oviedo 1959).

The failure to establish a permanent settlement and bungled administration on the island prompted the crown to send Fray Nicolas de Ovando as governor. In these early settlements the crown gave little direction, and Ferdinand's instructions to Ovando in 1501 state:

As it is necessary in the island of Española to make settlements and from here it is not possible to give precise instructions, investigate the possible sites, and in conformity with the quality of the land and sites as well as with the present population outside present settlements establish settlements in the numbers and in the places that seem proper to you. (Qtd. by Stanislawski 1947: 95).

Ovando arrived in 1502 with 2,500 settlers. When after two months a hurricane destroyed his capital, he resited on the right bank of the Ozama. Ovando developed a geometric layout that he used as the model for a master scheme of a network of towns on Hispaniola for which he "coordinated selected urban sites, controlled municipal appointments and determined the disposition of lots around the plazas" (Morse 1987: 171). Ovando's experiences with the laying out and administration of towns informed the crown's 1513 instructions to Pedrarias Davila that directed him to chose healthful places with good water and air, to divide plots for houses according to the status of the persons, and to arrange the houses in relation to the plaza, church, and pattern of streets. These instructions have been interpreted to imply a gridplan (Stanislawski 1947).

Gonzalo Fernández de Oviedo y Valdés describes Santo Domingo as superior even to Barcelona and all the other Old World cities that he had seen.

Since the city was founded in our own time, there was opportunity to plan the whole thing from the beginning. It was laid out with ruler and compass, with all the streets being carefully measured. Because of this Santo Domingo is better planned than any town I have seen. (Fernández de Oviedo y Valdés 1959: 11)

The earliest plan of the first permanent city in the New World (Bigges 1588) reveals the rather impressive settlement described by Oviedo centered around its plaza and cathedral. Straight, wide streets divide the town into rectangular blocks containing the homes of the settlers, warehouses, barracks, and buildings for religious orders. In the engraving the plaza's relationship to the cathedral is as a church sideyard. This cathedral-plaza relationship resembles the Patio des Naranjas sideyard of the Mezquita in Córdoba, Spain, and the church-plaza relationship of the bastides and Santa Fe, Granada, more than do the front-facing cathedral and plaza plans of later Spanish-American cities. Santo Domingo's plaza today retains this sideyard design.

Thus Santo Domingo's gridplan and plaza appears mostly derived from Spanish influence, primarily the design of Santa Fe, Granada, with some reference to the indigenous Taino cultural pattern. In the Santo Domingo example there is almost no direct evidence for the derivation of its plan, and one can only suggest possible Taino and Spanish models. Yet Santo Domingo becomes an influential urban model for later Spanish-American cities.

Mexico City. Tenochtitlán, the capital city of the Aztecs, was first encountered by Hernán Cortés and his men in 1519 when they entered the city and were given temporary quarters by the Aztec ruler Moctezuma II. At that time Tenochtitlán was probably the largest city in the world.

The descriptions of chroniclers emphasize the size and scale of the original Aztec city as well as the design and importance of the main plazas. Bernal Díaz del Castillo marvels:

Some of our soldiers who have been in many parts of the world, in Constantinople, in Rome, and all over Italy, said that they have never seen a market (plaza) so well laid out, so large, so orderly, and so filled with people." (Díaz del Castillo 1963: 235)

The Anonymous Conqueror writes:

There are in the city Temistitan (Tenochtitlán), Mexico, very large and beautiful plazas where they sell all of the things which the natives use. There was especially the great plaza which they call the Tutelula (Tlatelolco) which may be three times the size of the square of Salamanca. All around it are porticos where every day from twenty to twenty-five thousand people come to buy and sell. (Saville 1917: 65)

Cortés also is impressed by the city and writes to the king in his second letter that

The city itself is as big as Seville or Córdoba. The main streets are very wide and very straight; some of these are on the land, but the rest and all the smaller ones are half on land, half canals where they paddle their canoes. . . . This city has many squares where trading is done and markets are held continuously. There is also one square twice as big as that of Salamanca, with arcades all around. . . . There are, in all districts of this great city, many temples or houses for their idols. . . . Amongst these temples there is one, the principal one, whose great size and magnificence no human tongue could describe, for it is so large that within the precincts, which are surrounded by a very high well, a town of some five hundred inhabitants could easily be built. . . . There are as many as forty towers, all of which are so high that in the case of the largest there are fifty steps leading up to the main part of it; and the most important of these towers is higher than that of the cathedral of Seville. (Cortés [1524] 1986: 102–103, 105)

The conquest of Tenochtitlán and the siege of seventy-five days left the city destroyed. Cortés originally had wanted to rebuild the city on a better site but decided to rebuild "as the city was so renowned and was so important it seemed well to us to rebuild it" (Kubler 1948: 70). By occupying Tenochtitlán, the Spanish not only changed its pre-Conquest appearance but also identified themselves as the new political and governmental center (Kubler 1948: 71). This rebuilding has allowed the Aztec city plan to survive in that the same religious, administrative, and civic importance of Tenochtitlán's center buildings were maintained: the colonial plaza replaced the Aztec market, the cathedral was built on top of the Templo Major, and the National Palace covered the houses of Moctezuma II.

There is also some dispute about the master plan (*traza*) of Mexico City. M. T. Toussaint (Toussaint et al. 1938) states that Alonso García Bravo was the author of the plan following his expedition with Pedrarias Davila. He is said to have modified the Aztec plan by opening up new streets, widening some streets, and bringing in new streets at right angles (Toussaint et al. 1938; Boyer 1980). Kubler (1948), however, argues that the surveyor, García Bravo, was not called in to discuss land titles in connection with the assignment of municipal lands until 1524, and at the very least, the traza, or master plan, had not been established in 1523. So by the time the master plan was drawn, the cardinal thoroughfares had already been laid out, a year of building had taken place, and the preestablished pattern based on the Aztec design following the main arteries and house blocks of the Aztec city could not have been changed.

During the next hundred years Mexico City grew in importance and size to become a city visited by travelers whose accounts give a detailed description of its physical and social character. Thomas Gage's account of Mexico City describes the city during this period:

The chief place in the City is the Market place, which though it be not as spacious as in *Montezuma* his time, yet is at this day very fair and wide, built all with Arches on the one side where people may walke dry in time of rain, and there are shops of Merchants furnished with all sorts of stuffes and silks, and before them sit women selling all manner of fruits and herbes; over against these shops and Arches is the Viceroy his palace, which taketh up almost the whole length of the market with the walls of the house and of the gardens belonging to it. At the end of the Viceroy his Palace, is the chief prison which is strong of stone work. Next to this is the beautiful street called *la plateria* or Goldsmiths-street, where a mans eyes may beholdin sees then an hour many millions worth of gold, silver, pearls and jewels. (Gage 1655: 59)

By 1778, Monsignor Chappe D'Auteroche undertakes a scientific voyage to observe the natural history of the area, to record a Mexico City with well-developed plazas, buildings, and parks:

The streets of Mexico are very wide, perfectly strait, and almost all intersect each other at right angles. The houses are tolerably built, but not much ornamented w[h]ither within or without; their make is the same as in Spain. The city of Mexico contains three squares; the first is the *Major* or great square fronting the palace, the cathedral, and the market-place, which is a double square surrounded with buildings: This square is in the center of the city. The second, adjoining to this, is the square called *del Volador*, where the bull-feasts are held. The third, is that of *Santo Domingo*. These squares are tolerably regular, and each has a fountain in the middle. To the north of the town, near the suburbs, is the public walk, or *Alameda*. A rivulet runs all round it, and forms a pretty large square, with a bason and *jet d'eau* in the middle. Eight walks, with each two rows of trees, terminate at the bason like a star; but as the soil of Mexico is unfit for trees, they are not in a very thriving condition. This is the only walk in or near to Mexico; all the country about it is swampy ground, and full of canals. (Chappe D'Auteroche 1778: 40–41)

These accounts describe the physical evolution of Mexico City which to this day maintains the central plaza and cathedral on the site of the Aztec sacred ceremonial center.

Mérida, Yucatán. Mérida was built on the ruins of the Maya town of Tihoo near the Mayan sites of Uxmal, Chichén Itzá, and Tulum. It was the principal city of Spanish Yucatán and still remains the major city of the peninsula. According to the *Relaciones geográficas* (1890–1900) the first European to encounter this land was Hernández de Córdoba, who in 1517 reported fine cities of masonry houses, abundant populations, outlying plantations, and gold (Wagner 1942). Governor Diego Velazquez then sent Captain Juan de Grijalva in 1518 to explore what was to be called New Spain. Hernán Cortés passed through in 1519 on his way to Tenochtitlán, and finally Fernando de Montejo was sent in 1527 to settle the region.

In Peter Martyr's account of the discovery of the Yucatán he writes: "The Spaniards discovered a fortified town on the shore of such importance that they named it Cairo after the capital of Egypt. It possesses houses with towers, magnificent temples, regular streets, squares and marketplaces" (qtd. in Wagner 1942: 33). This description has been attributed to the site of Tulum. Other nearby sites also had a rectangular ceremonial plaza center and straight causeways leading to the plaza center. Chichén Itzá, a Postclassic site, is a hybridization of Toltec and Maya and is even more regular in plan, but while Tulum still functioned as a trading center, both Uxmal and Chichén Itzá were abandoned and appeared only as ruins.

Although there are few early plans of Mérida, there is rich textual material concerning its founding and development. The Maya resisted Spanish invasion and resettlement throughout the Yucatán region, and the city of Mérida was not founded until January 6, 1541. Diego López de Cogolludo, in his *História de Yucathan Compuesta*, published in Madrid in 1688, describes the founding of Mérida as following a great battle at Tihoo during which 60,000 Maya warriors were finally subdued (López Cogolludo 1688: 137). The Spanish replaced the chief of these people and built their new city on the same site, so that the people would know that their success would be permanent (López Cogolludo 1688: 137–138).

In 1548 Fray Lorenzo de Bienvenida describes Mérida in these terms:

after the beautiful buildings [Tihoo] contains: in all the discoveries in the Indies none so fine has been found. Buildings of big and well-carved stones—there is no record of who built them. It seems to us they were built before Christ, because the trees on top of the buildings were as high as the ones around them. Amongst these buildings, we, monks of the Order of St. Francis, settled. (qtd. in Hammond 1982: 33–34)

In 1605, with the birth of King Philip IV, Mérida was given the title of noble and loyal City of Mérida.

The Mérida of Spain was, in the manner of European cities, a clutter of overlapping social groups and competing activities, the plan of the old Roman city having been long obscured by centuries of casual growth. The new Mérida was a very conscious creation, neatly mapping its citizens' shared understanding of the right order of men and things, and carefully demarcating and framing those areas where what to the Spaniards were the crucial exchanges of social life were to take place. . . .

The centre of life and the city was the great plaza, the main stage for the sauntering display and the elaborate verbal exchanges which were the delights of town living. . . . The first site allocated, on the eastern flank of the plaza, was set aside for the cathedral. . . . To the north, the government buildings, royal and municipal, were soon under construction, as was the grandiose mansion built for Montejo, head of the royal government. (Clendinnan 1987:´39–40)

Charlene Alyce Browne (1988) argues in a study of the plaza that the Mayan plaza becomes the Spanish plaza; where the temple once faced the ancient plaza, the Spaniards located their church. Thus, even today as locals pass the day exchanging news and commentary on the plaza benches, one may interpret the meaning of this space as a confluence of Maya ceremonial center and Spanish secular and religious intentions.

DISCUSSION

These three cases illustrate the complexity of determining the origin and evolution of the gridplan–plaza design. Each plan is to some degree syn-

cretic, reflecting a combination of New World and Old World urban planning traditions.

Santo Domingo's plan by Ovando most closely resembles the Spanish
bastide-like garrison town of Santa Fe, Granada, although the plaza itself
is reminiscent of the sideyard of the Mosque/Cathedral in Córdoba, Spain.
There is some suggestion that the indigenous Taino towns may have influenced the presence of the plaza, but there is no direct evidence. Thus, Santo
Domingo's plan is mostly of Spanish derivation.

Mexico City's plan, designed by Cortés and executed by Alonso García
Bravo, is derived from the structure and foundations of the Aztec city of
Tenochtitlán. The *zócalo* of Mexico City lies directly on top of Moctezuma's
Main Temple Plaza, and the surrounding buildings retain the original order
of Aztec governmental and religious architecture. Cortés and García Bravo
had both seen Santo Domingo, but the evidence suggests that Mexico City
was of primarily Aztec design.

Mérida is another city that was built on top of the indigenous town of
Tihoo, but there is no evidence about the details of the indigenous town
plan nor archaeological excavations of the original site. There were Maya
models of nearby ceremonial sites with large ceremonial plazas, but by 1541
there were also a number of examples of Spanish-American town plans and
skilled surveyors. The design of Mérida, therefore, most likely reflects
elements from both indigenous and European architectural and planning
traditions.

Thus, it seems apparent that the gridplan town and central plaza design
of Spanish America must be interpreted in terms of both the indigenous
and European cultural meanings. Unfortunately, we have only limited evidence about the process by which this syncretism took place and few texts
that discuss the process of spatial appropriation other than the naming and
establishment of towns. It could be argued that especially for Mexico City
the spatial relationships that are maintained by building directly on top of
the Aztec ruins using the same stones, builders, and foundations allowed
for elements of the Aztec politicoreligious cultural system to remain. These
latent meanings were not necessarily acted upon publicly but may have been
useful in reinforcing aspects of indigenous identity, self-esteem, and spiritual
power that helped to preserve indigenous folkways, beliefs, and practices.

Today the tension between Spanish colonial and indigenous, particularly
Aztec, cultural authority and dominance can be seen in the current debate
over the allocation of space and excavation rights in the zócalo. The recent
archaeological excavation of the Temple Mayor of Tenochtitlán, stages one
through six—the seventh stage was destroyed by Cortés to build the current
colonial plaza and buildings—and the building of the new Museo del Templo
Mayor have caused considerable concern among architectural historians and
others interested in the colonial period. A number of important colonial
buildings were torn down in order to excavate the Aztec site and to make

room for the new museum that interprets the archaeological remains. Further, the archaeological excavations are said to have disturbed the foundations of a number of the remaining colonial buildings on the zócalo, including the cathedral and the National Palace, causing serious damage of the facades of some colonial buildings. The archaeological site itself is currently rising because of the removal of the weight of the colonial buildings and the expansion of the spongy soil of the original lake bed. Historians and architects are worried that with the continued excavation of the Aztec site there will be even more damage from the emerging Aztec ruins, so they are trying to stop or at least slow down the plans for other indigenous archaeology projects.

The irony is, of course, that again there is a struggle for the control of space in the symbolic center of Mexico City. The emergence of the Templo Mayor has created considerable cultural capital for the indigenous symbolism of Mexican identity. In response, the historians and architects who are involved in the cultural conservation of the Spanish colonial past and the preservation of the colonial symbolism of Mexican identity are attempting to reappropriate their zócalo, the most sacred—and political—of Mexican spaces. This struggle illustrates how important these symbolic spaces are for the formation and maintenance of cultural identity, as well as the ways in which meanings from the past are encoded in the built environment and are manipulated through spatial relationships and architecture to create the sociopolitical present.

NOTE

Funding for this project was provided by a National Endowment of the Humanities Research Fellowship at the John Carter Brown Library in Providence, Rhode Island, and by supplementary funds from the Graduate Center of the City University of New York. I would like to thank the John Carter Brown Library: Norman Fiering, librarian; Daniel Slive, reference librarian; Susan Danforth, curator of maps; and Richard Hurley, photographer; and resident fellows and faculty who participated in the weekly luncheon seminar series. I would particularly like to thank Lucile, Ken, and Frank Newman for their gracious hospitality. I would also like to thank Elizabeth Bakewell, Ellen Messinger, Joel Lefkowitz, Amos Rapoport, and Lauri Wilson for their suggestions and comments on earlier drafts of this paper.

7

Italian Urbanscape: Intersection of Private and Public

DONALD S. PITKIN

I first went to Italy in 1948 with a friend I shared a foxhole with in 1943, during the invasion of Kiska in the Aleutians. My friend was a painter and wanted to take the artist's pilgrimage to Rome. I was a second-year graduate student in anthropology who needed to decided where to do fieldwork. I had decided on either Micronesia in the Pacific or Colombia in Latin America. This trip, on a student ship to Europe, was to be my last fling. I was only slightly prepared for Rome.

We arrived by train in the Stazione Termine and found a room nearby on the Via Nazionale. I remember not being able to go to sleep, partly because of the excitement of having finally arrived in the Eternal City, but also because of the noise wafting into the room from the street below. I finally got up and joined the crowds outside, edging my way slowly down toward the Old City. Was it the heat of July that people were trying to escape, or was this a nightly embrace of the city by its inhabitants delighting in its beauty? Everywhere people were eating outside on tables often precariously perched, in seeming danger of being run over by the few motorized vehicles moving about. People acted as if the streets were their homes. Many years later, when I saw a similar street-feasting scene in Fellini's film *Roma*, I recognized that atmosphere of sensuality and spontaneity that I shared with those around me that evening.

When I finally arrived at the Piazza Venezia, I stared for some time at the balcony from which Mussolini gave his fateful speech, bringing Italy into the war. Newsreel images of Mussolini haranguing the crowds flashed into my mind as I tried to recall what I had read about piazza politics. The approbation Mussolini was able to achieve through manipulating crowds in confined urban spaces gave him a markedly different political opportunity for mobilizing consensus than the steps of the Old State House in Boston did to the governors of Massachusetts on ceremonial occasions I remembered from my childhood.

I turned my head to the left, away from the balcony, and thrilled to my first sight of the Colosseum, shimmering in the moonlight at the end of the Via del Impero. I turned back to the hotel, thinking as I moved away from the balcony and piazza of the continuity that has marked the political use of urban space in Italian history. The Emperor Vespasian built the ampitheater, later known as the Colosseum, in 80 A.D. for sating the Roman populace in their more carnal appetites, thus winning their support. One only has to think of the way the fourteenth-century dictator Cola di Rienzo used the public space of Rome as a stage by which to hold its inhabitants in thralldom (Hibbert 1985: 102). As I moved up the Via Quattro Novembre, those musings about Rome mingled with the caressing summer air, which bore a pungent and intoxicating odor, a mixture of urine, coffee, and tobacco.

Later in the week, we traveled around the Roman Campagna and into the hills, to Frascati and Rocco di Papa and beyond to Palestrina. It was at every turn an unfamiliar landscape, the sharp demarcation between town and country, the settlements perched on hilltops looking down upon a countryside almost bereft of habitation. Driving up the switchback roads into a town, even a small one, was like entering a miniature city. Nothing could have been more different from the New England town I grew up in. The buildings, streets, piazzas constitute one organic whole, often demarcated from that which lies beyond by a wall. When I left Italy to return to the States, I did so with the distinct impression that I was leaving an essentially urban society, although most of its population was still engaged in agricultural pursuits. I was not quite certain what reconceptualization, if any, of the idea of *urban* would be suggested if in Italy, at least in the part I had visited, many people lived in urban centers, agritowns, that were not at the same time cities in any conventional sense and certainly not metropolises.

What I was certain about, though, was that I was going to renounce my intention of going to either Micronesia or Colombia and instead undertake fieldwork in Italy. It was the juxtaposition of the ancient tradition of town/city primacy and the power subsumed within it to those millions of people regarded as peasants that I found particularly compelling. What definitely turned me in favor of Italy, however, was the reading, on my return to Cambridge, Massachusetts, of Carlo Levi's *Christ Stopped at Eboli* (1947). Levi, an anti-Fascist, was subjected, for his objection to Mussolini's war in Ethiopia, to a particularly Italian punishment, being sent "*in confino*," that is, confined beyond the pale of civilization, in a small settlement in the Lucanian countryside. His book was a vivid account of his exile in Aliano. Nothing to my mind connoted more fully the hegemony of the urban ideal in Italian high culture than the notion that in the hinterland beyond the provincial railhead city of Eboli, civilization, to say nothing of Christianity, had never penetrated. While Levi had not been trained as an anthropologist, I recognized that *Christ Stopped at Eboli* constituted a fine piece of anthropological writing. I returned to Italy with the intention of following in his footsteps.

In 1951 my wife and I settled in the town of Sermoneta, in the province of Latina, some sixty miles south of Rome. We remained there for eighteen months. My purpose was to undertake a community study for a doctoral dissertation in anthropology. A community study assumed that communities, like Sermoneta, Italy, or Scituate, Massachusetts (where I was raised), could be identified as autonomous territorially demarcated entities and made understandable by descriptive analysis. That, after all, was the assumption that informed Robert Lynd's 1929 investigation of Middletown or Horace Miner's 1939 study of a Canadian township. What such an approach failed to do was to take into account the extent of the beholdenness of such communities to larger metropolitan-based centers of power so that, in fact, much of my time was spent in delineating those connections (Pitkin 1959).

Despite the asymmetry in numbers between town and country dwellers, Sermoneta was identified with its urban village, as was the case with communities to the north, Norma and Cori; Bassiano to the east; and Sezze to the south. These, like Sermoneta, are intensely nucleated centers, situated on high ground dominating the countryside below. Sermoneta itself is surrounded by a wall attributed to the notable fourteenth-century architect of urban defensive structures, Antonio da Sagallo (Marchetti 1985: 22). Looming over the town is the massive Caetani castle dating from that papal family's hegemony in the southern Roman Campagna in the thirteenth and fourteenth centuries and refurbished by the Borgia Pope Alessandro VI during the Borgias' usurpation of Sermoneta from the Caetani in the sixteenth century. From the castle at the apex of the town's topography to its perimeteral wall Sermoneta is a maze of interconnecting narrow streets and piazzas. Like any urban reality and unlike the many homogenous rural settlements in other parts of the world, it is internally differentiated along class and economic lines. The large dwellings of the well-to-do are ranged along the Via Garibaldi, the main street leading into town from the principal gate. Most of the commercial establishments—shops, bars, trattoria—are to be found in and around the main piazza, Piazza del Popolo, while the administrative center, the town hall, and the employment office are adjacent to the castle. There was also a strong sense of competition between different neighborhoods, each carrying its own name, a rivalry that became intense when each faction would try to outdo the others in the size of its bonfire set on the night of March 18, in honor of St. Giuseppe. From subsequent trips to Sermoneta I have reason to believe that these old rivalries have abated, but in its essential physical structure Sermoneta has not changed any more than has the historic center of Rome; nothing has been torn down, no new building has taken place, only internal renovations have occurred, and all this despite the congestion and the inconvenience now caused by the ubiquitous automobile, moped, and lack of space to park them. It is as if those who experienced and continue to experience this kind of urbanscape by living in it appreciate the cognitive and sensual heightening of awareness that it affords by intersecting intimate and public spheres of life.

Very early on I was struck by the way the street in Sermoneta seemed to become an extension of the house. Chairs were readily brought from the inside and placed on the street or on the balcony overlooking it. Women spent time visiting with each other, sewing, knitting, talking, gossiping. Men usurped the space in front of the bars for card games or filled the piazza in the late afternoon, grouping in clusters for talk and bravura. Children ran freely here and there, playing or self-importantly running errands for adults. Then in the evening the main street of Sermoneta, and indeed of every other Italian town and provincial city that I visited, became itself a kind of great open-air *salotto*, during the ritual *passegiatta*, the stroll up and down in the hour before dinner, when everyone has the chance to offer a presentation of self and perform an assessment of the presentation of others.

In the ritual of the passegiatta the ordinary citizen is making a *figura*, an impression, in a manner analogous to that once undertaken by the circulation of the well-born and nobility in the grand salons of patrician palaces. That aspect of personhood which figura refers to is an expression of the interaction between personal aspiration and assessment by others. It represents, if you will, a kind of displacement of the interior self to the exterior where it becomes constructed as social fact. One is, for purposes of social discourse, what one is perceived to be. To make a *bella figura* is to burnish the image of self for the consumption of others. The derivation of the concept of the bella figura, to make the right impression, is not known to me and perhaps is unknowable, but I am of the opinion that its origin is to be found in ancient urban settings where a premium was placed on the appraisal of others for which propinquity selected.

The development of that social self, responsive to the authority of shame induced by the evaluation of others, is widespread in the Mediterranean world, precisely because of its relation to the emergence of the classical city-state. That early urbanscape where private and domestic were mediated by the exigencies of social and public afforded a crucible for the selection of an exteriorization of self, placing on such beliefs as the evil eye the onus of social control with its reliance on visual interaction.

If Greek culture and its larger manifestation, Hellenism, was the product of the city-state, so also Rome, when it stepped into its place, continued the Hellenistic urban tradition. For more than four hundred years, all of what we now call Mediterranean Europe was provided with a large degree of cultural coherence under the domination of Rome, which replicated its own essentially urban ideals to the furthest corners of the empire. In time the boundaries of the empire were hard pressed by peoples associated with, as Tacitus made known, forest and field, a land of tribes that sought virtue in a circumscribed existence of tillage and hunting except, of course, when they rampaged as Vikings to the west or to the south as Vandals. Yet even when they did overrun much of the empire, these northern people who by dint of myth and experience sought in nature the truth of their selfhood did not succeed in changing the convictions of those of the Latin world who by associating with urban existence legitimized themselves as civilized human beings. Some writers have suggested, as Ernst Pulgram points out, "that one notable reason for the failure of Germanic culture was that the Germans were mainly rural settlers and feudal lords who underrated and ignored the force of urban life in the South, applying tribal, rural and feudal conceptions in a country where the city, the archantagonist and eventual conqueror of feudalism was everything" (1958: 382). But if the incursion of Germanic peoples had surprisingly little long-range effect upon Mediterranean culture, the emergence of city life in the north did not succeed in implanting a classical urban preeminence at the expense of the pastoral experience. Urbanism came relatively late to the north, and when it did, it was implanted from the south in the form of a London, or a Frankfurt. And even when northern European cities assumed their own indigenous cast, they did not become a source of validation for a ruling elite who found rather in their association with the countryside the legitimation of their authority. In this regard the Italian humanist Leonard Olschki points out that "Italian travelers in England and France during the fifteenth and sixteenth centuries, Poggio Bracciolini, and the poet Toquato Tasso, were shocked to find the gentry living in isolated manors where they were unable to acquire courtly manners or lead the civilized life" (1949: 26–27).

The idealization of the rural in English thought and the mythification of nature in German consciousness would seem to have no pervasive counterpart in the Mediterranean. Indeed the valorization of landscape as opposed to urbanscape is associated with a process of individuation of selfhood related to different spatial referents than those found in the intensely social milieu of the southern city. If anything, the northern city has been experienced as an alien force, an intrusion. One can only be oneself with oneself unbeholden to others, free to find in nature the confirmation of an inner self. It is in the woods, *der Wald*, rather than in the piazza as it is in the solitary *Wanderung*, rather than in the teeming passegiatta, that one's personhood is found. The interioricity of guilt more than the exterioricity of shame charters the course for that Protestant persona that emerged within the spatial parameters characteristic of Northern Europe. The Protestant cleansed of the need for ecclesiastical intercession stood alone before his God unlike the Catholic, dependent as he was upon the society of others for his salvation.

It is in Protestant individualized space that the distinction is maintained between interior and exterior, between street and house, which characterizes those northern European cities bereft of life in the streets as opposed to familial Catholic space in which the domestication of public space is so palpable.

To speak of space as Protestant or Catholic is to fly in the face of conventional usage and invites that misplaced concreteness that inheres in all reification. Yet it is done here to suggest connections of considerable historical depth, intuitively understood to exist, between established institutions of belief, the structure of personhood and built form. Thus the pervasiveness of the classical political structure of *clientilismo* in modern Italy is to be understood as responsive to those formations of space, person, and belief that continue both because of and despite the ongoing contestation of meaning. By *clientism*, we mean that organization of power in terms of relations of dependency between patrons and clients. Clientism derives its efficacy not from the authority of party organization but by the subjective procedure of granting favors and exacting loyalty. Public arenas are ideally suited for that order of information exchange by which mobilization of support is obtained. Piazza politics begins or ends with the assurance that a patron has produced the advantage promised or that he has betrayed that trust granted to him. To be a player in that political process requires one to be personally present, to assume one's designated position in the piazza, in the bar, the street, wherever one can both observe and be observed, to make, that is, a presentation of self and to evaluate that of others.

The politicization of public space that Mussolini so skillfully managed from his balcony above the Piazza Venezia in Rome is the other side of the coin of the domestication of public space that my wife and I were daily witness to in Sermoneta in the early 1950s.

Central to this chapter is the distinction drawn between inner and outer, both in respect to space and to the individual, a dichotomy that in the last analysis locates its meaning in the eye of the beholder. When I first went to Italy, it was my own experience of space, socially informed, that invited me to take note of what I felt to be a transgression of the boundary between the inside and the outside. There is no reason whatsoever to believe that my perception of Italians living domestically in public space is a rendition of what they were doing and still do that they would subscribe to. *Al fresco*, in the sense of living outdoors, is made much of in Italian culture as long as it does not involve camping, but it does not mean that they are deliberately substituting an "outsideness" for an "insideness." Which is to say of course that all spatial constructions are experientially constructed and, of course, contested. Not all Romans who live in the old center, for instance, are in agreement with the trattoria proprietors who wish to put ever more dining tables in the street or piazza, for the pleasure of those who find them preferred places to eat at the cost of those who covet that space for walking. What I am saying here is in response to and in agreement with Margaret Rodman's assertion in her chapter (in this volume) that space is not given in nature but is socially constructed, continuously contested, and known experientially. In the same paper she admonishes against the use of "distinctions between . . . exterior and interior [which] still permeate many of our assumptions about the way the world works." I would contend, however, that what is conceptually regarded as inappropriate for the problem of understanding the flux that surrounds residential community spaces in modern cities may prove heuristic for thinking about the marked continuity that has characterized the construction of space in the north and south of Europe, the differential value attributed to that space, and the structure of the personhood that inhabits it.

8

Mapping Contested Terrains: Schoolrooms and Streetcorners in Urban Belize

CHARLES RUTHEISER

Several recent studies of schooling discuss the social dynamics of educational institutions in distinctly spatial terms, describing schools and, especially, classrooms, as "zones of conflict" (Willis 1977). Within these educational settings, students from subordinate groups resist or subvert the hegemonic messages mediated through the practices of schooling. Students are said to "carve out space" within these institutional settings for their own distinctive cultural identities and practices. The generative contexts for these oppositional student behaviors are usually qualitatively different sites within the urban landscape, such as the experienced or imagined adult workplace (for example, the "shopfloor culture" described by Willis 1977) or, more simply, "the streets" (McLaren 1986).

The formulations of Willis, McLaren, and other "resistance theorists" provide a powerful corrective to deterministic and agentless theories of schooling advanced by both modernization theorists and critics of neocolonial education alike (e.g., Inkeles and Smith 1974; Carnoy 1974; Watson 1982). Yet, despite multiple references to "arenas," "terrains," "sites," and "zones," resistance theorists pay little attention to schools, homes, or street corners as concrete, meaningful *places* within historically constituted urban landscapes. Both educational and oppositional settings are treated as passive and disconnected backdrops to the dramaturgy of authority and resistance, rather than as constitutive elements of cultural meaning and social activity. Variations among social sites are not examined, nor is consideration given to the wider urban environment in which these locales and their inhabitants are situated. These are crucial omissions, for not all street corners, much less all neighborhoods and all schools, provide the same kinds of generative contexts for belief and behavior, nor do they possess the same sociocultural meanings for the inhabitants of the city.

An understanding of the qualitative variability between and among social sites is essential not only for analyzing the dialectic of authority and resistance within schools, but for making sense of the differential constructions of social reality that inform the lives of all urban residents. A major concern of this chapter is to show how schools and their oppositional settings are situated within socially defined topographies that overlie and provide contrasting sets of identities and associations to the physical city for its inhabitants.

The city in question is Belize City, the largest and arguably, only "true" urban area in Belize, a small, multiethnic, and recently independent nation on the Caribbean coast of Central America. Drawing on fieldwork conducted during 1986–87 and 1991, this chapter first sketches the changing contours of the city's social and built environment, then looks at the "place"—variously conceived—of schools in the urban landscape before discussing the variable sense of place that these peculiar "social establishments" (Goffman 1961) create within urban settings. The final section focuses on a social site that has been identified as the locus of a distinct counterschool "street culture"—the "base."

THE CITY AS CONTEXT

Although it lacks the scale of Guatemala City, Kingston, or even Port of Spain, Belize City is unambiguously urban in its context. In 1991, approximately 50,000 persons inhabited a compact, densely populated area at the tip of a swampy peninsula that formed at a secondary mouth of the Belize River (Central Statistical Office 1991; hereafter CSO). The city's population is roughly five times the size of Orange Walk Town, the nation's second largest urban center. Together with the growing satellite towns of Ladyville, Hattieville, and Burrell Boom, Belize City is home to almost one in every three Belizeans (CSO 1991).

The city has a distinctive cultural orientation. Approximately three-quarters of city residents identify themselves as "Creole," a term generally taken to refer to English-speaking persons of African or Euro-African descent. Still, virtually every one of the nation's ethnic groups—Mestizos, Mayans, Garifuna, East Indians, Arabs, Chinese, and whites—is represented to some extent in the urban population.[1] This ethnic diversity is, however, mediated by intermarriage and cross-cut by divisions of class and political affiliation.

Belize City was founded in the latter half of the seventeenth century by English and Scottish buccaneers who turned from piracy to exporting the region's abundant supplies of dyewood and mahogany with the labor of African slaves. By the early nineteenth century the settlement achieved an urban primacy that endured even after the official capital was moved fifty kilometers inland to Belmopan in 1973 (Foster 1987). The city is still Belize's paramount economic, educational, and information center. All the main commercial enterprises are headquartered there, along with the production facilities for radio, television, and newspapers. Belize City possesses over half of the nation's secondary school places and the vast majority of post-secondary institutions, including Belize's only university, the University College of Belize (UCB). The city has also been, and remains, the principal channeling point for the import of foreign cultural influences and the export of migrants abroad. Until the 1960s, the dominant metropolitan referent was Great Britain. However, since then, the influences have been increasingly from the United States.

Owing partly to the intensity of foreign influence, Belize City occupies a contested place in Belizean popular consciousness. In a strained ambivalence not unlike that which characterizes the relationship between New York City and the rest of the United States, Belize City is alternately desired, disrespected, and detested. The contrast of meaning is epitomized in the response of a city newspaper editor to claims that Belize City "lacked culture": "Above all, Belize City has culture. It is a drug influenced culture, one which copies America too slavishly, and one which has no stomach for sacrifice. But it is the culture which gives Belize City identity and makes it flashy and attractive, like a Saturday night hooker" (Hyde 1986: 2).

For many of those who live in the district towns and rural areas, Belize City is spoken of as a sink of depravity—a squalid, crowded, and impersonal place full of lazy and hostile people. Still, the city receives a steady stream of migrants from these areas. For some nationalists, Belize City represents another sort of evil: a Creole-dominated neocolonial society linked in a dependent relation to the outside world. Although in large measure prompted by the city's vulnerability to hurricanes, the transfer of the capital to Belmopan was in part motivated by the desire of some nationalist politicians to make a clean break from the colonial past. This has not quite occurred, as many government workers, including top officials, continue to live in Belize City and commute to the capital. Only tourists, simultaneously pulled by the allures of the offshore cays and the interior and pushed by the not-so-thinly-veiled warnings of their guidebooks, tend not to linger more than they have to.

In the decade following the granting of independence in 1981, Belize City experienced substantial, and largely unplanned, change. Reclamation ventures turned mangrove swamp into housing sites on the city's northwestern margins and sparked a modest flight of the urban middle class from the city proper. A sewer system, funded by the Canadian International Development Agency, was completed after more than ten years of effort. New hotels were built and further ventures planned to serve a growing tourist trade. The government even constructed a new central market and a new bridge over the Haulover Creek.

These changes in the urban landscape were largely cosmetic, however. Only a third of the city's households were connected to the new sewer system by the summer of 1991. Under- and unemployment remained high: in 1990 it was estimated that some 40 percent of males and nearly 70 percent of females aged 16 to 25 lacked regular jobs. Overall, a large percentage of the city's population continue to live below the poverty line in crowded, substandard housing (Farazali 1987; UNICEF 1990). Since the late 1980s, as in other parts of the Caribbean and North America, crack cocaine has replaced marijuana as the drug of choice on city streets, while youth gangs and violent crime emerged as increasingly prominent features of urban social life.

The main physical feature of Belize City is the Haulover Creek, which divides the city into "north side" and "south side." The north side was the original locus of the seventeenth-century settlement, while the street grid of the easternmost half of the south side was the product of planned expansion in the early nineteenth century. The two sides are joined by three bridges, of which the oldest, and most important, is the southernmost, or "Swing," bridge. The bridge serves as the major crossing point for pedestrian and vehicular traffic within the central city and links Albert, Regent, and Queen Streets in a unified commercial corridor dominated by Indian and Arab merchants.

The Haulover Creek has historically been a first line of social differentiation and conflict within the city. With the exception of the Southern Foreshore section of Albert, the south side has tended, and continues, to be the poorer and more densely populated of the two regions (Urban Development Corporation 1989). Although the northern bank of the Haulover Creek has its share of crowded and impoverished neighborhoods, all of the highest status neighborhoods are located along the northern seacoast.

Administratively, Belize City is divided into nineteen "divisions," which serve primarily as electoral units (see Figure 8.1). Some of these units conform to distinctive neighborhoods as defined by residents, others are more arbitrary impositions of municipal authorities and encompass a number of popularly recognized areas. Neighborhoods displayed varying degrees of sharpness in their boundaries, as well as differing values in the geography of cultural respectability. All of the high-status urban neighborhoods—Fort George, Caribbean Shores, King's Park, and the Southern Foreshore of Albert—are situated along the ocean front. A major exception to this pattern is in the neighborhoods along the city's southern edge, such as Yarborough, Queen Charlotte Town, and Port Loyola, where tides directed the effluence from the city's network of drainage canals. These areas, not surprisingly, were among the city's poorest ([Urban Development Corporation, hereafter UDC] 1989; SPEAR 1989). On the south side of the city, these canals helped mark clear boundaries between similar, densely populated working-

Figure 8.1
Belize City Neighborhoods

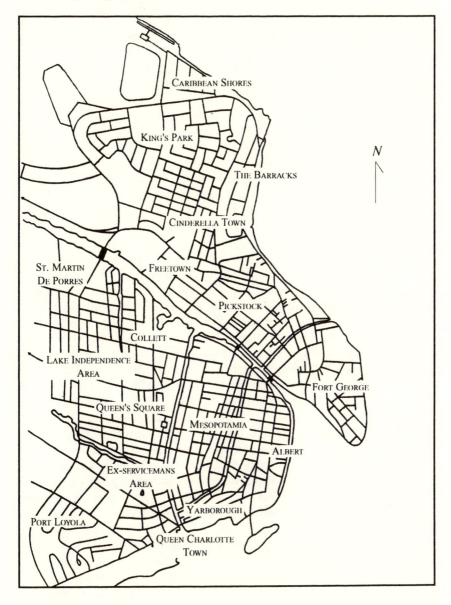

class neighborhoods, such as Mesopotamia, Queen's Square, Ex-Service-men's Area, and Collett.

Different phases of land reclamation, road construction, and systems of street naming also provided objective features that served as markers of urban zones. Boundaries between less-extensive neighborhoods were often fuzzy, with a loose sense of area radiating out from some central point—a street, alleyway, or other feature of the built environment. Residents of many neighborhoods developed alternatives to the official toponymy. Not surprisingly, upper-income residential areas had the most clearly defined senses of boundaries within the city. The borders of such areas as Caribbean Shores and northern King's Park are not only marked by the quality of housing but by the patrol circuits of private security guards. New elite areas that emerged outside of the city along the Northern Highway, such as Bella Vista, embodied the most extreme form of residential segregation by physical separation traditionally found in colonial cities.

Not all neighborhoods had unambiguous class identities, however. Even poor, densely populated areas like Mesopotamia and Pickstock had their share of socially respectable households. However, rising rates of violent crime in the late 1980s triggered an exodus of those families who could afford to do so.[2]

With a few exceptions, ethnic minorities tend not to cluster in distinctive residential zones but are distributed all over the urban landscape in largely Creole neighborhoods. The principal exception to the pattern of Creole dominance is found in the professional-commercial elite neighborhoods of Fort George, King's Park, Caribbean Shores, and Bella Vista. Mestizo families constituted the largest single group in these areas, with smaller numbers of Arabs, Chinese, and whites, as well as predominantly lighter-skinned Creoles. During the 1980s, the influx of impoverished Central American immigrants also served to increase the diversity of several lower-income neighborhoods, such as St. Martin De Porres and Port Loyola. Belize City lacks any comprehensive zoning ordinances; consequently all but the elite neighborhoods are characterized by a mix of residential and commercial uses. Even the poorest and most marginal areas possessed small stores selling basic goods, such as flour, sugar, cooking fuel, and the like. Some neighborhoods also are home to small workshops, although most of the city's limited industry was located along the Haulover Creek or on the extreme western edge of town. In nonelite areas, where houses tend to be small and families large, yards and streets are heavily utilized by persons of all ages, particularly children and adult women. Neighborhood social life for many adult men centers around the local bar or rum shop. Private clubs, such as the Pickwick, served a similar purpose for upper-income groups.

From solicitation of cognitive maps and by more informal investigation, city residents possessed highly variable levels of urban knowledge and spatial awareness. Age, gender, ethnicity, class, and occupation intersected to impose distinctive social topographies on the urban landscape for members of different groups. Most persons I interviewed had rather limited familiarity with areas outside their own residential zones and the central commercial core. In other words, there was lots of "empty space" in their cognitive maps (McDonogh, this volume). This was especially the case for the more privileged members of urban society. Residents of King's Park and Caribbean Shores, or for that matter even intermediate areas like Albert, were much more likely to visit Miami, Los Angeles, or New York than Port Loyola, Yarborough, or St. Martin De Porres.

Schools proved important but partial exceptions to these patterns of selective movement and association, as they both reinforced and cross-cut social and spatial divisions. The urban school system provided the major "stations" where the "time-space paths" (Hägerstrand 1975) of youthful residents crossed, albeit not always intentionally or without conflict. However, as will be discussed in greater detail below, patterns of circulation and sociospatial interaction by youth in and out of school both reflected and actively shaped existing patterns of social and cultural differentiation.

MAPPING THE ECOLOGIES OF URBAN SCHOOLING

In describing the functioning of schools and their relationships with surrounding communities, Belizean educators frequently used a set of metaphors drawn more from hydrology than pedagogy. "Catchment areas" and "streams" referred to, respectively, the sources of a school's students and the curricular channels they were directed into. Students who successfully negotiated the educational system found their way into different sections of the "pool" of skilled labor, where they were absorbed by the "employment sponge." Those who got lost en route constituted the "wastage rate." Consistent with the fluid imagery, the overall system was mapped on a "flow chart;" and, of course, there was the "brain drain" of the most-educated to metropolitan centers.

Such generative metaphors greatly reduce the sociocultural realities they describe—and, indeed, speak powerfully of the objectification and depersonalization of the consumers of education—but in so doing, they also crudely chart the trajectories of persons through time and space. They also provide a starting point for analyzing some of the linkages between schools and urban society. School catchment areas describe social rather than natural topographies that reflect, among other things, inequalities in the distribution of wealth and in the availability of educational opportunities, as well as qualitative differences between schools and among the students who pass through them.

The selective principles that define catchment areas vary considerably by the level, location, and institutional identity of the school. Primary education is both compulsory and free, as in the United States, but unlike that system, Belize defines no municipal school districts to organize the flow of youth through the system. In Belize City, where the majority of primary schools are managed by religious denominations but funded by the state, catchment areas have been historically determined by religious affiliation and family tradition, which tended to coincide with neighborhood residence. Increasingly, however, parental assessments of differential educational quality bring children in from outside these traditional areas, sometimes at the expense of neighborhood children. The status of a primary school usually parallels—but not necessarily—that of its surrounding locale. Several renowned primaries, such as Grace Chapel, are located in "bad" neighborhoods. Although precise figures are lacking, observation of the daily flow of uniformed schoolchildren through the streets indicates that a significant number of primary school students attend institutions outside their immediate neighborhood.

Although Belize City primary schools serve a public wider than denominational affiliation or neighborhood residence, they also serve as local community institutions to a much greater extent than do secondary schools. Several of the schools are located on the grounds of parish churches, such as St. Ignatius and St. Mary's; others take their names from the area in which they are located, for example, Queen's Square Anglican and Lake Independence Methodist. No matter their name or association, all primary schools serve as sites for a variety of important civic and social functions, from polling stations and meeting places to playgrounds for local youth. Since the advent of American-inspired youth gangs in 1988, schools have become key battlegrounds both during and after hours.

Outside Belize City, primary schools have a greater local importance, in both symbolic and practical terms. In the more remote rural areas of the country, the modest timber or concrete primary school buildings and their flagpoles are often the most tangible manifestations of outside authority. Even in the more accessible villages, the school building often doubles as the place of worship or locus for official civic activities, such as village council meetings (see Jesuit Mission 1944:3; Jones 1971; Ashcraft 1973).

Whereas primary schools are widely distributed over the Belizean landscape, secondary schooling is largely an urban and more selective affair. Nationwide, only half of primary school graduates go on to secondary education, and less than half of them will eventually graduate (Academy for Educational Development 1988). These rates of participation are much lower for the inhabitants of rural areas, as all but seven of the twenty-nine secondary schools are to be found within the boundaries of the eight centers of population classified as urban.[3]

Eleven of the urban schools, accounting for over one-half of the nation's secondary school places, are located in Belize City. These schools are far less likely to be formally identified with specific neighborhoods than primary schools, as they draw their students from all over town and, although to a much lesser degree, from the districts as well. With a few exceptions, secondary schools in Belize City have made little effort to orient themselves to the neighborhoods they are located in or near.

One factor that works against greater involvement of city secondary schools in their local environments is their spatial distribution. Five of the eleven schools, accounting for roughly half of the city's secondary enrollment, are located in an "educational zone" on the northwestern margins of the city, adjacent to the Belize College of Nursing, the Extramural Department of the University of the West Indies, and the University College of Belize (see Figure 8.2). They are adjacent to some of the city's wealthiest residential neighborhoods, among them Caribbean Shores and King's Park, but are not close enough to be considered in them. Only two of the schools in the zone, the elite St. John's College and up-and-coming Pallotti High School, regularly draw significant numbers of students from these neighborhoods. The three other secondary institutions, the E. P. Yorke, Gwendolyn Lizarraga, and Nazarene high schools, draw most of their students from a range of working-class neighborhoods.[4]

The six other secondary schools in the city are located in a variety of residential neighborhoods, ranging from elite St. Catherine's Academy in posh Fort George to lowly Excelsior High School in the marginal Port Loyola area. While the reputations of schools tended to coincide with their immediate surroundings, changes in neighborhood and academic reputation sometimes proceeded at different rates and in different directions.

A good example of the social tensions produced by the differing rates of change between the school and neighborhood is provided by Wesley College, Belize's oldest secondary school, which turned out several generations of Methodist Creole civil servants and professionals from its seaside Yarborough campus since its founding in 1882 (Methodist Church 1975). In the early 1970s, a progressive principal at the college initiated a program to assist residents of what had become one of the city's poorest neighborhoods at that time. However, protests from the Methodist board of education and the parents of the then mostly middle-class student body led to the end of the program and the firing of the principal.

Over the next two decades, Wesley's institutional image itself declined as it lost elite students to other, more modern institutions, especially Belize Technical College, and to emigration to the United States. By the late 1980s, Wesley was still an overwhelmingly Creole school, but the majority of students now came from working-class households from all over the city.

One school that possessed a much greater sense of community mission and had a greater proportion of students from its immediate locale than any other institution was Excelsior High School in Port Loyola.[5] Situated at the bottom of the educational status hierarchy, Excelsior was viewed by outsiders as an institution whose main function was not so much as education as keeping the kids off the street. A large percentage of its student body

Figure 8.2
Distribution of Secondary Schools in Belize City

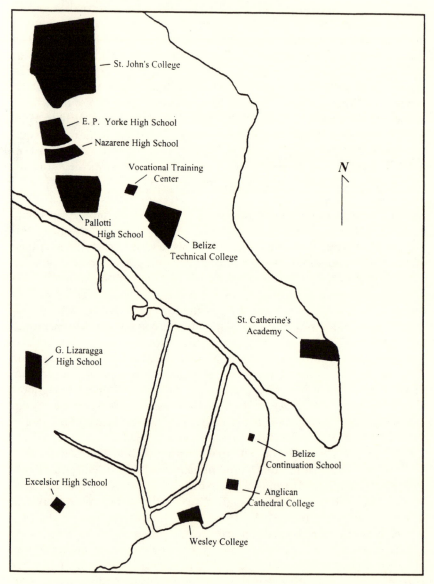

was composed of students who had been expelled from, or not accepted by, other city secondary schools. Still, it was one of the few city schools that saw itself as responding explicitly to the needs of its south-side neighborhood.

As the above examples indicate, the most decisive factor mediating the relationship between secondary schools and their adjacent neighborhoods is the selective order of community created by admission practices, which are themselves a mix born of parochial tradition and administrative vision. Grades, religious affiliation, and—as schooling beyond the primary level is neither free nor compulsory—ability to pay are the principal criteria employed by schools in shaping their student bodies. For their part, applicants are driven by perceptions of institutional prestige and curricular specialization as well as family tradition and religious affiliation. Each institution thus brings together different mixes of youth who tend to share such characteristics as class, ethnicity, religion, and perceived academic ability.

However, the social composition of student bodies is subject to considerable change over time and is not always in accord with the stereotypical ethnic, class, or religious identities associated with particular schools. In the late 1980s, for example, there were almost as many Catholic as Methodist students at Wesley College. Meanwhile, across town at elite St. John's and St. Catherine's—both typified as "Spanish" or Mestizo institutions—more than a third of the students identified themselves as Creoles. A number of them were from middle-class families that in the past had sent their children to Wesley, but the majority of Creoles at the two institutions were both Catholic and light-skinned (Rutheiser n.d.: 158–161).

THE SCHOOL AS CONTEXT

No matter their size or the scale of their physical plants, schools constitute a distinct kind of social space in Belize City. The institutional culture that all schools differentially shared was premised on an experiential break with the domains of home, neighborhood, and wider community. As Giddens notes, educational establishments derive much of their power from operating "within closed boundaries" (Giddens 1984: 135). This break is given quite emphatic representation in the built forms of school environments. These varied from the professionally planned, twenty-building, ninety-acre campus of elite St. John's to the solitary converted hurricane shelter on a small, swampy lot that comprised Excelsior's campus. The other school campuses ranged unevenly between the two extremes. The institutions in the "educational zone" all covered relatively large extents of land, but only Belize Technical College, which was located outside the zone, came anywhere near matching the facilities of St. John's. Belize Technical owed its large amount of open space to the fact that when the school was built in the 1950s, its Cinderella Town neighborhood then constituted the periphery of urban settlement (Everitt 1986).

However, school boundaries were not only spatial—for example, in the manner of fences, yards, and compartmentalized buildings—but temporal as well. Intersecting spatial and temporal boundaries not only demarcated the school from the outside world but structured the flow of social interaction within. In a related sense, educational philosophies and curricular boundaries frame differentially valued school knowledge and determine what will be taught to whom under what conditions (see Bernstein 1971; Bourdieu and Passeron 1977).

Although Belizean secondary schools can be said to share certain basic institutional forms and orientations, this culture of schooling is by no means homogenous or static. These schools have exhibited significant variation over time in their access to resources, their curricular biases, their prestige, their ethos. While all schools share the same general patterns of managing time and space, administering discipline, framing knowledge, and creating a distinctive sense of community, they do so to differing extents, with varying intensities, and with variable degrees of success. There are very clear relations between the ideology and status of a school, the people it serves, its access to resources, the elaborateness of its physical plant, and the "tightness" of its temporal and spatial boundaries. There are also differences in the adaptations of students to school regimes and in the kinds of challenges they direct toward school authority.

No matter the institution, however, school boundaries are quite permeable; the outside world intrudes in numerous ways. Even the most prestigious schools are only partially successful in directing the behavior of students within the classroom; they are even less effective when students are beyond the physical grounds of the institution. Even for the "best" and most committed of students—and young Belizeans are by no means unique in this regard—the demands of school culture are usually subordinated to the more pressing concerns of adolescent social life that arise from a multitude of nonschool settings.

One specific kind of nonschool setting is that which generates what ethnographers of schooling refer to as *oppositional behaviors*. One of the most important of these sites is the real or imagined adult workplace. As a postcolonial society with an economy geared to export agriculture and tourism, Belize lacks the kinds of workplaces necessary to produce an industrial "shopfloor culture" such as Willis (1977) describes for the English Midlands. Still, the cultural productions of the majority of urban youth denied access to the system of educational opportunity extol a similar sense of manualism and male bravado. During my first phase of research in 1986–87, Belizean popular discourse defined a distinctive social space that served as the symbolic locus of a distinctively urban, counterschool culture—the "base."

THE BASE

If schools are sites and symbols of cultural respectability and social opportunity, the street corners, alleyways, and playgrounds appropriated by the "crews" or "posses" of "baseboys" and "basegirls" symbolized the lack of both.[6] Bases were a ubiquitous presence in the city, found in virtually all commercial and residential areas, the notable exception being the wealthiest neighborhoods. Usually situated so as to afford a view of places where people congregated or crowds passed, bases also had to provide cover for some secluded "backstage" activities, particularly the sale or use of ganja (marijuana).

Bases had strong cultural and ethnic identifications. While Belizeans of all ages and origins "hung out" or engaged in some private appropriation of public space, bases were, as one youth explained to me, "Creole thangs," exclusive to Belize City. In addition to ethnoracial identity, base members tended to share a number of social characteristics. They ranged in age from twelve to the early twenties, although a few were as young as eight. They tended to come from "roots" neighborhoods like Trench Town, Yabra, and the Pink Jungle, and they either lacked an education beyond the primary level or had been expelled from secondary school. In many cases, both parents had emigrated, leaving them in the care of older siblings, other relatives, or family friends. Usually unemployed or engaged in short-term *ketch-an-kill* jobs (labor of an unskilled manual sort), they possessed vague or outrightly pessimistic notions of where their futures lay. Bases were also predominantly male domains, with basegirls possessing their own sites. Beginning in mid-morning, base crews passed their time listening to rap and reggae, smoking ganja and (more recently) crack, engaging in petty crime, and alternatively hassling passers-by or being hassled by the police, whom they referred to as "Babylon boops."

It is important to note that, in 1986–87 at least, "chillin" or "hanging" at a base was not automatically equivalent to gang membership in the same sense as belonging to the Crips or Bloods. Indeed, there was considerable ambiguity in what the terms *baseboy* or *basegirl* referred to. At times they were used by the more socially respectable Belizean citizenry to refer to any unemployed or impoverished youth, whether or not they actually belonged to a base or engaged in criminal activities.

The meaning of the label was further confounded as I found that between 15 to 20 percent of male Creole and Garifuna[7] students in Belize City secondary schools reported that they frequented bases on at least a weekly basis (Rutheiser 1991). Most, but not all, of student-baseboys were from working-class Afro-Belizean backgrounds. However, students were rarely core members of a crew, as the temporal demands of schooling competed directly with those of the base. When commitment to the base won out over the demands of schooling, expulsion was usually the eventual result. By contrast, female Creole students and non–Afro-Belizean students of both genders rarely participated in base activities and possessed extremely negative opinions of baseboys and basegirls.

Contrary to perceptions of the media and the more privileged members of Belizean society throughout the 1980s, bases were not necessarily dens of vice and iniquity, but sites of sociability and solidarity for those youths who found themselves excluded from the system of social opportunity. Even without outward manifestations of illegal behavior, the mere idle lounging of youth was viewed by the respectable public as a delinquent activity. Nor did the majority of Belize City youth who lacked more than a primary education necessarily belong to a base crew, use drugs, engage in crime, or lack a job.

Although they occupied the margins of respectable society, baseboys and basegirls nonetheless possessed considerable influence in defining a citywide youth culture. Being keen observers of the latest trends manifested both locally and in the transnational mass media, the inhabitants of the bases were frequently the prime arbitrators of what was "most fresh" or "inna de style" among Afro-Belizean youth, especially, but not limited to, the areas of music and fashion. The principal venues for the diffusion of "street style" were the dance clubs and discos that anchored the social lives of city residents between the ages of 16 and 25. Although discos were nominally off-limits to students, on pain of suspension or expulsion, many went regardless. Through street style, the influence of base culture extended considerably beyond out-of-school youth to reach even some of the scions of the respectable Creole middle class, particularly the males.

TRANSFORMATION AND CONFLICT

While bases remained a ubiquitous feature of the Belize City landscape in 1991, they had undergone a qualitative shift in identity. While in the past many base crews had functioned and identified themselves as gangs, they tended to be isolated and localized networks of association. As recently as 1987, bases—and their crews—derived their identity primarily from their locality: for example, Church Street Base or Pink Jungle Base. Four years later, bases were not so much discrete, individualized outposts for local youth as "chapters" in a hierarchical network of gangs divided into two citywide confraternities called Crips and Bloods.

The definition of gang territories partially reproduced the historic north side–south side divide within the city, with the Crips claiming the north and the Bloods the south. These territories are far from homogenous, however, as the much larger Crip organization "ruled" over parts of such southside neighborhoods as Port Loyola and Mesopotamia. Nor is place of residence coterminous with gang identity, as members of both groups live all over the city, creating numerous irruptions and points of potential conflict.[8]

The official interpretation voiced by police and government officials insists that Belizean Crips and Bloods "are not real gang members, but only use the name" (Branigan 1989). They claim that gang identification is largely a copycat effect produced by films like *Colors* upon impressionable Belizean youth.[9] Another school of interpretation agrees that movies like *Colors* and a steady diet of U.S. television intensified the local popularity of gang identity after 1988 but that the gangs themselves were first introduced by returning Belizean youth who were gang members in Los Angeles (Branigan 1989). A third interpretation emphasizes that "all of this is bigger than just young people" and that the gangs are merely a front for the activities of older Belizeans engaged in the domestic and international trafficking of cocaine (Ewens 1990: 20).

All of these contain an element of the truth. It is undeniable that the gang craze "exploded" after the showing of *Colors* in 1988, sparking a flood of "wanna-bes." However, as one youth explained to me, wanna-bes "just get fucked up by true gang-bangers." It is also clear that the gangs are intimately linked to the transition from a marijuana- to a crack-cocaine-based local drug economy. Gang and chapter turfs delimit territories within a centralized system of drug dealing. Numerous bases of the mid–1980s had become dedicated crack houses by 1991.

Despite police denials, and for whatever the causes, the gangs are indeed quite real. For the residents of Belize City, it makes little difference if they are chartered franchises of "real" North American gangs or creative appropriations of metropolitan forms by local youth. By one estimate, the north-side-based Crips and south-side-based Bloods have 1,000 and 300 members, respectively (Branigan 1989). These figures are nearly impossible to confirm, however, and do not distinguish between hard-core members and supporters. Still, one only has to observe an all-too-frequent procession for a gang member's funeral to realize that the numbers are far higher than the total of seventy-five estimated by former Minister of the Interior Curl Thompson (Branigan 1989).

Nor are gangs a phenomenon limited to out-of-school youth. Students whom I talked to in the summer of 1991 reported considerable pressure either to side with a particular gang or pay protection in order to guarantee their safe passage to and from school. The previous year many students commuting to schools in the educational zone were mugged or beaten by gang members. The police subsequently stepped up patrols in the area, but students were, quite rightly, skeptical of the ability and/or commitment of the police in dealing with a gang problem that they officially claim does not exist (see esp. Ewens 1990). Periodic sweeps by police, such as during Operation Thunder in 1990, provided only a temporary—and from a civil rights standpoint, highly questionable—respite.[10]

Gangs have also become an increasingly common aspect of life within schools, both at the primary and secondary levels. As of 1991, gang activity was more frequent and widespread in primary than in secondary schools. However, this is changing as the primary school cohorts enter secondary schools. Although many gang-bangers will be selected out by academic, financial, and other barriers, a significant number will make the transition to secondary schools, especially those institutions that cater to lower-income students. At Excelsior High School, for example, a number of the older students claimed that as many as one-third of the first-year students had gang affiliations.[11] Similar claims were made for Wesley College and Belize Continuation School, a vocationally oriented secondary school for female students who, for the most part, had been expelled from other institutions.

Low-status schools are not the only ones troubled by gang activity: even more prestigious institutions like Belize Technical and Anglican Cathedral College had Crips and Bloods in their student populations. Gangs and street culture do not affect all schools or all students to the same degree. On the contrary, the scions of the light-skinned Creole and Mestizo elite who attended St. John's College, St. Catherine's Academy, and Pallotti High School constituted a distinct social network that eschewed contact with students from other schools and nonstudents alike. Throughout the 1980s, they preferred the forms of white North American popular culture and rejected the Afrocentricity of street style. Whereas students from Excelsior or even Technical or Anglican Cathedral College were more apt to spend their out-of-school time with their friends on the streets and bases of Belize City, St. John's kids were more likely to be playing school-organized sports activities or clustered in their living rooms playing Nintendo. At their most extreme, the practices of the St. John's/St. Catherine's/Pallotti axis seemed predicated on a complete denial of their Belizean provenance, a tendency nowhere more apparent than in their musical preferences for North American heavy metal in favor of the pan-Afro-Caribbean rhythms of reggae, soca, and rap.

Nonschool environments, such as the home, the playground, or the streets, are usually thought of as being less regimented spaces than educational establishments. Behavior and deportment on the street corner is "looser" and in every way counterposed to the achievement ideology of the school (McLaren 1986). Schools are characterized by institutionalized patterns of spatial, temporal, and disciplinary organization that make them specialized "power containers" (Giddens 1984). There are different kinds and modalities of social power, however.

Students, for example, have the power, within limits to be sure, to resist or otherwise evade school authority as manifest in the teacher or any other aspect of the environment of schooling. This power is nurtured through social collectivities generated at other sites—the home, the neighborhood, or the base. The influence of baseboys and basegirls on the definition of a citywide youth culture is also a kind of social power. However, the power that Belizean Crips and Bloods possess is of a different order than the previous two examples: it is in some ways more similar to the power associated with institutional environments, such as schools.

The emergence of a citywide network of gangs adds yet another selectively defined topography to an already-crowded urban landscape, one that is characterized by quite regimented notions of space and deportment. Whatever the police or more respectable society might think, gang culture is all about discipline, identity, and the command of space. There is nothing loose about the stylized gestures and symbols that define identity, nor about the control of activity within territorial boundaries. What is truly powerful about this appropriation of space is that the general public, not just gang members, must heed it or ignore it at their peril.

This chapter has tried to convey some sense of the urban realities faced by the youth population of Belize City by focusing on how two radically opposed sites are situated within the urban landscape and the different patterns of sociospatial relations that they create and sustain. Of course, there are other social sites besides schools and bases that shape the beliefs, identities, and behaviors of Belize City youth. For student and nonstudent alike, the most crucial social learning is encountered not in the classroom, but in the course of their daily encounters with the forces of parental authority, law, and capital, their experiences of sex, play, and work, and, increasingly, in the satellite television they watch "beamed dareck from Babylon" (the United States). Future research will concentrate on how these local, national, and transnational domains intersect to reproduce cultural identities and patterns of social activity in the urban environments of postcolonial states like Belize.

NOTES

This chapter is based on research conducted in Belize during 1986–87 and 1991 with support from IIE/Fulbright, the Inter-American Foundation, the Johns Hopkins University, and the Faculty Research and Creative Activities Support Fund of Western Michigan University. I would especially like to thank Paulette Broaster and Leslie Gillette for their valuable assistance in the field and Gary McDonogh, Robert Rotenberg, and Meredith McGill for their many helpful comments in the preparation of this manuscript.

1. The term *Creole*, while subject to some variable definition, is usually taken to refer to a person of African or Euro-African ancestry. For a more in-depth discussion of the dynamics of Creole identity, see Rutheiser (in press).

2. One survey conducted by the University College of Belize found that 64 percent of Belize City households surveyed had experienced a robbery or some form of violent assault against one of its members in 1990.

3. Belize City, Orange Walk Town, Corozal Town, Dangriga Town, San Ignacio/Santa Elena, Belmopan, Benque Viejo del Carmen, and Punta Gorda.

4. The Belize Vocational Training Center is also located in this area. While it is officially classified by the government as a "secondary school," it only provides a one-year training program.

5. As at the primary level, district towns present more intimate operating environments for secondary schools. After a wave of mergers and amalgamations in the 1970s and early 1980s, only one town possessed more than one secondary school. Underscoring the more focused connection between the school and the surrounding community, the institutions in three of the largest towns are known as "community colleges" and are managed by a local board of governors. The sense of community so-defined in district high schools goes beyond the limits of the towns they are located in. Significant numbers of their students come from adjacent rural areas, although limited public transport and the high cost of boarding in towns constrains the accessibility of secondary education for rural youth.

6. While I have been unable to trace the genealogy of the term *base*, the term *posse* presents an interesting case of cross-cultural flow and influence. It appears to have first originated among "rude-boy" gangs in Jamaica, who had appropriated the label from American Westerns. Reintroduced by Jamaican gangs to the United States, it was in turn appropriated by urban African-American youth. It is unclear whether the Belizean usage stems from the "original" Jamaican context, or was imported, like so much else, with other metropolitan subcultural forms. In anglophone Eastern Caribbean societies like Barbados and Trinidad, a similar appropriation of social space is referred to as "liming" (Lieber 1981).

7. The Garifuna were formerly known in the ethnographic record as the Black Carib and are the product of the intermarriage of escaped African slaves and aboriginal Carib Indians on the eastern Caribbean island of St. Vincent. Deported to the Caribbean coast of Central America by a victorious British army in the late eighteenth century, they comprise approximately 7 percent of the total Belizean population.

8. Further complicating the situation is the existence of gangs like the Rolling 60's that broke away from the Crips and are equally antagonistic to the Bloods and their former colleagues alike. One source notes that there may be as many as eight, rather than two, principal gangs in the city (Ewens 1990).

9. Released in 1988, the movie *Colors* dramatizes the multifaceted conflicts among gangs and between them and the police in 1980s Los Angeles.

10. Responding to public pressure, the police and the Belize Defense Force conducted a joint operation "to take back the city streets" in the fall of 1991. While initially successful in curtailing gang activity, its medium- to long-range consequences are unclear.

11. During the summer of 1991, an Excelsior Crip was killed in a drive-by shooting. The only difference from one in Los Angeles was that the shooter rode on a bicycle, rather than in a car.

Part III

Planning and Response

9

Beyond Built Form and Culture in the Anthropological Study of Residential Community Spaces

MARGARET RODMAN

Puzzling over the relationship between architecture and community formation in Toronto social housing prompted me to reflect more generally on the relationship between built form and culture. How well do buildings actually work to foster or discourage residential community? How do residents' communities affect the creation and experience of space in the buildings they live in? Answering these questions, it seems to me, requires a clearer understanding of just what it is we are trying to study. No doubt some reflection on this subject should lead in an architectural direction, for example, to a reconsideration of elite–mass culture relationships and of participatory design. But that path I leave to architects. Here I want to reconsider the relationship between built form and culture from an anthropological perspective, with an emphasis on how we study contemporary urban residential space and community in our own society.

What are we trying to understand? The creation and experience of place. The creation of place is at once so simple—planting a tree in a co-op courtyard—and so complex, as anyone studying the creation of urban space recognizes. Any experience of place weaves together space, built form, behavior, and ideas, at individual and collective levels. And it does so within particular social, economic, political, and historical contexts. There are serious limitations on experience as a basis for analysis of place, which I will consider later. But both the experience of place and its social construction seem to be key anthropological dimensions of what we are trying to understand. They link culture to built form, or rather dissolve the separation between place and culture.

As Miles Richardson (1989: 142) has observed, "place remains an underdeveloped concept in anthropology." So for me, the discovery in 1986 that there was an interdisciplinary group of people who specialized in the study of culture and built form was exciting. The group that attended the conference in Kansas that year on culture and built form was delightfully interdisciplinary. Geographers, historians, architects, and urban planners (among others) brought points of view that I found refreshing and stimulating. Yet, ultimately, I think many of us are unsatisfied with the kind of analysis that seems possible within the field of built form and culture. It is largely static, and either intuitive, functionalist, or structuralist in orientation. This dissatisfaction, I suggest, is partly a realization that what seemed divergent points of view on a common topic are in fact *not* very different. And they reflect other shared problems in conceptualizing the study of built form and culture.

In this chapter, I first outline my dissatisfaction with some of the analytical options that have been used in the study of built form and culture. I then discuss recent innovative approaches in other fields that have implications for the anthropological study of space. I hope to suggest how more powerful analyses of place might result from interdisciplinary rethinking of what we are trying to understand as anthropologists. The chapter goes on to consider material from my research with Matthew Cooper on Toronto housing co-ops in a way that combines both experience and social production of place.

BUILT FORM AND CULTURE

The idea that there is a relationship between "culture" and "built form" deserves critical attention. There must be a conceptual separation between the two for a relationship to exist in the first place. Culture in such a relationship must be separable from physical form.

Disciplinary separations have made this distinction seem natural. Architects, for example, can season their work with a cultural perspective: cultural considerations are nice if they are available, but they are not essential or intrinsic to conventional architectural training. Culture as a symbolized system of meaning becomes a domain separable from the principles of modern building construction.

For ethnographers in social anthropology, as Denise Lawrence and Setha Low note (1990: 457), built form has played a "relatively passive role." It provided the material context or framework within which to analyze household relations and symbolic orders. As such, descriptions of the built environment and its construction often were published separately from monographs in the 1940s and 1950s.

Richardson (1989: 142) suggests that nineteenth-century definitions of culture are to blame for the neglect of place in anthropology. They also help us to understand the conceptual separation of place and culture as part of the disciplinary distinction between geography and anthropology. Edward B. Tylor's ideational definition of culture asserted that it "was the intellectual property of people everywhere. . . . Since people everywhere had culture, and since culture was a product of thinking, the specific places societies inhabited had little bearing on general cultural development. . . . The concept was place free (Ibid.)."

Richardson claims that place has been a crucial concept in geography. "Indeed, place, in the sense of 'why things are where they are' is synonymous in the minds of many with the rise of geography as an academic discipline" (Ibid. 143). But some disagree. One of the co-editors of the volume that includes Richardson's paper argues that "within much social science two other concepts, those of community and class, have dominated to the extent that thinking and talking in terms of place has been largely impossible" (Agnew 1989: 9).

Those of us who advocate the inclusion of cultural considerations in the study of built form, then, are seeking to bridge this separation. For example, we may, as I started out to do here, explore the relationship between designing buildings in certain ways and the development of residential communities. But I have come to think that this idea of linking separate spheres of culture and built form is mistaken. In fact, it may be a major stumbling block. I will argue in this chapter that the gap we seek to span between the study of built form and the study of culture keeps us from more powerful analyses of place.

Some of the most influential studies of the relationship between culture and built form have approached the former through the latter (e.g., Bourdieu 1977; Glassie 1975; Lawrence 1982; Rapoport 1969). That is, they have approached the relationship between culture and built form through vernacular architecture, objects, spaces, and zones. Characteristically, the importance of cultural and social practice is emphasized, but analysis starts with material forms as a way of getting at the less tangible habits, beliefs, categories, and so on that order houses and other buildings.

In this respect, Roderick Lawrence's work on the study of contemporary urban housing is notably important. He (1987: 145) introduces a perspective that treats "the affective and spatial characteristics of houses" as complementary. He suggests (Ibid. ch. 5) a reorientation of housing research based on reciprocal relations between spatial forms and values (cultural, social, and personal). In this view, "people and built environments are linked in an active and reactive sense (Ibid. 200)."

Lawrence's position is innovative, but it is hindered by some of its own assumptions. Some limitations of Lawrence's work arise from personifying buildings as pseudoindividuals and from his reliance on structural analysis. He is in good company. For example, William Whyte (1988) in his penetrating analysis of urban spaces, *City*, observes that some sealed high-rise buildings get "sick," just like people. In attributing agency to buildings, Lawrence rewrites the relationship of built form to culture as one of people to people (or people to peoplelike buildings). While this is clearly reductionist, Lawrence's personification of buildings hints that he too may find the separation of culture and built form limiting.

Lawrence's reliance on structuralism presents a more serious problem. "Ambiguous zones" (Ibid. 172) straddle oppositions between, for example, public and private, interior and exterior. For Lawrence, domestic space can be analyzed cross-culturally in terms of "bipolar codes for the classification of space" (Ibid. 107): frontstage-backstage, upstairs-downstairs, dirty-clean, and so forth. Domestic spaces, on the one hand, and activities, on the other, are related to this scheme through spatial codes, which are seen to vary cross-culturally. He explains that his

intent is to illustrate how the home and household life can be considered in terms of a structural framework, using the word *structural* in the sense used by Levi-Strauss (1968). The rationale, in essence, for adopting this framework is as follows: if the spatial form and use of domestic space (or another sociocultural phenomenon) has a social meaning, then there ought to be an underlying system of constitutive rules or conventions which make this meaning possible. (Ibid. 85)

Anthropological critics of Levi-Straussian structuralism have found many faults. Lawrence and Low's recent article in *Annual Reviews in Anthropology* (1990: 467–469) summarizes these criticisms with regard to the study of the built environment. One problem is with the indeterminacy of the relationship between structuralism's "underlying systems" and the reality these systems allegedly explain. The static analysis produced by arraying oppositions also is widely seen to be unsatisfying. In such an analysis there is no room for conflict or contest, no explanation for how one gets from objects to meanings—or from built form to culture—and back again.

Despite these limitations, Roderick Lawrence's work holds great promise for the study of place, especially for the study of boundaries. His emphasis on a temporal perspective and on viewing housing as a process are particularly compelling. But the reorientation he advocates needs some modification in light of recent developments in other fields that call into question such distinctions as those between built form and culture, or between objects and meaning. We have misconstrued relations based on resemblance (similarities and differences that produce context). We have identified them inappropriately as relations between objects (buildings) and their meanings or between symbols and the ideas they represent.

REPRESENTATION AND THE STUDY OF BUILT FORM

In a recent historical study of the Middle East, Timothy Mitchell (1988) has much to say that, I think, should be applied to the study of built form and culture. Like Mitchell, geographers (e.g., Ley and Olds 1988) and anthropologists (e.g., Clifford 1988) interested in place and spectacle have studied the world-as-exhibition that emerged during the nineteenth century. What Mitchell makes especially clear, though, is that European notions of representation and reality elaborated a distinction between objects and what they mean that still preoccupies us.

Mitchell starts with the accounts of Egyptian visitors to the 1889 World Exhibition in Paris and their encounters with imitation bazaars, mock palaces, and displays of the world's commodities. The exhibition displayed the products of capitalism on a global scale, emphasized the importance of unrestricted international trade, promoted the transformation of the world to modern capitalism, and symbolized that transformation. Mitchell uses the world-as-exhibition motif to explore the peculiar systems of order and truth that characterize Western thought.

One of these peculiarities is the conceptual separation of people from the physical world, which Mitchell argues is fundamental to our concepts of representation and objectivity. Europeans by the mid-nineteenth century had come to view the person as set apart from the physical world, and as one who observes and controls it. This was certainly evident in the concepts of culture and place that emerged in nineteenth-century anthropology and geography. Even Karl Marx accepted this distinction in viewing mystification as the source of the power of commodities. For Marx, as for European capitalists, there seemed to be a natural distinction between representations and reality. Neither recognized the novel idea of "continuously creating the effect of 'external reality' as itself a mechanism of power" (Mitchell 1988: 18).

Representation seemed a universal condition. But it was not. At least not yet, as the confusion of Europeans who visited Egypt attested. These visitors brought with them images of Egypt from what they had seen at the exhibition. This was especially evident in European responses to Egyptian built form.

Mitchell borrows the concept of "enframing" from Heidegger to discuss the colonial imposition of "model villages" and a new order, which was in part spatial. This order claimed to be the essence of order, the only "real" order there could be. "Enframing" is the effect this order produces,

a method of dividing up and containing, as in the construction of barracks or the rebuilding of villages, which operates by conjuring up a neutral surface or volume called 'space'. . . . In reconstructing the village, the spacing that forms its rooms, courtyards, and buildings is specified in exact magnitudes, down to the nearest centimetre. Rather than as an occurrence of walls, floors, and openings, this system of magnitudes can be thought of apart, as space itself. The plans and dimensions introduce space as something apparently abstract and neutral, a series of inert frames or containers. (Ibid. 44–45)

Enframing is a disciplinary mechanism in Foucault's (1975) sense that can be effective in a colonial process partly because of its flexibility as a method of containment. In Egypt, the model village was a harmonious system in which networks of cellular housing could be varied to accommodate different family sizes, for example, all the while effectively controlling its inhabitants.

Model villages and the invention of space as containers of people sought to replace vernacular Mediterranean–Middle Eastern housing, one form of which is Bourdieu's (1977) Kabyle or Berber house. Mitchell offers a re-analysis of Bourdieu's structuralist interpretation of the Kabyle house. He notes that the Kabyle house differs from the European notion of enframing space in several crucial ways, one of which I present here because of its implications for the study of built form and culture.

Nothing in this vernacular house form is made to stand apart as a frame. Instead of the interlocking central house post and beam "symbolizing" sexual union, as Bourdieu describes, Mitchell argues that "since the building of a house always takes place when a son is married, the interlocking of its parts is a direct reenactment and repetition of the union that forms the new household. The sexual union and the assembling of the house echo and resemble one another. Neither is a mere symbol of the other" (Ibid. 52). The Kabyle house, in Mitchell's view, is a process "caught up" in the lives, births, growths, and deaths of those who dwell in it. It is not an apparently inert framework, not seemingly separate from its inhabitants. Similarly, the building process is not one of following a plan; instead it is an interactive process related, as Bourdieu recognized, to cycles of emptying and filling, abundance and decay. The division of space inside the house and between the house and the outside is contextual and relational. It is based on resemblances and differences, not on codes or symbols separable from the physical world:

So the dividing of male and female space, outside and inside, varies with the time, the season, the work to be done, and other forces and demands. It is such unstable forces and demands that polarise space, and each polarity occurs only as the temporary exclusion or postponement of its own opposite. (Ibid. 55)

Resemblance and difference express this housing process: "Nothing stands apart from what resembles or differs, as the simple, self-identical original, the way a real world is thought to stand outside the exhibition" (Ibid. 61).

If we apply Mitchell's critique to our own work, I think it should be apparent why it is difficult to analyze the relationship between built form and culture very powerfully. We have failed to see that the origins of our separation of built form from culture lie in our Western acceptance of representation. Structuralists are not the only ones guilty of trying to pin down meanings presumed to stand apart from, and behind, the "real" world of objects.[1] Distinctions between spectacle and spectator, original and the copy, object and meaning, material and symbolic, exterior and interior, still permeate many of our assumptions about the way the world works. What I am suggesting is that, in the study of housing processes, we must recognize the limitations of these assumptions and rethink them.

DYNAMICS OF PLACE

Social scientists have, of course, historically studied housing as process. Some have implicitly blended built form and culture. As an example, for Anthony King (1984) the history of the bungalow is a play of similarity and difference expressed in changing architecture, dwelling practices, and political economy, each of which implicates the other.

Jordan Adams (1984: 515) proclaimed in an address to the American Geographical Association that housing is an interactive process that makes social and cultural categories visible. But he maintained the opposition of built form to culture: "a house is a structure; a home is an experience."

Christopher Alexander has made a poetic case for studying the vitality of space. No neutral frame, a building in Alexander's view is alive. Patterns—a pattern language—are the source of what he calls a nameless, living quality.

The total pattern, space and events together, is an element of people's culture. It is invented by culture, transmitted by culture, and merely anchored in space. But there is an inner connection between each pattern of events, and the pattern of space in which it happens. For the pattern in space is, precisely, the precondition, the requirement, which allows the pattern of events to happen. In this sense, it plays a fundamental role in making sure that just this pattern of events keeps on repeating over and over again, through the space, and that it is, therefore, one of the things which gives certain buildings, or a certain town, its character. (1979: 92)

Like Mitchell, Alexander views buildings and people, form and content, as bound up in each other, elements in a practice of resemblance and difference.[2] He intuitively recognizes the contextual interplay of form and activity that defines spaces as places. He defends this holism staunchly, admonishing the reader to read the whole book quickly (and telling the reader how to do it!) rather than reading a chapter out of context. Through the notion of a pattern language Alexander tries to analyze the quality that makes buildings "live" in terms of codes and meanings. The connection between the two is unclear and ultimately mystical. The problem, it seems to me, is of his own making. The task he sets himself of specifying the structure of this pattern language is impossible; the symbolic structure of language is at odds with the holistic experience of place that intrigues him.

How he could get from the whole to its parts, from the meanings we can see in space to the codes that allegedly generate them remains a mystery.

EXPERIENCING PLACE

Tony Hiss's journalistic account of *The Experience of Place* (1990) is intuitive and impressionistic phenomenology. But it is provocative, like Alexander's work, because it implicitly dissolves the built form–culture distinction and draws attention to experience in understanding place.[3] Hiss observes that we experience place with all our senses, not just the visual. He calls this holistic appreciation of places "simultaneous perception." Experiencing places with all our senses can create a feeling of "connectedness." This is a feeling of being part of a place rather than aloof from it. Connectedness also involves consciousness of the simultaneous perception that is usually an unconscious influence on our experience.

For Hiss and Alexander there is no dichotomy between built form and culture.[4] People, culture, buildings, and design are all dimensions of places that can be understood through experience. They grasp the phenomenological complexity of the way place is experienced.

Unfortunately, they seem unconcerned by differences of class, gender, or ethnicity that affect the experience of place. Hiss, for example, asserts the universal applicability of simultaneous perception but writes from an unreflectively middle-class point of view and deals almost entirely with New York City in this section of his book. Perhaps it would be more fruitful to see places, like other symbols, as socially and culturally created, but individually experienced in many different ways. That is, different people construct their meaning differently in different experiential contexts (Darnton 1990: 330). But this does not transcend the individualistic limitation of experience as a concept. It is also necessary to contextualize experience in terms of the political economy of space. We must shift our focus "from the nature of the relationships between social form and physical form to how these 'physical surroundings' are produced in the first place" (Lawrence and Low 1990: 486).

BUILDING FOR COMMUNITY—EXAMPLES FROM HOUSING COOPERATIVES

I have claimed that both experience of place and its socially contested construction are crucial to understanding the kinds of problems that have interested us in the field we have called, unwisely, "built form and culture." But where do we go from here? Perhaps this will be clearer with a practical example concerning social housing and community drawn from research Matthew Cooper and I have conducted in Toronto.

Kevin Lynch (1981: 36) uses the language of form and function to express an idea that transcends both. He points to the possibility for integrative analyses of socially constructed and experienced space:

City forms, their actual function and the ideas and values that people attach to them make up a single phenomenon. Therefore, the history of city form cannot be written just by tracing the diffusion of the rectangular grid pattern . . . [or] solely by reference to the impersonal forces of the state and the market. . . . One must penetrate into the actual experience of places by their inhabitants, in the course of their daily lives.

People's experiences of place in Toronto housing cooperatives are entangled in and contribute to the social (and sometimes the physical) construction of those places. In part, this is because residents do not simply live in a building, they belong to the co-op. And the co-op as a social form encourages the formation of a residential community.

The relationship between buildings and community is particularly interesting in the context of these housing cooperatives because of the apparent contrast between the built and social forms. On the one hand, these co-ops offer some people a real social alternative. Here one has a form of tenure in which people are individually tenants but collectively landlords. In Canadian nonequity co-ops people do not own their units. But they still enjoy some of the benefits of home ownership, such as security of tenure and greater control over their housing. Co-ops actively seek to include diversity in terms of the members' backgrounds, incomes, and household composition. They encourage members to work together "cooperatively" to achieve a quality of life in co-ops greater than they might find in other rental accommodation, or even in private home ownership. And an important aspect of this quality of life is a stronger sense of community.

The concept of community deserves discussion here.[5] Larry Lyon surveys approaches to the study of community in *The Community in Urban Society*. He concludes (1987: 86–87) that three dimensions of community emphasize respectively (1) area, (2) common ties, and (3) social interaction. That is, approaches to the study of community can focus on the spatial or ecological dimensions. Alternatively (or additionally) they can address issues of identity. Networks and interactional fields are a third dimension, which is concerned with questions of power, interpersonal relationships, and community development. The spatial and social interaction dimensions are especially important to understanding the pros and cons of community action in controlling urban places. These are particularly evident if one applies the concept of community to new housing co-ops where common ties between residents are generally weak, both because they are new neighbors and because of the diversity of their backgrounds.

Community formation in housing co-ops may involve the neighborhood and larger community beyond the co-op. But to a great extent the focus is on development of a sense of community and frequent social interaction among people who live in the same co-op. One way of encouraging community formation is through participation in running, or controlling, the co-op. Much of this occurs in committee meetings. In part, the importance of meetings in co-op community development arises from the way co-ops work. That is, participation on co-op committees is essential to keep a co-op running smoothly. In part, meetings assume particular importance in shaping co-op communities because there are relatively few other opportunities for residents to interact. There are summer evenings spent with neighbors in the courtyard, casual greetings in the elevator, and the occasional party. But meetings are the most regular occasions that bring people together.[6]

If we consider the experience of place in the context of socially constructing community space at meetings, one of the underlying tensions in Canadian co-ops appears. This tension relates to the striking contrast between the way the co-ops look and the way they work. But we can learn more by seeing it as a tension expressed in the creation and experience of space than in the static juxtaposition of the built form (conventional apartment building or townhouse) with co-op culture.

Control over the amount of space available for community use, as opposed to private household units, rests with the governmental institutions that set maximum unit prices (MUPs). Low MUPs associated with non-profit housing for people in need of "affordable" places to live mean that little space is left over for community use within a co-op. Ironically, the social construction of a co-op community must be achieved in buildings in which little in the built form encourages community formation.[7]

The limited community space in co-ops is used for meetings. I would argue that much of the community development that occurs is shaped through the experience of place, and that such experience also shapes the co-op community. Specifically, people's sense of the co-op as a community, and of their role in it, is shaped by holding meetings in these community rooms. These meetings, of course, also affect the operation of the co-op.

In the new co-ops we studied, committees did not meet in people's apartments but on the neutral or common ground that meeting rooms provided. The fact that the meeting rooms were there allowed the cooperative social form to take the shape it did. People experienced meetings in ways that were perhaps more formal and more democratic than if they had met in the chairperson's home. In the meeting room, participants were on a more equal footing. A meeting in a common room was far less revealing of the chair's personal life than one held in his or her living room would have been. This does not mean that the playing field was level in co-op meetings. Anyone who has lived in a co-op has tales to tell of political wrangling. But it does suggest ways in which the experience of place and the social production of space reciprocally affected each other.

What Lynch calls "place control" is another way of exploring this relationship. Lynch advocates congruence of use and control. That is, actual and potential users should, by and large, control spaces in proportion to their stake in them. This is in effect congruence of experience with control over the social construction of space. Control, for Lynch, has a number of dimensions (1981: 205–207). First, there is the right to be present in a place. Other dimensions include rights of use and action, appropriation, modification, and disposition. In Western society all are associated with ownership, but as Lynch points out, place control is cross-culturally variable insofar as "these rights are separable, and not inevitable" (Ibid. 207).

There would seem also to be variation according to scale. By this I mean that control of places within a co-op, for example, can be contested along the same dimensions as a neighborhood or larger community.

Lynch (Ibid. 272) advocates a fine "grain of control." By this he means a mixing and diffusion of different interests, classes, income levels, and so on. Along with density and the access system, grain creates the texture of a city. A good city, he feels, presents "a fine mosaic of public and private places, group commons, children's turf and no-man's land."[8] But this is not a still picture; its composition may be hotly and continually contested. Lynch recognizes that control by those whose experience of local places is most direct may run counter to the goal of mixing urban uses and users.

One problem with localization of control is a problem of scale. Many problems that affect local people are not purely local in origin, nor can they be solved by communities acting alone. Environmental problems are an obvious example.

Another drawback to local control, Lynch notes, is an ethical one: "Control of the local turf slips easily into exclusion or expulsion of the unwanted" (Ibid. 247). NIMBY ("Not In My Backyard") syndrome is one aspect of this problem. Should barriers to neighborhoods, such as entrance gates or bypasses, be created? Is "community" desirable when it encourages social homogeneity? Planned social physical homogeneity, Lynch concludes (Ibid. 247–249), may be defensible and even desirable at the level of neighborhood (<100 households) "since they improve social cohesion, fit, control, and sense without seriously damaging anyone's access. But they are more dangerous at the community scale."

Ambivalence about community control is especially relevant to understanding built form and community in co-ops because co-ops house some of the kinds of people middle-class communities would like to keep out— for example, low-income immigrants or single female-headed households. Co-ops house what are sometimes regarded as unconventional households, although increasingly the "traditional" nuclear family is the unconventional one. Moreover, they house these unconventional households in very conventional housing, in which the built form may be ill suited to the needs of the household, including its need for community.

To explain what I mean by this, let me return once more to the concept of community, this time in a contemporary context. It is easy to understand how built form can be incompatible with the development of a sense of community. The Pruit-Igoe project in St. Louis and countless other public housing projects demonstrated how negatively a building could affect residents' quality of life, including their sense of community. It is also clear that conventional housing may poorly fit the needs of "new" households (Franck and Ahrentzen 1989; Hayden 1984) who may require more flexible spaces, work space in the home, accessibility features, and so on. So what is unusual about the need for community among people in unconventional households living in all too conventional buildings? Nothing. What *is* unusual, and interesting to study, are two things: first, how strongly the desire for a "traditional" sense of community is grounded in the experience of place; and second, how clearly the desire for community is not what it seems. It is not a desire for a traditional community, leaving aside the question of whether such a thing ever existed. The kind of community co-op residents want, and seek to form, is something new.

The nontraditional community sought through invocation of a traditional model is not peculiar to co-ops. It is just particularly easy to see it there. Similarly, this sense of what might be called the irony of community was apparent to Raymond Williams in the context of Welsh nationalism. "Society," he points out, once was used to contrast with "the State." In the eighteenth century, "society" was strongly associated with face-to-face relationships, with social contact, in contrast to the impersonal power structures of a state. But the term *society* has taken on many of the meanings it once opposed; it "became the general abstract term for a whole social-political system (Williams 1989: 115)." This reflected historical changes, especially to the mode of production, "which put certain of the basic elements of our social life beyond the reach both of direct experience and of simple affirmation" (Ibid. 116). Williams believed that attempts to extend the traditional meaning of community in contemporary society are similarly doomed by systematic obstacles. Community is always seen as a positive thing, and that may be the reason that the petty tyranny of community control over zoning bylaws and such provokes such mixed feelings. As Williams observes,

Community is unusual among the terms of political vocabulary in being, I think, the one term which has never been used in a negative sense. People never, from any political position, want to say that they are against community or against the community. . . . I think on the one hand we should be glad that this is so, on the other hand we should be suspicious. A term which is agreed among so many people, a term which everybody likes, a notion which everybody is in favour of—if this reflected reality then we'd be living in a world very different from this one. So what is the problem inside the term, what is it that allows people to at once respond very positively to it and yet mean such very different things by it? (Ibid. 112–113)

The kind of community that co-op residents speak about is neither the rural community of mutual responsibility that grows out of living in the same place and sharing a sense of identity nor an industrial community forged in common struggle and conflict. Yet, like these, it grows out of (and is expressed in) the experience of place. That is, it is connected to the form of ownership, social organization, and physical space of co-op housing. And like the rural and industrial forms of Welsh community that intrigued Williams, the kinds of communities to which co-ops aspire are very limited in scope. The direct experience of place that is so important to the concept of such a community is self-limiting.

It is not self-limiting simply because such experience is available only to the relatively few who live in co-ops. Rather it is limited because the simple extension of such a community is impossible on two counts: first, the systematic complexity of modern society precludes simple extension of shared, place-based identity and interaction; second, we each carry within our thinking about community (and within our endorsement of it in the abstract) elements of that larger, depersonalized system. As Williams puts it, "Right back in your own mind, and right back inside the oppressed and deprived community [in rural Wales], there are reproduced elements of the thinking and the feeling of that dominating centre. These become the destructive complexities inside what had once seemed a simple affirmative mood" (Ibid. 117).

These tensions associated with "community" are evident in the experience of place in housing co-ops and in the social production of their built form. First, they are a response to the "destructive complexities" of communities dominated by conventional housing. This is evident in at least four ways: (1) They are havens of secure tenure amidst a crisis of affordability in which rental conversions to condominiums are common and many middle-income households cannot afford to buy a home. (2) They offer residents considerable control over their housing conditions and allow for control without also encouraging the kinds of discrimination that can accompany control by local communities. (3) Co-ops also protect households that are different from those of the dominant forces in society—the poor, people with physical or mental disabilities, senior citizens, among others. (4) Co-ops are potentially counterhegemonic in their advocacy of collective ownership and management in a capitalist economy.

Second, the tension between co-ops and the institutional context in which they exist also is apparent. These tensions flow in two directions—first, into concerns over what kinds of buildings to build and second, into conflicts over who should live in them. The former leads us back to the matter of MUPs. If we view cultural dimensions as contested in the production of built form, it becomes evident that the maximum unit price is closely associated not just with how much money governments and developers are willing to invest in social housing. It is also connected with views of what the minimal conditions are for adequate housing in this culture. Separate bedrooms for parents and for opposite-sex siblings are a minimum, for example.[9] The institutional imposition of MUPs is, in Foucault's sense, the imposition of power through spatial order on the residents. The co-op movement resists this power in arguing for a redefinition of MUPs to allow for more community space. But it is a measure of how limited the co-op housing sector is as a counterhegemonic force that this is the extent of its argument. No attempt, for example, is made to argue for communal dining space or teenagers' rooms in a block at some distance from parental units.

One reason Canadian housing co-ops offer a social form of organization that is much more different from conventional housing than is their built form concerns the funding of the co-ops. They have been heavily dependent on financial assistance (especially through mortgages and rental subsidies) from the public sector. Innovative built forms of collective housing are much more apparent in Scandinavian private-sector projects, for example (McCamant and Durrett 1988).[10]

Conflicts over who should live in co-ops revolve around the issue of mixing incomes in nonprofit projects. Metropolitan, provincial, and federal interests lie in housing the poor in nonprofit housing, including co-ops, while providing less visible assistance to developers and middle-income homeowners. While the negative examples of housing only the poor in public housing are not forgotten, there is always a trade-off between providing affordable housing for those in greatest need and attending to issues of the quality of life in such projects, including the sense of community. To an extent, then, "community" becomes a frill. In Toronto, and presumably elsewhere, the housing conditions believed to encourage community formation are continually negotiated and contested. This is so, of course, in the high as well as the low ends of the housing market as arguments over density and NIMBY issues illustrate.

In co-ops, such wrangling is quite literally built into the production of the space, as Matthew Cooper and I have shown in our analysis of the building of a "fully accessible" co-op (Rodman and Cooper 1989). The meanings we identified were often hotly contested in the design, construction, and occupancy processes. The building, then, was not simply a built form from which one could read out cultural meanings. These meanings did not "stand behind" the physical form. They were part of it. For example, consider the idea that people with disabilities could be integrated into the co-op community by living anywhere they wanted in the building. Acceptance of this principle is still evident in the wide hallways, low electrical outlets, and large bathrooms of every unit. This is so even though many of the apartments occupied by residents with disabilities in fact required further modifications to make them "fully accessible." Moreover, the real freedom of choice applied only to the initial rental. Today any applicant, able bodied or otherwise, has a much more limited choice of units. In other words, the cultural dimensions of the building were not separate from the building itself. They were not static ideals. Instead, they were contested and embodied in the production of the built form.

This contest continues in the experience of space once a co-op is occupied. Elsewhere, Cooper and I have considered the conflicts that arose over the assertion of private ownership over collective property and tensions between people receiving rent subsidies and those who pay full housing charges that arose over setting aside part of these fees for future repairs (Cooper and Rodman 1990). We have heard conflicting views of what a co-op community should be all about (Cooper and Rodman 1992, ch. 4). And we have seen confusion over community expressed in space, as for example, in the extension of some people's property into hallways (Rodman 1990). There is a continuing tension in the co-ops we studied over the ways in which a co-op should and should not be "more than just a place to live."

In this chapter I have advocated a synthesis of experience-based approaches to understanding place with those that treat space as socially constructed and contested. The experience of place in the Kabyle house or a Toronto co-op is not simply an ebb and flow of life that defines categories, boundaries, and domains. It is part of a constructed, created, contested social and physical form. This process can be harmonious or confrontational. It can involve an extension of the self, the state, or many interests, individuals, and institutions in between.

The socially constructed nature of space is generally accepted in urban studies and in anthropology.[11] But the emphasis has been much more on the social, political, and economic dimensions of this process than on the experience of place. There are few examples in the literature on the social construction of buildings to make certain kinds of experience possible; nor is there much on the conflict that can accompany such a process. I have tried in this paper to give some examples from research on new Toronto housing cooperatives. Many more are possible; the whole question of boundaries as negotiated zones is one aspect among many that could be explored, developing Lawrence's (1987) work beyond the limitations of structuralism.

In Toronto co-ops or precolonial Egyptian houses we should not see buildings as "frames" standing apart from social life. They are contested, created processes, not the simple products of plans. Divisions of space inside buildings and between houses and streets or neighborhoods are not dichotomous. Oppositions between inside-outside, private-public, and so on are too simple. So is the opposition between built form and culture. Instead, I have argued that we can best apprehend relationships between buildings and the communities they foster or inhibit, create and house by approaching them through the experience of place and its social production.

NOTES

1. Those who see spectacle as exemplifying the hegemonic power of consumption-driven capitalism also regard the masses, if not certain elites (including architects?), as duped, or at least confused, by a proliferation of signs. A good example of a postmodern approach to the study of place that follows this approach is John Dorst's *The Written Suburb* (1989) about Chadd's Ford, Pennsylvania.

2. Marilyn Strathern (1991) would call these "partial connections." Questions of comparison and of the future of comparative method in anthropology are much the same as those I address here to the study of place.

3. See also Walter (1988) on place as a location of experience.

4. But there is a difference between space and place, at least for Alexander, as the quotation cited (1979: 92) suggests. For him, culture creates places that are only anchored in space. Place, in other words, is a cultural product; space is merely a physical reality.

5. See also Hummon (1990, esp. ch. 1) for a discussion of the role of place imagery in conceptualizing cities, suburbs, and small towns in the contemporary United States of America.

6. There are courtyards in some co-ops and other spaces where considerable activity related to community formation occurs informally. But a survey of the differences between these co-ops and some cohousing projects in Scandinavia is striking and instructive. Such European projects, designed to encourage community, often include collective cooking and dining facilities, shared recreational areas—for example, a teen music room and interior streets (McCamant and Durrett 1988).

7. An even greater irony is that new social housing in Toronto such as the Fred Victor Mission includes features—for example, dining facilities—intended to encourage a sense of community among residents who are more homogenous—again for example, in their homelessness—than co-op residents.

8. Jane Jacobs (1961) and others have also advocated this kind of mixed use.

9. See Ellen Pader (1988) for documentation of Mexican-Americans redefinitions of bedroom space in reaction to institutional regulations in Los Angeles. Her concern, following Giddens (1979), is with structuration and domestic space.

10. It would be interesting to study the results of Canadian projects (for example, in Vancouver) built without government assistance.

11. Lawrence and Low devote much of their review article on "The Built Environment and Spatial Form" to an overview of literature on the social production of built form (1990: 482–493). They single out Bourdieu, Castells, Foucault, Giddens, Harvey, King, and Rabinow as having made especially important contributions to anthropologists' work on the social production of space. Further, they argue that "the most promising new direction for anthropologists lies in the area of social production theories" (Ibid. 491).

10

Housing Abandonment in Inner-City Black Neighborhoods: A Case Study of the Effects of the Dual Housing Market

SUSAN D. GREENBAUM

Academics, researchers and planners supposedly deal in facts, but in the politics of housing, facts are what you can persuade people to accept.
(R. E. Mendelson and M. A. Quinn 1976: 247).

The phrase *urban black "ghettos"* evokes in many people images of blight and despair, of diminished lives and destructive life-styles. Dilapidated housing and garbage-strewn lots frame a material context, in which unappealing zones of habitation complement unattractive stereotypes about African-Americans and their communities. The belief that black Americans are to a large extent responsible for blighted conditions in their neighborhoods is deeply rooted. A corollary assumption in housing economics, also with deep roots, is that black occupancy devalues property and dooms neighborhoods to a rapid process of decay.

The long history of slavery, racial discrimination and unequal treatment of American blacks adversely influences behavior in urban poverty concentrations in which they predominate. Therefore, it may be the concentration of both poverty and race and the larger community's reactions to it that produce the "critical mass" of undesirable neighborhood characteristics found in many large cities. (Downs 1981: 54–55)

For many decades, and continuing still, housing theories and policies have reflected strongly the belief that race is an important explanatory variable. These convictions originate from the "invasion-succession" model (Gillette 1957; Grigsby et al. 1987; Park et al. 1925), with more contemporary refinements under the labels of "filtering" and "arbitrage" (Birch 1971; Blair 1972; Downs 1981; Leven et al. 1976; Little 1976; Rose 1971;

Sternlieb and Burchell 1973; White 1971). Neighborhood decline is viewed as a quasi-biotic process, in which the entry of new and alien populations drives out the incumbents and undermines stability. Aging structures, lowered incomes, and the cultural dysfunctions of newcomers combine to accelerate physical decay. In this process, race is like cancer, the darker the invaders, the more virulent the strain.

Policies inspired by the "invasion-succession" model have become self-fulfilling prophecies (Rent and Lord 1978). Few ideas derived from social science have had such far-reaching influence (see U.S. Department of Housing and Urban Development 1975), or such unsalutory effects. The process is simple, almost mechanical. If a banker believes that a property has less value solely because of the race of the occupant, then the real valuation of that property is less in fact. If academic research offers apparently scientific support for this discriminatory assessment, then the banker would be violating fiduciary responsibilities to risk loaning depositors' money for houses in black neighborhoods. Prospective buyers in these areas have difficulty securing mortgages, and insurance companies are reluctant to write policies, a practice known as "redlining" (Fefferman 1976; Helper 1969). Capital is withdrawn, maintenance is deferred, and deterioration accelerates. Unmarketable properties are abandoned. The blighting effects of abandoned buildings spurs further vacancy, and more abandonment.

An excursion through the predominantly black district of any large city will, initially at least, tend visually to confirm the image of blight as a contagious disease. Empty buildings, weedy lots, quantities of unsavory litter, and angry graffiti suggest profound maladies. Windshield examinations by motorists rushing through the main corridors of places they are anxious to leave, however, produce blurred and distorted perceptions. Like other affluent Americans, most housing economists have spent little or no time in these neighborhoods, whose fates they have pondered and determined. If they did, they would confront some anomalies, among them, well-kept yards surrounded on both sides by overgrown vacant lots, clusters of neat houses centered around churches, blocks where the only problems are in vacant houses, blocks where there are no problems at all.

Ghetto is a monolithic concept, describing districts that may be ethnically uniform but which reflect a large degree of variability, both internally and among different cities. Many prominent researchers on race and real estate have failed to consider this variability (Schwab 1987) or to test their assumptions about the cultural/behavioral characteristics of black and white residents (Massey 1990). Further, to denote black neighborhoods as ghettos—places where undesirables are shut off from the good people—shapes a powerful metaphor for the intent, as well as the consequences, of housing discrimination. When folk categories, like *ghetto*, are reified and made respectable in the models and taxonomies of scholars and analysts, consequences and intentions become viciously intertwined.

This chapter offers a case study in neighborhood decline. It focuses on the rapid process of housing abandonment that affected black neighborhoods in one midwestern city during the 1960s and 1970s, an especially volatile period in urban housing markets. Throughout the country, the ratio of white to black urban residents altered dramatically, and previously sound neighborhoods experienced precipitous decay (Ashton 1978; Bradford 1979; Frey 1979; Galster 1990a; Taeuber & Taeuber 1965; Taub et al. 1984). White flight became black blight. There is a conventional wisdom about this change, which this account seeks to contradict. It is a modest challenge, based on only a single city. This particular case has singular virtues, however. It offers an example where at least two of the presumptively causal variables are naturally controlled, providing a limited test of the assumptions of the invasion-succession model.

This model posits a direct relationship between the urban influx of black rural migrants and the suburban exodus of middle-class white families (Birch 1971; Downs 1981; Gillette 1957; Grigsby et al. 1987; Leven et al. 1976). Tandem events, which had their origins in the post–World War II era, these two phenomena seem inescapably linked. The invasion of large numbers of rural black peasants unsettled urban housing markets, already softened by suburban expansion. Neighborhoods turned over like dominoes, as occupancy switched from stable working families to distressed, unskilled refugees. Social pathologies, especially crime, drove away businesses and any residents able to escape. The housing stock deteriorated rapidly in the hands of new residents who were unfamiliar with maintenance requirements and too poor to carry them out. Of course, other factors were associated with the spread of blight in inner-city neighborhoods, such as fiscal problems from declining tax revenue and redlining by banks and insurance companies. But the germ of this malady, the pathogen that sparked the epidemic, is thought to reside in the social characteristics of black newcomers.

An opposing view, centered on political economy rather than social pathology, argues that housing problems in black neighborhoods are due largely to the existence of a "dual housing market" (Bradford 1979; Kain and Quigley 1975; Massey 1990; Molotch 1969; Taub et al. 1984). The dual housing market defines neighborhoods as either black or white, and by tacit agreement real estate brokers "steer" their clients to one or the other, depending on their race. Few conventional lenders or insurers are willing to do business in the black submarket. Housing choices of black consumers are thus more limited, and distinctions in neighborhood services can be defined easily according to the race of the residents. Less powerful constituents are spatially bundled and bounded by the dual housing market.

The dual housing market has starved black neighborhoods of capital needed for maintenance. Preservation of older housing requires more, rather than less, investment compared with newer housing. Because inner-city black neighborhoods typically are also old neighborhoods, the downward spiral proceeds very rapidly once maintenance begins to be neglected (Bradford 1979; Galster 1988; Kellogg 1983). The spatial ecology of racism has situated properties at risk in the neighborhoods where African-Americans live.

Dividing the housing market into two mutually exclusive sectors, one white and the other black, also complicates the nature of supply and demand. Overall equilibrium rests on a complex balance between numbers of buyers and sellers in both markets. When in- or out-migration disturbs this equilibrium, complex adjustments are required. In the period following World War II, most cities witnessed a dramatic revision in the boundaries of these two submarkets.

Neighborhood transition often has been characterized as a natural response to oversupply in the white sector and unmet demand in the black sector—a process known as *filtering* (Blair 1973; Leven et al. 1976; White 1971). White families move to better neighborhoods in the suburbs and leave their still-good houses to a growing population of black families. Housing production in the white submarket trickles into the black submarket through chains of household moves, and all of this theoretically results in improved housing conditions across both markets (White 1971). However, the entry of black residents into houses in previously all-white areas generally had the unwieldy effect of filtering entire neighborhoods out of the white submarket and into the black one, a process known as "arbitrage" (Downs 1981). Although efforts were made to target the changes, free enterprise made this process impossible to control.

Blockbusting, the practice of deliberately introducing black residents into white neighborhoods slated for transition, proved highly profitable for real estate entrepreneurs during the 1950s and 1960s (Bisceglia 1973; Farley and Allen 1989; Galster 1990b; Helper 1969). In a panic, white owners sold out at below-market prices, and new black residents were willing to pay a premium to move into their houses. The discrepancy yielded a tidy profit for real estate brokers. Once underway, however, this process had a life of its own, continuing long after the market had dropped out. White families continued to leave, and neighborhoods became resegregated. During the 1960s and 1970s, huge tracts of urban landscape transferred from white to black submarkets, and ghetto districts expanded enormously within the urban core. By the 1980s, cities had stopped growing, and their populations had become dramatically poorer, and darker (Farley and Allen 1989; Kellogg 1983; Massey 1990).

Loss of manufacturing jobs and the restructuring of urban economies contribute to the impoverishment of those who are trapped in inner cities, but poverty alone does not explain the blighted conditions of urban housing (Massey and Eggers 1990; Schwab 1987). Racial discrimination in housing and lending affects stable working families as well as troubled welfare families. When banks assess risk, they consider the condition of neighborhoods, as well as the creditworthiness of borrowers. Even in the absence of outright discrimination, this disadvantages black residents, especially those who live in areas with visible blight.

Abandoned properties are a principal source of blight, a collective liability that devalues surrounding houses, however well taken care of these other units may be (Sternlieb and Burchell 1973). Empty buildings are unsightly, and they invite vandalism and harbor criminal activities. Excessive vacancies in urban black neighborhoods have been cited as one indication that black occupants are hard on housing, that they wear it out at a rapid rate and scare away investors (Downs 1981; Sternlieb and Burchell 1973; Stull 1978). The interaction of demography and the dual housing market offers a simpler explanation. If the size of the black population fails to match the number of housing units that fall within the black submarket, vacancy is inevitable.

STABILITY AND ABANDONMENT

With the aim of elucidating this argument, this chapter focuses on residential abandonment in inner-city black neighborhoods in Kansas City, Kansas (KCK), in the period between World War II and the late 1970s. KCK is an independent municipality, contiguous with Kansas City, Missouri, but situated on the other side of the state line. It has had a very separate history, the origins of which date to the pre–Civil War period when Kansas was a free state and Missouri was not. This distinction was particularly significant for the growth and character of the African-American community in KCK. Because KCK played a role in the antislavery struggle, its black population was already large and well established prior to the turn of the century, especially in comparison with other midwestern industrial cities (including KC, Mo.). Schools were relatively better for blacks living on the Kansas side of the line, as were political rights and opportunities to develop viable community institutions. Packinghouses and the railroads, which were the primary industries in KCK, offered relatively dependable employment for unskilled black workers (Greenbaum 1980).

Historical factors resulted in a rather atypical community development process for the black population of KCK. More recent history also reflects a departure from the pattern observed elsewhere. In particular, there was very little absolute growth in the post–World War II period in KCK's African-American population. Relative to the white population of the city, the percentage of blacks actually decreased by more than ten points during the 1950s. A flood in 1951 destroyed the packinghouses, the most likely explanation for KCK's failure to attract new black migrants during the postwar period. The result, however, was that during a period when most cities were experiencing a large influx of black migrants, KCK's black population grew by slightly more than 1 percent a year.[1]

KCK's somewhat unique racial demography helps disentangle conflicting issues in competing hypotheses about why black neighborhoods are particularly vulnerable to the problems of abandonment. From the perspective of those who argue that rural habits and rapid influx were leading causes of housing decay, the relative stability of KCK's African-American population would lead one to predict that problems of abandonment would be less serious there than in other cities. The "invasion" dimension is lacking. The black families who were already living there in the 1950s and 1960s were well adapted to their environment; 90 percent of the black residents in 1960 had been born in KCK, and 58 percent had lived in the same houses for more than five years. Two-thirds were homeowners. Only 3 percent were southern migrants.[2]

These facts notwithstanding, by the late 1970s, KCK's inner-city neighborhoods reflected a very high rate of abandonment. Within the northeast quadrant, which by that time was nearly 90 percent black, 17 percent of all housing units were vacant. Almost one out of five houses was empty, averaging about four or five per block. Over half of these vacant units had not been occupied in more than two years and in all probability never would be again. Why should this problem be so bad in a city where major presumed causal factors (that is, rapid influx, southern habits) had been almost completely absent?

My answer is that the stability of the black population of KCK was actually the underlying cause of the widespread abandonment of houses in their neighborhoods. More accurately, the causes of this problem were the wholesale flight of white homeowners to the suburbs during this period, combined with the unsettling practices of real estate dealers who encouraged them to leave. When white residents began moving out of the northeast section of KCK, it was in response to the growing supply of new affordable suburban housing, not because they were pushed out by newcomers. Blockbusting did occur, and black residents were eager to improve their own conditions by moving into the houses being left by new suburbanites. Numerous real estate agents, both black and white, were involved in this process.[3] They competed with one another for opportunities to profit from the initial stages of transition. Once the dust had settled, and the panic subsided, they had busted more blocks than there were black residents to occupy. Vacancy and abandonment were the predictable results. Had there in fact been a large influx of new black residents during the same period, the problem arguably would have been much less severe. There at least might have been a market for the houses that white owners fled.

The rather unremarkable insights that vacancy results from oversupply, and that demand is tied to the size of the consumer population, receive relatively little attention in the literature on housing abandonment (for exceptions see Galster 1990a; Molotch 1969). Although science generally favors parsimony, in this case simplicity has been obscured by the political baggage of generations of housing theories. My own conclusions in this regard were more the result of ethnography than of quantitative analyses, although the explication ultimately relied on quantitative data.

NORTHEAST AREA STUDY

In the late 1970s, I had a contract with the KCK Community Development program to conduct two separate but related studies of the predominantly black northeast section of the city. The first was a community history; the second was an assessment of housing problems. These two efforts intertwined, and it was only through an understanding of the history of the neighborhoods of the Northeast Area that I was able to gain a clear picture of what was happening to the housing stock.

The historical research was done in collaboration with an eighty-year old man who had grown up in the Northeast Area and was its unofficial "griot."[4] Our initial activities involved traveling through the neighborhoods, during which he pointed out and explained all the pertinent landmarks. Sites of early black settlement, areas where the Irish and Germans had settled, churches, schools, businesses, all were recorded and mapped. He took me to the ruins of an abolitionist town (named Quindaro) and the post–Civil War black settlement that grew up on its site. His grandfather had escaped across the river into that town in the early 1860s. Also part of his family history was an area called Juniper, where more than a thousand ex-slaves from Mississippi had sought refuge from the Ku Klux Klan in 1879 in a mass movement known as the Kansas Fever Exodus (Painter 1976). His maternal grandmother was among these refugees. Two other sites were noteworthy. Rattlebone Hollow was the name given to a settlement begun in the 1880s by packinghouse workers, both black and German. Most of the Germans had moved out by the turn of the century. The final area was known simply as the Third Ward. Established shortly after the Civil War on what was then the western edge of the downtown area, this area hosted the two oldest black churches in the city—one Baptist, the other Methodist. These four areas comprised the principal sites of early black occupation in the city. Widely dispersed from each other, they were located in the four corners of what is now the black ghetto of KCK (see Figure 10.1).

In between, there were working-, middle-, and upper-class white neighborhoods. This section of the city, which was immune to flooding because of its elevated terrain, was historically considered the most desirable for residential development. In the early 1900s, a luxurious subdivision (named Parkwood Estates) was developed about twenty blocks east of Quindaro. The white sections of the northeast area were heterogeneous, but generally prosperous, and for a long period remained quite stable. Along the edges, especially in the older eastern section, continued growth in the black pop-

Figure 10.1
Historic Black Settlement Sites

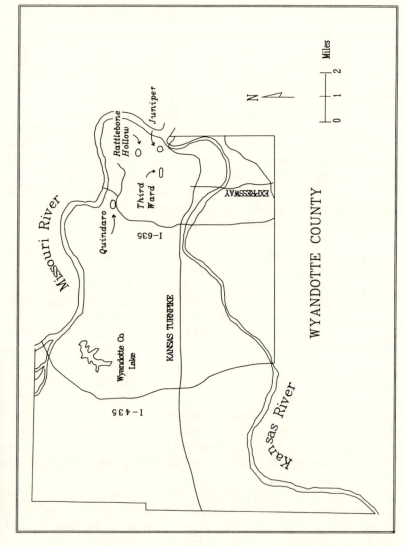

ulation expanded the boundaries of traditional black neighborhoods. Rattlebone Hollow and Juniper eventually merged, forming a long corridor of concentrated black settlement. Until the 1950s, however, the white core of the northeast area remained virtually solid, bolstered by overt housing discrimination. When I began my research in the late 1970s, the overwhelming majority of the residents of the entire area were black.

In the course of many excursions through the Northeast Area, I not only learned about specific historical events, I also began to focus my perceptions of housing and neighborhoods. There was a pronounced gradient in the quality of the housing, from east to west, but blighted conditions existed throughout. The large number of vacant and boarded-up houses, even in neighborhoods where the housing was intrinsically good, seemed anomalous. As I learned more about the social characteristics of the community, the longevity of its institutions, and the stability of the population, these neighborhood conditions seemed all the more inconsistent.

In the wake of the suburban exodus, KCK's African-American community had fallen heir to a large supply of quite good housing, including the prized Parkwood Estates. Why had this ironic windfall not fulfilled the promises of the filtering hypothesis? Not only was the community unusually stable and cohesive, but the black institutions of the city included both a bank and an insurance company. KCK should have offered an ideal site for demonstrating the efficacy of trickle-down economics.

POPULATION LOSSES AND ABANDONMENT

Neighborhood observations failed to confirm this rosy scenario. Numerous empty houses conveyed the impression of an area that was simply too large for the population that inhabited it. This, in turn, led to an examination of the scope and magnitude of population losses in the preceding decades. The data derived from federal and county censuses, and the *Polk's Profiles of Change* data. Data were also collected on housing loans in 1977.[5]

The district known as the Northeast Area contains thirteen census tracts. In 1960 the total population was 41,336, 47 percent of whom were white. By 1978, there were only 29,089 people still living in these tracts, and only 13 percent were white. Within eighteen years, the overall population had declined by 30 percent. The white population had dropped by 79 percent, and the black population increased by only 13.7 percent. Net loss amounted to 12,247 people. In 1960, the vacancy rate had been 4 percent; by 1970 it had jumped to about 7 percent, and by 1978 it was a whopping 17 percent.[6]

Filtering still might have occurred if the vacancies had been concentrated in the most undesirable neighborhoods. To examine these effects, the tracts were subdivided into two categories—established black areas (EBAs) and transitional areas (TAs) (see Figure 10.2). In 1960 the EBAs were 95 percent black, and the TAs were 78 percent white. Eighteen years later, the EBAs had risen slightly to 96 percent black, and the TAs had dropped to 18 percent white.

Vacancy rates in 1978 varied among the 13 tracts between 9 percent and 24 percent. Rates for the EBAs and the TAs were approximately equivalent (17.1 percent and 16.3 percent, respectively). Even more comparable were rates of two-term vacancies (9.5 percent and 9.0 percent), that is, those which had remained vacant for two or more successive years. Chronic vacancies offer a better measure of abandonment. Average 1970 housing values were 28 percent higher in the transitional compared with the established tracts. Housing in the formerly white neighborhoods also tended to be newer. In the EBAs, 95 percent of the houses were built before 1939; in the TAs only 78 percent were that old (see Table 10.1). High vacancy rates in the overall area thus were not simply a function of the population's shifting from older substandard housing into neighborhoods where the houses were newer and better.

The dispersed pattern of abandonment in the Northeast Area suggests market problems unrelated to quality. Interviews with residents and realtors indicated that many of the better-quality abandonments were "heir" properties. The older white neighborhoods of the Northeast Area had contained a large number of elderly residents, many of whom were unable or unwilling to join in the suburban flight. When these residents died, however, orderly transfer of their houses was often problematic, especially if heirs did not live in the area. Delinquent taxes and damage to properties that remained vacant for any period of time conspired to put the price of reclamation beyond reach. Mortgages and rehabilitation loans were difficult to obtain. So these properties tended to remain vacant, while low- and moderate-income black families continued to occupy substandard housing. The presumed rationality of the filtering process was confounded by financial practices that prevented residents from optimizing their choices. Moreover, those who had managed to move into newer neighborhoods did not escape the blight associated with abandoned housing.

BLACK VERSUS WHITE TRACTS

Perhaps these problems stem from an inner-city location and were not a direct consequence of race. Redlining reportedly also occurs in white ethnic neighborhoods, and in older neighborhoods in general (Bradford 1979). Similar processes might have been operating throughout the older sections of the city. To assess this possibility, the thirteen Northeast tracts were each paired with a predominantly white city census tract within the older part of KCK (see Fig. 10.2). These pairings were based on comparability in housing values and household income.[7] KCK has a large white working-class population (mainly of Irish and Slavic descent), a fact that facilitated this comparison (see Table 10.2).

Figure 10.2
Northeast and Southcentral Census Tracts

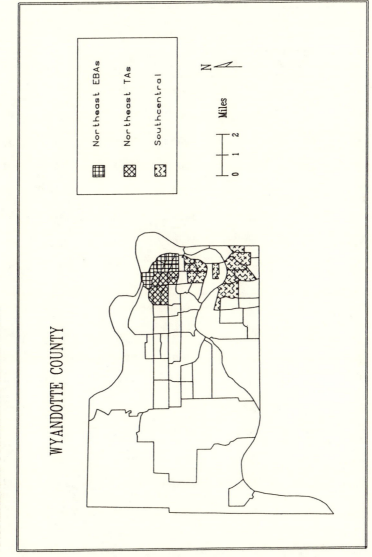

Table 10.1
Northeast Area Census Tracts: Vacancy Rates and House Values

Tract	% Black		House Value	% Vacant	% 2-Term	% Built pre-1939
	1960	1970				
Established Black Areas						
408	93	98	9000	14.0	7.0	96
409.01	94	95	7900	19.0	10.0	93
409.02	94	97	7300	19.0	11.0	93
410	99	97	7900	15.0	9.0	96
411.01	94	90	7900	17.0	7.0	96
411.02	94	99	9500	20.0	13.0	96
Total	94	99	8250	17.3	9.5	95
Transitional Areas						
402	6	92	9500	24.0	12.0	90
403	50	97	9700	19.0	10.0	63
404	0	7611	000	12.0	6.0	69
406	0	5812	700	9.0	4.0	50
407	29	90	9700	13.0	7.0	96
412.01	47	96	8100	18.0	10.0	88
412.02	47	64	9200	20.0	14.0	88
Total	26	82	9986	16.4	9.0	78

Source: U.S. Census for Wyandotte County Kansas, 1960, 1970 (house values); Polks Profiles of Change for Kansas City, Kansas, 1978 (vacancy rates).

Table 10.2
Northeast Tracts Compared with White Tracts in Southcentral KCK

Tract	House Value (1970)	% Owners (1978)	Income index (1978)	% Black (1974)	% 2-term Vacant	
Northeast Tracts						
402	9500	72	91	92	13	
403	9700	71	84	97	9	
404	11	000	80	92	76	6
406	12	700	83	96	51	4
407	9700	76	88	94	7	
408	9000	73	79	99	7	
409.01	7900	77	80	99	9	
409.02	7300	66	75	99	11	
410	7900	54	74	99	9	
411.01	7900	24	90	99	7	
411.02	9500	55	77	99	14	
412.01	8100	68	83	99	10	
412.02	9200	61	83	53	14	
Total	9185	66	84	87	9	
Southcentral Tracts						
419	9800	66	85	6	9	
420.01	8700	64	86	18	11	
420.02	7300	52	76	3	6	
421	9500	65	89	3	6	
423	8700	59	84	2	7	
424	8100	67	83	8	8	
426	7000	63	87	2	7	
428	13	000	42	86	9	1
429.01	9800	78	92	2	7	

Table 10.2 (*continued*)

Tract	House Value (1970)	% Owners (1978)	Income index (1978)	% Black (1974)	% 2-term Vacant	
Southcentral Tracts						
429.02	8300	61	85	7	5	
431.01	10	600	28	76	2	2
431.02	9100	38	83	37	7	
433.02	10	300	79	90	3	8
Total	9246	60	85	8	6	

Source: U.S. Census, 1970; Wyandotte County Census, 1974; Polks Profiles of Change, Kansas City, Kansas, 1978 (data on vacancy, ownership, and income are from Polks).

Rates of two-term vacancies reflect rates of abandonment. In the Northeast Area, this rate for 1978 was 9 percent. By comparison, the white tracts had a rate of 6 percent. The latter is only 1 percent higher than the rate for KCK as a whole (5 percent), including new suburban areas. Rates in the northeast area were almost double those of the city and one-third higher than in the older white neighborhoods.

Housing values in the black and white tracts were comparable (mean of $9,185 and $9,246, respectively). Family income was also controlled. Rates of ownership were actually higher in the Northeast tracts, and rates of residential turnover were substantially lower.[8] There was a major distinction, however, in the magnitude of recent population losses. Between 1970 and 1974, losses in the all-white tracts had amounted to only 2 percent, compared with 10 percent in the Northeast Area during the same period.[9] The comparatively higher vacancy rates in the Northeast Area were a direct reflection of differential rates of population decline. Visual effects of this discrepancy, however, contributed to a widespread impression in KCK that lower-income white neighborhoods were better taken care of than those inhabited by blacks.

Lending practices constitute another important difference between KCK's black and white urban census tracts. Although bankers may be reluctant to grant loans in all older neighborhoods, patterns of racial discrimination were quite evident in this setting. Mortgage disclosure data for 1977 indicate that despite the fact that housing values and family income were approximately the same in the two sets of tracts, the all-white neighborhoods attracted almost five times as much mortgage and rehab investment in 1977. Residents in the white tracts succeeded in obtaining more loans, bigger loans, and were serviced by a larger number of lending institutions (see Table 10.3). Had it not been for the existence of a black-owned bank in KCK, which granted 20 percent of all the loans in the Northeast Area, the discrepancy would have been much greater.

Blaming the victim is a familiar device in the epistemology of social control (Ryan 1972). Models of neighborhood decline, which posit the residents' behavior as the primary agent of destruction, conform to this paradigm (Massey 1990; Schwab 1987). Such interpretations admittedly have been difficult either to verify or disconfirm (Grigsby et al. 1987: 58). The historical intersection between postwar suburban development and the massive migration of southern rural blacks confounds understanding of cause and effect. Were white residents fleeing the onslaught of a population whose poverty and cultural shortcomings made them unacceptable neighbors? Or were they lured away by suburban life-styles and generous federal subsidies? Would they have left anyway, or were they pushed out of neighborhoods where they would have preferred to remain? What was the role of institutions and brokers whose profits were fattened by neighborhood transition?

In most places, answers to these questions remain elusive. Co-occurrence of all the relevant factors makes the chain of causation difficult to ascertain. KCK's unique demography reduces the uncertainty, however, and shifts the burden of explanation away from the characteristics of black families. In KCK there was no postwar "invasion"; assumptions based either on sudden housing competition or the behavior of maladapted rural black migrants, do not apply. The city did experience a boom in new housing construction in this period. Postwar prosperity and low-interest loans, especially for veterans, made these houses affordable, enabling a large-scale movement of white families to the suburbs. Real estate brokers in KCK followed the example of their counterparts elsewhere by capitalizing on opportunities this exodus presented. As elsewhere, blockbusting was a short-run entrepreneurial gambit. The long-term equation between buyers and sellers was not assessed by these agents, nor was it a matter of concern.

Spatial ecology of the Northeast Area offers an added explanation for why the process of neighborhood transition resulted in a ghetto too large for the city's black population. The parameters of arbitrage in the white neighborhoods of the Northeast Area were set by the historical locations of black neighborhoods in that section of the city. Because the nuclei of black settlements were dispersed, rather than concentrated, multiple borders existed. Transitional neighborhoods encircled and ultimately engulfed the all-white neighborhoods caught in the middle. White residents of those neighborhoods tended to be more affluent than inhabitants of the white

Table 10.3

Mortgage and Rehabilitation Loans for 1977: Northeast Tracts Compared with Southcentral Tracts

	Northeast			Southcentral	
Tract	Total $ (thousands)	Number	Tract	Total $ (thousands)	Number
402	17.32	4	419	96.21	10
403	4.41	2	420.01	47.09	6
404	81.52	7	420.02	17.05	5
406	109.60	8	421	333.59	27
407	27.62	4	423	125.18	16
408	--	0	424	87.76	12
409.01	5.11	3	426	71.69	12
409.02	--	0	428	509.10	23
410	64.40	2	429.01	38.84	6
411.01	21.16	2	429.02	44.50	6
411.02	2.20	1	431.01	66.35	5
412.01	3.16	1	431.02	42.6	5
412.02	--	0	433.02	36.45	3
Total	336.38	34	1516.41	136	
Average	25.86	2.6	116.65	10.5	

Source: Data supplied by banks and savings and loans in Wyandotte County in response to the Mortgage Disclosure Act; information collected by the Kansas City, Kansas Dept. of Planning & Development.

working-class neighborhoods located in the southern sections of KCK's urban core, hence financially better able to leave. This factor helps account for the relatively lower rates of population decline in the thirteen white neighborhoods in the comparison.

According to proponents of filtering theory, the housing market is like a game of musical chairs. But when the music stops, someone has to lose. Individual choices have aggregate effects. Filtering might work in a market that is free, flexible, and rational enough to allocate these choices in an optimal fashion. The dual housing market is none of these things. Group-determined disadvantages severely handicap black consumers and have done unaccountable damage to the older housing stock in our cities. Added to this injury is the insult of labels like *ghetto*. In the political economy of urban housing, the concepts of filtering and arbitrage represent sophisticated versions of social Darwinism, which simultaneously sanction oppression and denigrate the oppressed. A solution to the failed cycle of destructive urban policies, from which homelessness and abandonment have grown in direct proportions, demands a radical reappraisal of these models.

NOTES

1. U.S. censuses for 1930–60 indicate that the African-American population of Wyandotte County, Kansas (a stable boundary throughout that period, since over 90 percent of the county's population resides in the city of Kansas City, Kansas), grew by 7 percent the first decade, 28 percent the second, and only 5 percent the third, for a total of 40 percent in thirty years. By contrast, Cleveland's black population grew by 163 percent during that same period and Detroit's by 187 percent (Taeuber and Taeuber 1965).

2. In 1960, the U.S. census enumerated 14,610 African-Americans over five years of age in the Northeast Area of Kansas City, Kansas, only 492 of whom had been living in the South in the prior census.

3. The Northeast Area Project, from which the data for this study were derived, included about forty in-depth interviews with persons knowledgeable about the community. These included two black realtors, the presidents of the black-owned bank and insurance company, and several white lenders and realtors.

4. The term *griot*, creolized in Haiti, derives from a West African word for storyteller, or conservator of oral traditions.

5. In addition to data from the U.S. census, I also had access to more current demographic data, *Polk's Profiles in Change*, packaged by the R. L. Polk Company, which publishes city directories. I also availed mortgage lending disclosure data compiled pursuant to the Home Mortgage Disclosure Act of 1975.

6. Vacancy data for 1960 and 1970 were obtained from the U.S. censuses for those years; 1978 figures derived from *Polk's Profiles in Change*. The discrepancy between 30 percent population losses and only a 13 percent rise in vacancies is explainable by demolitions that took place in the mid–1960s and early 1970s.

7. Housing values for these twenty-six census tracts were derived from the U.S.

census for 1970; family income data were drawn from the *Polk's Profiles in Change* for 1978.

8. Data on owner occupancy and residential turnover were taken from the 1978 *Polk's Profiles in Change*. The Northeast tracts had an average of 66 percent owner occupants, compared with only 60 percent in the Southcentral tracts. Much of the ownership in the Northeast Area is through "option contract," rather than conventional mortgages. Rates of turnover for the Northeast tracts were 31 percent in 1978, compared with 36 percent in the Southcentral tracts. Citywide figures for ownership and turnover in that same year were 70 percent and 31 percent, respectively.

9. Based on the 1970 U.S. census and 1974 Wyandotte County census, the population in the Northeast Area dropped from 35,815 to 32,265 (10 percent); in the Southcentral tracts population declined from 33,425 to 32,695 (2 percent).

11

Access to the Waterfront: Transformations of Meaning on the Toronto Lakeshore

MATTHEW COOPER

The central waterfront of Toronto has been the focus of controversy since the mid–1970s. Debates over the scale and kind of development that should take place persist, with no signs of abating. Concerns about public access have been a key part of the issue. Waterfront redevelopment has been a genuine political football, passed back and forth among the federal, provincial, metro, and city governments.[1]

Such redevelopment expresses and reflects the changing meanings of this peculiar urban space. Changes in its use depend in part on the ways in which it is thought about and described. Such discourse, however, is neither static nor uncontested. It crucially informed and is itself affected by political-economic and technological change.

At a general level, I consider changes in the built environment and the use of space in relation to changing meanings. Kevin Lynch (1981) has described how access, in its different forms, can be crucial to the control of space. In this chapter, while considering the history of the Toronto waterfront, I focus on how the meaning of *access* has changed.

Geographers have pointed to a common theme in the development of Toronto and other port cities. They liken the waterfront to an urban "frontier." Its redevelopment, they argue, fundamentally depends on external forces, interests, and actors (Desfor, Goldrick, and Merrens 1988, 1989). The course of waterfront redevelopment thus reflects more pervasive changes in the city and in the larger political economy.

Looked at somewhat differently, frontiers may be thought of as edges between two zones, whose use and users differ markedly. Frontiers may be "crossed," "pushed back," or "opened up." Central to the idea of a frontier, I would suggest, is the sense of potential. On the frontier, the ordered and the known give way: anything is possible.

On the waterfront of port cities, the experience of open possibilities comes to residents in many ways. Shipping gives a sense of connection with far-away places. The open vistas of large bodies of water contrast sharply with those of modern cities. The rectangular and vertical give way abruptly to the undifferentiated and horizontal. The waterfront puts the city dweller, whose experience increasingly is of managed environments, face-to-face with uncontrollable nature.

The image of the waterfront as an urban frontier thus highlights discontinuity. In an almost structuralist manner it picks out series of oppositions, controlled versus uncontrolled, constrained versus unconstrained, closed versus open, actual versus potential, civilized versus wild. The list easily could be extended, in this well-known parlor game.

Instead, one might think about the waterfront in terms of continuity and broadened context, both historical and ecological. Spatially, that means seeing the waterfront not as an edge but rather as a variable zone of transition. Historically, it implies viewing the waterfront as an ambiguous zone, one whose meaning has shifted in relation to diverse interests, technology, changing patterns of use, and often has been contested. Thus, a second purpose of this chapter is to suggest that focusing on boundaries, borders, and zones of transition may be a useful tactic in studying the course of development beyond them.[2]

In the case of Toronto such a view might begin with the open lake, move to the Toronto Islands, then to the inner harbor, the water's edge, and finally perhaps to Front Street (several blocks inland) (see Figure 11.1). In the other direction, especially from an ecosystemic perspective, it could begin miles inland and include the entire watershed (as the Royal Commission on the Future of the Toronto Waterfront proposed in its 1990 interim report).

Michael Hough (1990: 198) provides a relevant example. In discussing design plans submitted for the Harbourfront redevelopment area on Toronto's central waterfront in 1987, he asked:

What makes the waterfront special? The urbanized shoreline of the old port, with its docks, warehouses, and industrial buildings, and the wooded pastoral landscape and soft edges of the Toronto Islands, give Toronto's central waterfront a powerful image as a memorable place. The relationship between these two contrasting landscapes, separated by and enclosing the inner harbor, provides the key to its regional identity.

With the construction of a wall of high rises along the waterfront in recent years, the contrast of hard and soft edges has grown even stronger. Hough goes on to propose regional design principles that would strengthen this

Figure 11.1
Toronto's Changing Waterfront

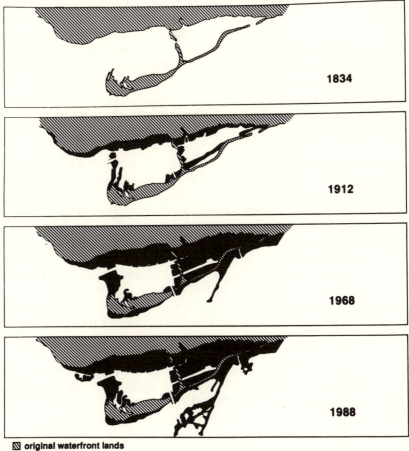

N original waterfront lands
■ created lands

identity: attention to context and the environment, linkage to the rest of the city, the waterfront as a place of work, continuity with past uses, diversity of spaces and built form, diversity of use and users.

Yet, as Edward Relph (1990: 26) pointed out, the landscape we see today did not always appear as it now does.

Probably the most distinctive-thing about Toronto's geomorphology now is how much of it is artificial, or has been profoundly altered by humans—streams buried, ravines filled, lakeshore extended, spits constructed. Even the Islands . . . have been raised and extended with landfill. The Leslie Street spit to the east of [the] Islands is an entirely artificial geomorphological project, one of a series of pseudo-spits intended to change the patterns of erosion and deposition along the lakeshore.

SPACE ON THE CENTRAL WATERFRONT

For the purposes of this chapter I will divide the history of Toronto's waterfront into several periods: (1) prerailway (before 1850); (2) the railway era (1850–1909); (3) commercial and industrial dominance (1909–mid–1960s); and (4) the era of consumption (early 1970s–present).[3] The landscape, uses, and meaning of the waterfront have differed during each period but in ways that reflect the different interests and perceptions of those most concerned with it.

The Prerailway Era

Much of the land that makes up Toronto's present central waterfront did not exist prior to World War I. The old shoreline lay about one-quarter mile inland from where it is today. In the early nineteenth century, the settlement of Toronto spread northward from the shores of Lake Ontario. The waterfront itself played a crucial role in the development of this commercial and administrative center. In Toronto's hinterland, wheat for export to Britain was the economic focus for the first half of the nineteenth century. As this hinterland expanded at the expense of other nearby centers, Toronto's port took on heightened importance.

The general public had a diffuse interest in the enjoyment of the waterfront lands. In the prerailway era, as the Royal Commission (1989b: 11) pointed out:

Sailing, rowing, fishing, and swimming were popular in the summer, as was promenading along the treed embankment that followed the shoreline. Skating, sledding, curling, and ice-boating were enjoyable pastimes when the bay froze over. Among the more unusual winter attractions were horse-racing and even fox-hunting across the slick ice fields.

The first lands south of the original shoreline were created in the 1850s. The land and water lots that formed The Esplanade, a carriage way and promenade along the shore, were granted by the crown to the City. One of the conditions laid down was that its development should serve the "healthfulness of the City" (Royal Commission 1989a: 15).

The Railway Era

Critical to Toronto's later preeminence was the growth and centralization of the railways there in the 1850s and thereafter. Thus arose several of the issues that continue to exercise Torontonians: public access, environmental quality, and whose interests were to be served. The railways transformed the area, laying track and building terminals directly on the waterfront. As the railways developed, they tried also to destroy lake shipping as the primary mode of regional freight transportation.

A recent report for the Royal Commission on the Future of the Toronto Waterfront (1989a: 11) remarks that

before the turn of the century, every street leading from downtown Toronto to the waterfront and Port had a level crossing—in some places as many as 16 tracks wide! The railway companies themselves actively worked to sever traffic between the city and the waterfront by parking rolling stock at crossings. Frequent accidents drew attention to the fact that the crossings were not only inconvenient but dangerous.

While the public sought better access to the lakeshore, the railways tried to block it. Commercial and civic groups called for many years without success for the railways to build a viaduct, so that trains would not enter Toronto at grade. For much of the railway era the central waterfront was cut off increasingly from the rest of the city.

Furthermore, "healthfulness" did not rank high on the railways' agenda. Indeed, as visiting poet Rupert Brooke (quoted in Royal Commission 1989b: 13) lamented in 1913, although Toronto lay on the shores of a

lovely lake . . . you could never see that because the railways have occupied the entire lakefront. So if, at evening, you try to find your way to the edge of the water you are checked by a region of smoke, sheds, trucks, wharves, shore houses, "depots", railway lines, signals and locomotives, and trains that wander on the tracks up and down and across streets, pushing their way through pedestrians and tolling as they go.

The ambiguity, even in perception, of this transitional zone became obvious in the economic and political struggles over it. For the railways the image of the waterfront was linear, a corridor running east-west along the shore. But for the rest of the city the railway lands were a wasteland to be crossed at one's peril, blocking the city's natural north-south connection to Lake Ontario. To a large extent, during this period *access* thus meant simple physical reachability.

Commercial and Industrial Dominance

In 1909, antirailway interests finally won out. The city looked forward to improved access to the waterfront. Construction of a viaduct was ordered, although it was not finally completed until 1930. But commercial and industrial interests, especially those associated with the Toronto Board of Trade, eagerly awaited the redevelopment of the Port, as well as the development of the waterfront lands for industry.

Redeveloping the waterfront fell to the newly created (1911) Board of Toronto Harbour Commissioners. A federal agency with appointed members, the THC became the major player on the waterfront stage. As Desfor, Goldrick, and Merrens (1988: 97) argue,

the Commission was to be much more than the harbour-minding authority signified by its name. With broad powers to control land, with extensive land holdings *ab initio,* and with the opportunity of creating a land bank through the mechanism of landfill, the Commission quickly began to function as a land-development agency.

In 1912 the Commission published a comprehensive waterfront development plan, influenced in part by the recent redevelopment of Chicago's waterfront. The key to this plan was the creation of a new waterfront for industrial, commercial, and recreational purposes. Much of the new land was to be reclaimed marshland in the Eastern Harbour. But the central waterfront would be extended as well, south of the lands taken over by the railways during the nineteenth century.

Thus, throughout the early part of this century three major players, each with its own interests, contended for control of the Toronto waterfront. To the railways the Harbour Commission's land-creation plans meant loss of access and riparian rights. Negotiations over these issues took place throughout the 1920s and 1930s. The City of Toronto had transferred its ownership of the waterfront to the Harbour Commission in 1912. But it attempted to maintain some control over it. In 1917 the Harbour Commission agreed not to dispose of any of the lands transferred to it without the City's express consent (Royal Commission 1989a: 13).

Desfor, Goldrick, and Merrens (1988: 97–98) summarize the Harbour Commission's success as a developer. By 1929 about 182 hectares had been created for industrial sites, of which 52 hectares had been sold or leased to industrial firms. These included ship builders, coal processors, ice storage companies, grain elevators, metal fabricators, sewage treatment facilities, fishing companies, construction firms, oil and gas storage companies, and so forth. Development continued through the 1940s, by which time most of the goals of the 1912 plan had been realized (Merrens 1988).

The Harbour Commission attempted to solve the long-standing conflict between public access and commercial development. But its solution involved pushing recreational uses to the periphery. The Toronto Islands were enlarged, although plans to link them to the mainland by bridge or tunnel never were realized. To the west of the central waterfront, a strip of parkland nearly five kilometers long was developed along the new shoreline. This included Sunnyside Park, which attracted large numbers of people to its pool, boardwalk, and amusements. As the Royal Commission (1989a: 15) noted, it also served the Harbour Commission's own interests: raising public awareness of the Commission's contributions and, more important, producing revenue from the western waterfront.

Another access issue arose in the 1930s with the Harbour Commission's plans to develop a small airport in Toronto. The site finally chosen was at the western end of the Toronto Islands, opposite Bathurst Quay. The key to the access issue was whether the Islands would be permanently linked to the mainland (Royal Commission 1989a: 14; see also 1989c). Residents of the Islands and members of the public who enjoyed them for recreation felt that a tunnel or bridge ultimately would destroy the Islands' parklike character. In the event, a small ferry was used. Coincidentally, the ferry's limited capacity restricted expansion of the airport.

Thus, by the 1950s Toronto's waterfront bore little resemblance to the pleasant harbor of a hundred years earlier. The water's edge lay about 300 meters south of the original shoreline. The headquarters of the Harbour Commission no longer stood on the shore. Wharves, elevators, terminal buildings, heavy industry, and railway yards occupied the central waterfront. The inner harbor served commerce and industry, not recreation. To the east the reclaimed marshes had begun to be developed for port facilities. Recreational uses of the waterfront had moved to the peripheries. Ferries from the central waterfront took residents to the Toronto Islands, which still had parks, beaches, and an old residential community.

The next barrier between the city and the central waterfront went up in the 1960s. The Gardiner Expressway, opened between 1958 and 1966, runs along the waterfront at heights of up to twenty-three meters. Below it lies Lakeshore Boulevard, with six to eight lanes of traffic and numerous ramps to the Expressway. Along with the tunnels under the railway viaduct, this physical and psychological barrier helped create the "dark, confusing ground-level approach to the lake so often reviled today" (Royal Commission 1989b: 14).

Thus, the meaning of *access* had become more complex over this period. When the Harbour Commission first was formed, it meant simply people's ability physically to reach the waterfront. As industry developed on the newly developed lands, conflicts over land use and water access emerged among commercial users and the railways. In the late 1930s, the controversy over a fixed link to Toronto Island Airport revealed another side of the access issue. Providing improved access for airport patrons potentially threatened Island residents and recreational users. Conflicting rights of private property and public enjoyment, itself hard to define, provided other levels of meaning.

Questions arose about *how much* access, of *what kind,* for *whom,* to *what,* for *what purposes*? Conflicts over these issues revealed how complex the access question really was. With later development, such issues became more complicated still.

In the 1960s, container ships became more common, and the old port facilities fell into disuse. New port facilities were developed in the eastern part of the inner harbor. Meanwhile, Metropolitan Toronto undertook a major waterfront planning exercise. This lead to waterfront development at the eastern and western sides of Metro. It also produced a futuristic recreation complex built on artificial islands just to the west of the central waterfront. The central waterfront, however, had been excluded from the 1967 plan. A high-rise development of offices, hotel, and luxury apartments rose massively at the very center of the waterfront. But the rest of it was deserted and rapidly became derelict.

Developing the Landscape of Consumption

In 1972, the federal government expropriated a thirty-five-hectare stretch of the central waterfront and gave it to the people of Toronto, some have suggested, as an election campaign present. Initially, the government envisioned a long stretch of green space along the waterfront with a mix of cultural and recreational activities.

The Harbourfront Crown Corporation was created to redevelop and administer the area. Its board of directors saw it as "an urban meeting place with a waterfront flavour, providing opportunity to display, enrich and share the diverse cultural traditions of the people of Toronto" (qtd. in Harbourfront 1978). This early park plan gave way in 1980 to a scheme approved by the Toronto City Council and the Ontario Municipal Board that "would bring the city to the water's edge" by including a mix of recreational, commercial, and residential uses.[4]

According to Desfor, Goldrick, and Merrens (1988: 100–102; 1989), the Harbourfront plan was a response to the interaction of complex political and economic forces affecting the redevelopment of the waterfront. Toronto's economy had become more oriented toward services in the 1970s and 1980s, especially finance and information processing. Furthermore, high-order information-based services tended increasingly to concentrate in the Central Area of the city. Thus, the city's occupational structure also changed, with rapid growth of managerial, technical, and administrative jobs.

Many of these relatively affluent white-collar workers preferred to live near their work places. Thus, extensive gentrification occurred in older, working-class districts near the Central Area, and many expensive condominium projects went up. At the same time, established middle-class residential areas were able to win exclusionary zoning regulations to protect themselves against redevelopment. The upshot was rapidly rising land rents throughout the Central Area and adjacent parts of the city. One of the few areas that could be redeveloped was the waterfront. Given the general level of land rents, only the construction of high-density, luxury commercial and residential space made economic sense to developers.

In this wider context, Harbourfront Corporation sought to define both its own mission and a new meaning for the area. The need for improved public access remained. "Bringing the city to the water's edge" now implied more explicit concern with public transportation, parking, and roadways. As well, it entailed thinking about *visual* access to the waterfront from the city, not just its physical reachability.

The idea of an "urban meeting place" rested on assumptions that were quite different from those that had informed earlier waterfront development. To develop an urban meeting place implied a concern with design that would encourage social interaction. It also entailed concerns about the kinds of activities that would contribute to such interaction. Should the area become a park, or should it include a mix of recreational, residential, and commercial uses? How much of the housing should be "affordable"? The reigning assumption was that *urban* meant *diverse*. Mixed use would make the area more interesting and vital. It also would encourage continuous use and thus would promote safety.

Further, the area had to exhibit and enrich the cultural diversity of the city. This principle implied a rather different conception of public access. Physical access was crucial, but now the area had to be made accessible socially. The "public" could no longer be thought of as being more or less homogeneous. It was differentiated economically, socially, and culturally. Social diversity was good; it too added to the vitality of the city. But what this diversity actually was and how it was manifested needed to be defined. Did it simply imply programming Japanese movies, a Swedish food festival, and Philippine dances, for example?

It soon became apparent that Harbourfront lacked the financial resources to fund its ambitious plans. In order to defray the development and main-tenance costs of its own facilities and the multimillion-dollar cost of some 4,000 cultural events annually, Harbourfront Corporation became a devel-oper. It leased rights on its property for the private development of rental apartments, condominiums, hotels, marinas, and shops. Such revenues went into a fund that had reached about $30 million by the late 1980s. Along with commercial fees and receipts from events, interest on the fund was supposed to pay for Harbourfront's programming.[5]

Trouble struck first in 1981. With the worst recession since the 1930s, developers became leery of investing in waterfront development. To fund its programs, Harbourfront entered into agreements with a developer to construct three large apartment towers: two of thirty-one stories and one of nineteen stories. As the buildings went up, the public and politicians began to complain that the "site was becoming an ugly concrete canyon" (Taylor 21, 1987). Besides the ugly high rises, luxury condominiums, ho-tels, and upscale shopping facilities began rapidly to occupy the area.

Slightly less than two-thirds of Harbourfront's retail, residential and office space was allocated for housing in the 1980 plan.[6] (Residential and office densities were reduced following the 1987 architects' report, but they remain live issues.) But most of this housing consists of expensive condominiums, as do projects in the immediately adjacent areas. Given that part of the revitalized waterfront was devoted to housing, *who* should have access to *what type of housing* became contentious issues.

Harbourfront was required in its plan to provide affordable housing. As Dale Martin (qtd. in Dale 1990: 83), former member of Metro Toronto Council for the downtown area, put it,

The official plan says fifty percent of housing should be for the bottom fifty percent of the population. Harbourfront has a thirty percent commitment... What we've seen is Harbourfront's attempt to get out of that... commitment, and as a result we're at around ten percent of the units being affordable. That's simply not good enough for publicly owned land.

Most of the space Harbourfront allotted for this housing is peripheral, on Bathurst Quay, as far as possible from the central area of upscale hotels, condos, and shops. Bathurst Quay, created by dredging in the 1920s, had been a derelict waterfront industrial area like the rest of Harbourfront in the early 1970s. It was connected by ferry with Toronto Island Airport.

From 1926 until 1968, Maple Leaf Stadium, named after the minor league baseball team that played there, occupied the area where one of the Quay's four nonprofit housing cooperatives now stands. One of the earliest industrial occupants (1926) was the Canada Malting Company, whose monolithic elevators still fill the eastern pier. During World War II, Bathurst Quay became the site of barracks and a training camp for the Norwegian Air Force. The barracks later were used for emergency wartime housing. After 1954, the site fell into disuse until the mid-1970s. Then Harbourfront turned what had become a dump into adventure and creative playgrounds. Today, the playgrounds too have disappeared, replaced by Little Norway Park, which commemorates the wartime training camp.

No one lived in the Bathurst Quay area before the co-ops arrived in the 1980s. Since 1986, four housing cooperatives and two Cityhome projects (nonprofit, assisted housing provided by the City of Toronto) have all been developed. With a total of 660 units, these projects had a population estimated at just over 1,500 in 1989 (Bradbee 1989: Appendix A. 6, 7).

Residential development meant the creation of new interests in the area. Residents were interested principally in expanding and protecting the use values they derived from living there (Cooper and Rodman 1990; Logan and Molotch 1987). For the residents, Bathurst Quay meant home, not a profit opportunity, tourist mecca, or institutional power base.[7]

As the residential community grew, so too did its concern with the pattern of development around it. Neighborhood associations developed to defend resident interests. Residents lobbied the City for better transportation, community facilities, and to forestall development of more condos nearby. In opposition to Harbourfront Corporation, they joined with the wealthier residents of the expensive condos. They resented Harbourfront's often heavy-handed attempts to control their projects, which extended to the trees they planted and the colors they painted their buildings.

Continual changes in policy on the part of the various interested government agencies, described in the sections to come, made it hard for residents to know what was happening. So too did the actions of private developers, airlines, and other economic actors. Many residents came to feel that their neighborhood was under siege.

Harbourfront: The Plot Thickens

As Colin Vaughan put it, "Harbourfront foundered on three key decisions: the need to break even financially in seven years; Harbourfront's partnership in development on the site; and the construction of that east-west highway down the centre" (Vaughan 1987: 54). The first decision forced excessive development at breakneck pace. The second created a conflict of interest on Harbourfront's part between planning and profit-generation goals. Finally, the road heightened the scale of development.

For Stephen Dale, Harbourfront's early history reflected a mix of structural and circumstantial factors:

Buffeted by antagonistic currents . . . Harbourfront was shaped by conflict and defined by compromise, as several levels of government vied for position on a shifting constitutional landscape; as the grandiose conceptions of an affluent age met an incoming tide of fiscal conservatism; as an emerging urban reform movement faced off against an entrenched federal bureaucracy.[8]

In 1987 a panel of architects had been asked to draw up recommendations to salvage plans for the area (Baird/Sampson Architects 1987). Their work was constrained in that 50 percent of Harbourfront already had been spoken for. Essentially, they concluded that Harbourfront should be urban in character rather than pastoral. While there should be less intensive development, a continuous wall of buildings still would be acceptable (Freedman 1987).

But events overtook the panel. In 1987, first the City and then the federal government froze all projects already planned. Responding to public concerns, in 1988 the Toronto City Council revised its official plan for the central waterfront, the area including Harbourfront and adjacent lands (Royal Commission 1989a: 54–92). The new plan aimed to extend mixed residential, commercial, and institutional development in the central waterfront. Too, public access to the area, especially for recreation, was to be improved, as were the aesthetics of development there. Unfortunately, the City did not stick to its own planning guidelines. Developers, for example, were allowed to build the required assisted housing part of their projects off site rather than integrating them into their waterfront developments.

In 1987, a Federal Royal Commission was charged with reviewing development along the Toronto region's entire waterfront. Former Toronto Mayor David Crombie, well regarded for his concern with neighborhoods and quality-of-life issues, was appointed the sole commissioner. In an interim report issued in the summer of 1989, the Royal Commission recommended that the Harbourfront Corporation should get out of property development and management (Coutts and Smith 1989).

Meanwhile, though, the City of Toronto entered into a deal with Harbourfront to lift its development freeze in return for cash and additional parkland on the site (Fine 1989; Slotnick 1989). When the City freeze was about to expire in December 1989 and before the new deal could take effect, however, the Ontario government stepped in with its own indefinite freeze (Allen and Polanyi 1989).

Proposals to expand Toronto Island Airport and to improve access to it exercised nearby residents. They were concerned about increased noise levels, more traffic, and safety. Although the City of Toronto also opposed expansion, the plans of the airlines and the Toronto Harbour Commission (which owns the facility) won out (Polanyi and MacLeod 1989; Anonymous 1990).

In May 1990, a federal-provincial agreement was announced that would take all land development out of Harbourfront Corporation's hands. Darcy McKeough, a former Ontario politician and businessman, was appointed by the federal government to resolve Harbourfront's problems. This agreement proposed that the City would get the additional parkland and cash it had earlier agreed to. Harbourfront's cultural activities would be supported by income from an endowment fund set up by the federal government. Finally, four condominium projects caught in the various freezes would be allowed to go ahead. But the projects would be moved to different sites, away from the water's edge. Less positive was the proposal to sell off the remaining development sites rather than leasing them (Allen 1990; Allemang 1990).

In August 1990, the Royal Commission recommended again that Harbourfront Corporation should get out of the development business. It also proposed that the Harbour Commission should be restricted to managing the Port. No longer should the Harbour Commission act as a developer and landlord.

Perhaps most optimistically, the Royal Commission adopted an entirely different perspective on the waterfront and its problems. Earlier studies had dealt with waterfront redevelopment segmentally as separable issues of access and transportation, housing, parks, airport expansion, cultural facilities, environmental quality, and the aesthetics of the built environment. Now, it adopted an ecosystemic perspective and a set of principles summarized as "clean; green; useable; diverse; open; accessible; connected; affordable; attractive" (Royal Commission 1990: 51):

In future, policies and proposals along the waterfront should not be judged solely on their economic merits, or their contribution to recreational, housing or other objectives. They must also be judged on whether they contribute to rehabilitating ecological health and public use and enjoyment of the waterfront, or simply continue the pattern of past abuses. Applying these principles forms the foundation for such a judgement.

In its principles and recommendations, the Royal Commission brought together many of the different meanings of access discussed earlier. It stressed that waterfront development must not create visual barriers. Users of the area must be able to see the water from nearby activity areas and the city more generally. Further, the water's edge should be open to public physical access. Design barriers should not restrict or inhibit such access. People should be able to "escape from the confines of the urban form" (Royal Commission 1990: 65).

As well, the Commission recognized that physical accessibility of the waterfront depends not only on whether, but on how it can be reached. Thus it stressed the need for improvements to several modes of transportation: public transit, private automobile, bicycle, and pedestrian. It also discussed problems of social, economic, and psychological accessibility. Such concerns "are particularly crucial for children, the elderly, and the physically challenged," as well as women concerned about their safety (Royal Commission 1990: 69). In economic terms, the waterfront should be accessible to "people at all income levels and of all family types," both for housing and for recreational opportunities (Ibid. 76).

In late November 1990, Darcy McKeogh issued his report on the future of Harbourfront Corporation. He called for turning it into a nonprofit cultural organization whose commercial assets should be disposed of. After paying debts of some $50 million, about $80 million would be left for an endowment fund. Income from the fund would underwrite Harbourfront's activities (Harris 1990a; 1990b). Although the report seemed definitive, it was immediately rejected by the Toronto City Council (Vincent 1990).[9]

By early 1991, Harbourfront Corporation had been dismantled to create three new bodies: a nonprofit organization to run cultural and recreational programs, a charitable foundation to manage Harbourfront's endowment, and a federal corporation charged with selling off most of Harbourfront's assets to developers. A three-year plan was established to try to provide some stability at least for the short term (Harris 1991).

At this time, some development issues seemed to have been resolved. But many problems remained. Public confidence in planning for the waterfront was at an all-time low. The approach taken by the Royal Commission represented a giant step forward—if its recommendations are followed.

Assessing Harbourfront's short history, one finds sharply polarized views. For some, Harbourfront had succeeded in turning a derelict water-front area into a neighborhood that is interesting, diverse, and filled with people at all times of day or night. Yet for others Harbourfront had come to embody the public's worst fears about the city. For one resident it had taken an opportunity for waterfront parks and turned it into "an investment opportunity for private developers and wealthy speculators" (Platiel 1989). "The story of Harbourfront," one critic wrote, "is the story of Toronto in the eighties right down to the last, quivering grab for profit and power" (Freedman 1987).

This brief survey of the history of Toronto's central waterfront has focused on two main points. First, I have suggested that transitional zones are useful areas in which to study the ways in which the meanings of urban space change. Their open and ill-defined quality makes them the object of parties whose visions of them can differ radically.

Second, I have shown how the meaning of *access* has changed, growing considerably more complex. Those changes have reflected shifts in the larger political economy and ideological trends. They have been intimately associated with changes in use and a shifting landscape of variably powerful interests.

The number and variety of such interested parties seems steadily to have increased on the Toronto waterfront. Today, the overlapping jurisdictions of four levels of government plus several semiautonomous agencies have produced a policy nightmare. The struggles of developers, commercial interests, airlines, arts organizations, and residents, to name only a few, have compounded the confusion. At a more general level, therefore, I urge that the meanings of space and the built environment should be studied, not as static givens, but as they are created, manipulated, and fought over.

NOTES

1. The City of Toronto and a number of surrounding municipalities formed the Regional Municipality of Metropolitan Toronto in 1953. Both levels of government deal with similar issues of planning, for example, roads and education, though at different scales. Metro Toronto is supposed to coordinate the activities of the member municipalities. In this chapter, I use *City* to refer to the City of Toronto and *city* to refer more generally to Metro Toronto and the area.

2. The history of the waterfront in a major port city cannot necessarily be generalized to other parts of that city or others. Yet this example may be helpful in understanding transformations of use and meaning in urban settings. It suggests that focusing on boundaries, borders and zones of transition may be useful. Studying these zones may help clarify the course of development beyond them.

That is, one should look historically at the development of the transitional spaces and at the development of discourse having to do with them—in relation to the attempts of different groups or individuals to control those spaces. All of these are moving targets, changing over time.

As well, the technology of control changes as does its nature. What sort of access is at issue—physical, visual, auditory? What sorts of rights and privileges do people claim or attempt to claim in respect of the spaces? How can access or the right to modify or dispose of the space be achieved (that is, the actual "technology" or "instruments" of control)? How does their doing so affect the spaces themselves?

In a Foucaultian sense, one would have a political economy of boundaries. But it would be one that tried to integrate structure and agency, partly through consideration of discourse.

3. This account of the early history of Toronto's waterfront is based chiefly on Desfor, Goldrick, and Merrens (1988), Royal Commission of the Future of the Toronto Waterfront (1989a, 1989b, 1990), and papers presented at a conference entitled "Toronto's Changing Waterfront: Perspectives from the Past" sponsored by the Toronto Harbour Commissioners (November 3–4, 1989).

4. *Toronto Globe and Mail,* April 21, 1987. The plans also were influenced by the success of the waterfront redevelopment in other North American cities. See, for example, Tunbridge (1988) and other articles in Hoyle, Pinder, and Husain (1988). The Ontario Municipal Board is an appointed provincial body that oversees the activities of the municipalities. It often is called upon to adjudicate disputes between developers and residents or municipalities.

5. Dale (1990: 84, 86) suggests that interest from the development fund actually accounted for only a small part of the programming expenses. For example, in 1988 Harbourfront spent more than $13 million on programming expenses. However, only $867,845 of that came from the development fund.

6. Housing issues along the entire waterfront are discussed in Royal Commission (1989d).

7. On the growth of tourism in the Harbourfront area, see, for example, Francis, 1990. The Metro Toronto Convention and Visitors Association lists Harbourfront as one of the city's top ten attractions and growing.

8. Dale (1990) provides an excellent account of the twists and turns in the history of the Harbourfront.

9. Overlapping jurisdictions have continually bedeviled waterfront planning. Harbourfront's land is *federally* owned; constitutionally, harbours are under federal jurisdiction; McKeogh was appointed by the federal government. But land-use planning is a municipal responsibility. However, because municipalities in Canada legally are creatures of the provinces, the Province of Ontario also has an interest. Through several provincial ministries and agencies it regulates municipal affairs and planning.

12

Public Access on the Urban Waterfront: A Question of Vision

R. TIMOTHY SIEBER

Revitalization of urban waterfronts is a seemingly ubiquitous process in North America, and increasingly common in Europe and Australasia as well. Generally, waterfront revitalization emerges in port cities experiencing postindustrial transitions, where port trade and manufacturing have declined in local economies in favor of growth in the service, information, and high technology sectors. Obsolete industrial and commercial space and facilities on waterfronts undergo redevelopment into new mixed-use office and residential complexes, and accompanying upscale retail services, festival marketplaces, leisure areas, and public amenities. Redevelopments typically involve gentrification and the transformation of long-standing blue-collar, sometimes roughneck, zones into middle- and upper-income enclaves, occupied or frequented by a mix of resident professionals, suburban commuters, and tourists (Sieber 1991). In North America this redevelopment pattern is most visible in the showpiece seaport cities like Toronto, where it has been analyzed by Cooper and Rodman (Cooper and Rodman 1990; Rodman and Cooper 1989; Cooper, this volume), Boston (Sieber 1991), Seattle, Baltimore, Vancouver, and San Francisco. The pattern is also apparent, however, in waterfront cities of all sizes, at all levels in the urban hierarchy, located on inland waterways as well as on the sea (Heritage Conservation and Recreation Service 1980: 1; Hoyle 1988: 15).

As urban waterfronts become redesigned and redeveloped and knitted more closely into the fabric of post-industrial cities' residential and commercial life, a major aim of planners and designers has been the promotion of public access to waterfront locations. Whatever the moral or political ramifications might be, public access is necessary to the economic vitality of most revitalized waterfronts, since retailing, tourism, and leisure are central components to their economic programs. Public access is also important politically in building a climate of public support for general downtown and waterfront redevelopment efforts and for the usually costly public capital outlays necessary for infrastructural improvement in these sites.

Increasingly in newly redeveloping port cities a central component of public access to waterfronts is being defined as *visual access,* the provision of places that allow the public to view the water—often, as we shall see, in recreational contexts. As one planner explained about Boston, "People can't feel connected to the Harbor, can't feel like they have access, unless they can see the water." Provision and enhancement of water views are not only concerns in public zones—such as parks, walkways, plazas, hotels, restaurants, and markets—but also extend to private places, especially residences, but also offices. Writing on the history of Toronto's waterfront since the 1970s, Matthew Cooper (this volume) noted that in that city's recently emerging postindustrial "landscape of consumption," public access has come to be defined in predominantly visual terms.

This chapter will focus on Boston, Massachusetts, as a case city, in order to examine this largely, if tacitly, accepted feature of new waterfront developments: the prominence of consideration of vision in the way that waterfront places are designed, constructed, marketed, and used. More specifically, the focus will be the overriding concern that those places are designed so that people can *see the water* from them, in fact, *must look at the water* from them. The working assumption is that this pattern results not simply from the widely noted tendency of designers to "stress vision to the exclusion of other senses" (Rapoport 1977: 184) but that a deeper cultural predilection—shared by designers, officials, and large segments of the public—is at work here and requires cultural interpretation. It is not the visual aspects of architecture and design that are at issue, in other words, but the visual connection that design promotes between people and the water or, as we shall see, between the city and nature.

To examine and interpret this preoccupation with viewing water, this chapter will consider discourse and imaging about waterfront places, the structure of the built environment itself, and social activities along the waterfront—particularly recreational ones. First, as evidence for the preoccupation and how it has been realized, I will discuss existing official guidelines for waterfront design in Boston and some critical related features of the built environment that are coming to exemplify those design principles. Second, both as further evidence of preoccupation with viewing water and as a way of tapping the symbolic meanings of water views to people on the waterfront, I will examine representations of waterfront places in real estate advertising and promotional materials, a strategy suggested by Amos Rapoport in his own analysis of environmental preferences (Rapoport 1977: 62–63). The next section of the chapter will present a cultural interpretation of this new preoccupation in terms of the social and historical development of contemporary port cities. Once gritty working ports peopled by blue-collar workers, increasingly many of today's urban harbors are being designed to serve the leisure needs of more bourgeois groups; the emphasis on vision speaks to the cultural sensibilities of these newcomers and to the new kinds of relationships they have to the water. As water and waterfronts are increasingly invested with recreational and aesthetic meaning by their designers and users, they serve as the focus for newly emerging urban "pastoral" visions. The conclusion suggests that while today's waterfront developments are novel in their presence in urban harbors, they articulate ideas about relations between city and nature that are long-standing in Anglo-America and possibly cities cross-culturally.

Boston, my case study city, is a trendsetter nationally and internationally for urban waterfront redevelopment. As is so in many other postindustrial cities of its type, such as Pittsburgh (Plotnicov 1987) and Toronto (Cooper, this volume), over most of the twentieth century Boston's economy has shifted from reliance on port trade and manufacturing to service and information industries. In Boston, this has recently opened for redevelopment miles of obsolete finger piers, immediately adjacent to the central business district. The result has been a "globally prominent" waterfront revitalization, one which "might claim pre-eminence [in North America], in so far as it . . . is both multi-faceted and intricately interwoven with probably the most successful inner-city revitalization in the USA" (Tunbridge 1988: 70). Boston waterfront projects have also received many design awards, particularly from the Waterfront Center of Washington, D.C., in its annual Excellence on the Waterfront competition.

THE EVIDENCE: THE FIXATION ON VIEWING WATER.

Promotion of public and especially visual access to the sea is a central principle in regulations governing all waterfront planning, design, and construction in Boston. The state's coastal zone management plan, its Public Tidelands Law (embodied in the Public Waterfront Act, or Chapter 91, of the Massachusetts General Laws), and accompanying harbor zoning regulations administered by the Boston Redevelopment Authority under its Harborpark Program (Boston Redevelopment Authority 1990) have all been made generally consistent with one another in their guidelines for waterfront design and development. Standards and interpretations are still evolving, but over the last decade or more development has been moving in a consistent direction, particularly with regard to visual access to water.

The emphasis on establishing visual connections is evident in a number of planning and zoning domains, in guidelines and plans, as well as in the built environment (see Exhibit 12.1).

1. In terms of the massing of waterfront structures at the water's edge,

Exhibit 12.1. The downtown waterfront area, adjacent to Boston's financial district and Faneuil Hall Marketplace, often called simply the Waterfront, showing the "stepping down" of building heights as structures approach the water's edge. The 1971 twin multihistory Harbor Towers in the center of the picture initiated gentrification of the downtown waterfront and predate recent planning guidelines. Because of their size and the barriers they offer to public physical and visual access, the towers today are considered design mistakes. (Photograph by Jonathan Klein)

guidelines currently in force call for keeping "building heights . . . relatively low to . . . allow maximum views of the Harbor. Building height will be allowed to increase with distance from the water" (Boston Redevelopment Authority 1984:16). Avoiding a curtain of high rises ringing the water has been considered particularly important in the downtown waterfront, since it is adjacent to the city's financial district, the major site of recent downtown office tower development. As Exhibit 12.1 indicates, buildings all along the downtown waterfront are "stepped down" in height as they approach the water. This precludes the construction of high visual barriers at water's edge and allows maximum viewing from inland locations, particularly from upper stories of office towers and high-rise apartment buildings (see Exhibit 12.2).

2. The centerpiece of the public's access to the water is a continuous pedestrian walkway, called Harborwalk, which when completed will provide an eight-mile perimeter pathway along the central city's shoreline. Already four miles are in use. The walkway must be at least twelve feet wide and appointed with appropriate street furniture, mainly benches,

Exhibit 12.2. Viewing telescope pointed toward Boston Harbor from the twenty-third-floor lobby of a law firm in Boston's financial district.

which typically orient users toward water views (see Exhibit 12.3). As will be explained below, most of the leisure activities appropriate for these walkways are passive ones, in which the observation of water is a critical component.

3. As in most redeveloping postindustrial seaports, the Central Boston shoreline is still lined with finger piers (see Exhibit 12.4), which are being retained—and even extended—in new construction so as to maximize valuable shoreline and water access. Walkways are expected to follow pier perimeters too, and the pier ends, those shoreline spaces extending furthest into open water, are key areas. At pier ends, regulations call for increased setbacks of thirty to fifty feet, large open observation areas, and viewing platforms or other open structures that do not impede water viewing (see Exhibit 12.5). Restaurants and other commercial public accommodations located on piers are expected to, and do, promote harbor viewing through appropriate windows and terracing (see Exhibit 12.6).

4. Guidelines call for building features that promote or accentuate harbor views, that orient users to the water: "Rooftop domes, galleries, and pent-houses that offer public views and public amenities will be encouraged. . . . Buildings on the pier ends that frame the harbor views through porticos or glass and frame structures will be encouraged" (Boston Redevelopment Authority 1984: 16). Designers note that water views appropriately framed

Exhibit 12.3. A section of Boston's Harborwalk, located near Rowes Wharf, show-ing characteristic water-oriented public benches.

through human-made structures "can visually create the illusion of infinity" for viewers (Boston Redevelopment Authority 1984: 25) (see Exhibit 12.7).

5. Guidelines call for preservation of sight lines, termed "view corri-dors," between buildings and through streetscapes so that water views are left open to pedestrians in locations distant from the waterfront. In the heart of the city, or at least from major nearby streets, city dwellers can thus still glimpse the ocean (see Exhibit 12.8). Planning for more than twenty years has observed such view corridors.

6. Boston Redevelopment Authority plans for waterfront redevelopment call for consolidation of a series of prominent public observation towers along the downtown Waterfront, set back from the piers, to allow the public additional vantage points from which to view the harbor (see Exhibit 12.9).

Public discourse and imaging regarding waterfront places also reflect a preoccupation with water views; in Boston this is highly evident, for ex-ample, in waterfront real estate marketing, particularly that related to private residential properties. Boston Harbor spans seven municipalities—Win-throp, Chelsea, Quincy, Hull, Weymouth, and Hingham, as well as Bos-ton—and the 1980s witnessed a massive building boom of residential properties along the entire waterfront, mostly condominium apartments and townhouses at middle- or upper-income levels of affordability. What-

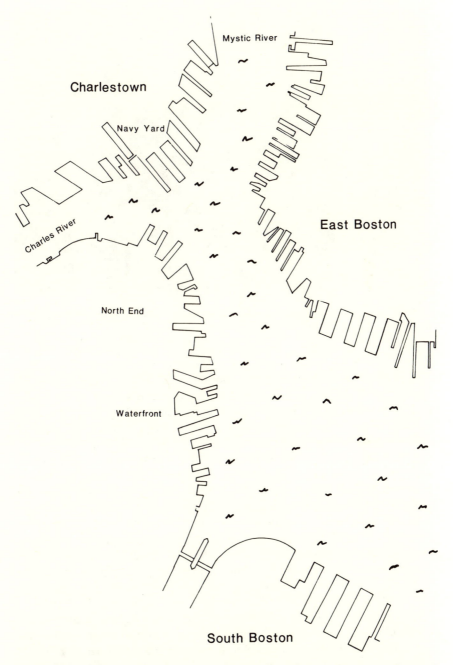

Exhibit 12.4. Map of Central Boston and the Inner Harbor, showing outlines of current finger piers in the downtown Waterfront, North End, Charlestown, East Boston, and South Boston areas. (Map by Christopher R. Eck)

Exhibit 12.5. Open observation area and viewing structure at pier's end, completed in 1990, located at the end of Long Wharf, Boston.

ever the setting and whatever the community, however, water views are usually listed as the primary amenity in real estate advertising and promotional materials and in personal sales pitches to prospective buyers or tenants. Many buildings, in ways that almost defy geometry (and that are publicly acknowledged to create otherwise ugly exterior shapes), are designed to afford each unit a water view. These are in some sense buildings designed from the inside out. The most salient design feature is not how the building itself looks from the outside, or in relation to its site, but rather how the outdoor environs look from interior space.

In advertisements, to be able to see the ocean from one's private residence is always described as an out-of-the-ordinary experience. Views are always "spectacular," "breathtaking," "dramatic," "striking," "exciting," "sublime," or full of "splendor" or "beauty." In keeping with the preoccupation with vistas, many advertisements, rather than picturing the property itself, instead show the view outward toward the water (see Exhibit 12.10).

To enable views, a standard feature of the typical waterfront unit is always a balcony viewing platform, as well as large windows on the water side (see Exhibit 12.11). At Marina Bay in Quincy, for example, each unit is advertised as having a "private balcony and wide expanses of insulated glass offering panoramic ocean views." At another development, potential buyers are encouraged to "take the Balcony Test. Trust your sensibilities—and

ROWES

*Restaurant
&Cafe*

WHARF

WATER SERVED WITH EVERY MEAL

Fresh native seafood
Regional American cuisine
Distinctive service

Exhibit 12.6. Waterfront restaurants, like these at the Boston Harbor Hotel on Rowes Wharf, maximize water viewing through terrace cafes and extensive windows. Water views are also promoted in their advertising.

your senses. Lean back, put your feet up on the balcony rail and *experience* life at Seaside Marina." In yet another condominium project in Dorchester, a sales agent stood on an apartment terrace, looked out to the nearby marshes and harbor, and encouraged a sales prospect with these remarks: "It's an exquisite view. I can visualize morning coffee here in the summertime. It's soothing, so relaxing. It's a wonderful feeling. Sometimes it's hard to leave here. It's so quiet and peaceful." House tours of waterfront properties also show that the hundreds of tour goers spend as much time looking out

Exhibit 12.7. Framing of harbor view, from the city side, by Foster's Rotunda at Rowes Wharf.

windows and balconies, and evaluating views, as they take to notice interior furnishings or layout.

Not all views are equal, of course, and this is reflected in different market values. Apartments with water views in more than one direction cost more, as do those in buildings closer to the water. In most developments, a premium is also put on units on upper floors, realtors explain, because they generally offer less obstructed views. At the Harbor Point Apartments in Boston's Dorchester neighborhood, for example, the rent differential is $900 per year for units on the top three floors of seven-story buildings. In some downtown projects where half a building looks cityward and not all units have a water view, we can get another sense of the value of water views.

Exhibit 12.8. Designer's conception of "view corridor" from inland streets to the sea. (Source: Boston Redevelopment Authority's manual of waterfront design standards [Boston Redevelopment Authority 1984: 27]).

At the Mariner in Boston's North End, for example, same-sized studios with a terrace and water view in 1989 cost $27,000, or 21 percent more than those without. A water view and a fireplace together allowed a one-bedroom condo to command $289,000 or 45 percent above the one-bedroom with neither amenity. Aside from the question of views, the greater value given to higher-floor units is consistent with the traditional association of status with elevation in Western culture (Rapoport 1977: 61).

THE SOCIOHISTORICAL CONTEXT

Why has this preoccupation with visual access to the water arisen at this time? What does it signify about the direction of change in North American postindustrial cities in the late twentieth century? Here I would like to suggest that the emergence of the visual connection to water, as an aesthetic value, arises as part of a general transformation in the public culture of postindustrial cities at this time. The new public culture is a largely "in-

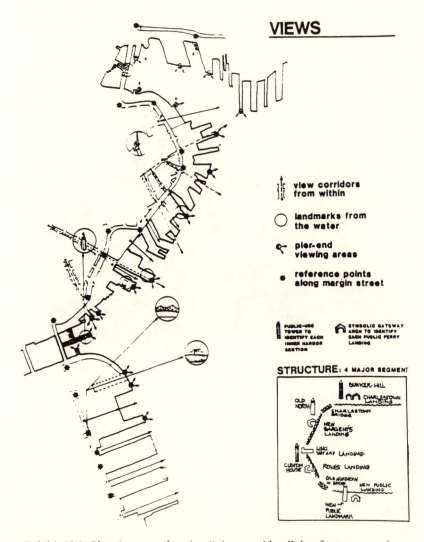

Exhibit 12.9. Planning map showing "view corridors" that foster water views from inland marginal streets; also showing a network of public observation towers in different waterfront area. (Source: Boston Redevelopment Authority's manual of waterfront design standards [Boston Redevelopment Authority 1984: 23]).

Exhibit 12.10. Typical waterfront real estate advertisement showing sunrise over the Atlantic Ocean. Here the water view is promised as the chief amenity, and the advertisement interestingly markets the view from the sale property, rather than the view of the sale property.

vented" one (Hobsbawm 1983) that serves the new constituencies now inhabiting and visiting redeveloped downtowns: urban professionals, sub-urban commuters, and tourists (Sieber 1990, 1991). This emerging public culture, I believe, seeks to create a sense of authentic belongingness—a connection to place, local environment, and local traditions—among these groups, all of whom have typically been strangers to the city in recent generations and who are largely ignorant of its ways (Sieber 1990). This emerging culture is a deeply class-based one, speaking mainly to the interests and condition of middle- and upper-class people who constitute today's influential user groups.

The full meaning of the new preoccupation with visual ties to water, its class implications, and its peculiarities as a form of public access to water can best be illuminated through a consideration of what sorts of access the new forms are in fact historically replacing. We also need to understand,

Exhibit 12.11. Waterfront real estate advertisement, one of a broad range, displaying commoditization of ocean views and emphasizing the property's outdoor terrace and vista as selling points.

as Alan Dundes (1975) has pointed out, how seeing is not really an issue of sense perception but a metaphor for worldview. Basically, as people in Boston have *used* the water less and less as a source of economic livelihood, they have emphasized *looking* at it more and more as an aesthetic object. This shift signifies the ascendancy of bourgeois, over working-class, constructions of the meaning of water and the growing importance of water's exchange value over its use value. This transformation is also reflected in the high level of commoditization of water view so evident in design and marketing. Commoditization and increased aesthetic valuation of water views, in other words, go hand in hand. Manifestations of these changes can be seen in a number of areas.

First, contemporary definitions see public access to the water as an issue of recreation rather than jobs. The domination on waterfronts of explicitly defined leisure areas—or parks—itself carries a message about what kinds of activity are appropriate there, since as Galen Cranz has noted, "in all eras, the park has been kept free of connotations of work, to serve as a balance to ugly, stressful work environments" (Cranz 1982: 253). In earlier generations, however, urban waterfronts in such cities as Boston, Baltimore, San Francisco, and New York supported vital marine-related industries—fishing, shipbuilding, and cargo handling—that employed legions of blue-collar men and gave waterfronts their flavor as active, rough, gritty, working-class places. In Boston, working-class people from neighborhoods ringing the waterfront, such as Charlestown, East Boston, and the North End, walked daily to jobs on the waterfront as longshoremen, fishermen, ship welders, and the like. These are all industries that have mostly collapsed in Boston and other postindustrial port cities; if not, they have at least been pushed out of now-pricey downtown waterfront areas to more distant locations. Most of today's waterfront parks are located on former worksites—for example, Boston's prize-winning Christopher Columbus Waterfront Park adjacent to Faneuil Hall Marketplace, which now occupies the sites of the famed Packard's and "T" wharves, once the home of Boston's fishing fleet. In waterfront land use, the displacement of workplaces by parks has been a key process in the city's deindustrialization and in the closing of many traditional working-class economic niches.

Today, water more and more is cast as a recreational or aesthetic resource. When people talk about looking at water, they usually emphasize its relaxing, soothing, or calming effects—seeing it as an antidote to the stress and tension of the normal workaday world, or to urban life in general (see Exhibit 12.12). Viewing and contemplating water is essentially a leisure activity, and if images of the water do contain human constructions, they are virtually always marinas, sailboats, and other recreational vessels, not working boats, like freighters and tugs. The focus on vision, in other words, legitimates on an aesthetic plane the transformation of the waterfront from an industrial, blue-collar location to a postindustrial, white-collar one.

The emphasis on quiet, respose, and expansive vista echoes traditional bourgeois—and urban—conceptions of the "pastoral," a tradition in English landscape architecture applied to urban park design, chiefly during the late-nineteenth century Progressive Era (Schuyler 1986: 141). On today's redeveloping waterfronts, a similar sort of aesthetic applies, only this time directed at seascape. Interestingly, as in the case of the older pastoral, today's peaceful waterfront vistas are also justified as healthful, a palliative to urban bustle, confinement, and what Frederick Law Olmsted called the "special enervating conditions of the town" (Olmsted 1973: 126). Today is also a time, as was the Progressive Era, marked by a dramatic new urban political

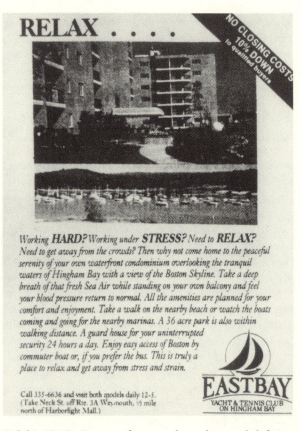

Exhibit 12.12. As part of a general trend toward defining waterfronts as places of play and leisure, advertisements like this one present the message that seaside living is a leisureful, relaxing experience that functions to relieve work stress and offers a release from the pressures of urban living.

and cultural ascendancy of white-collar professionals over working-class ethnic populations.

A related issue we must consider is the *kind* of leisure that revitalized waterfronts promote: this, too, has changed significantly. The new recreational places are designed for more passive or low-technology forms of leisure, particularly those enjoyed by the middle and upper classes—quiet viewing of water, as well as walking, bicycling, jogging, and picnicking. Forms of waterfront leisure more traditional among working-class city residents in harborfront neighborhoods, on the other hand, are ocean swimming, powerboating, family and other collective socializing, fishing, and shooting and hunting. Cars, amplified sound, gasoline-powered motors, noise, and alcoholic beverages are common accompaniments to these kinds of activities. Despite the expansion of leisure areas on the waterfront, little public or private capital investment is going to improvement of conditions for these traditional working-class activities that, moreover, are increasingly subject to restrictions, since they are viewed as noisy, polluting, disorderly, or dangerous (Sieber 1989). Redevelopment has made it harder than ever before to find a place to launch or moor a boat in Boston Harbor, for example; basketball courts in some areas have been removed to make way for waterfront parks and walkways in which quiet contemplation of nature is the main activity; and restrictions against public drinking increasingly constrain the kinds of socializing that can occur on public parklands. In many respects, these shifts in conceptions of appropriate leisure also echo the older pastoral notions. The true pastoral setting, as Olmsted argued in the last century, excludes "exertive" and "gregarious" forms of recreation in favor of "receptive" and "neighborly" (quiet, small-group) ones (Olmsted 1973: 126—129; Schuyler 1986: 141).

It is not clear, however, that the working-class people who have worked and played in the harbor unit recently have always made so sharp a distinction between work and leisure as the new urban professionals, and their planners, do. People have frequently played—fished, socialized, and swam—in working areas not officially set aside for recreation, and they still do so. The Charlestown Navy Yard is a case in point. At its height employing 4,000 workers, the shipyard was deactivated in 1975 and is now undergoing a $500 million redevelopment into offices, research facilities, and housing under the direction of the Boston Redevelopment Authority. Working-class people visiting the Yard for recreation believe that their leisure opportunities to fish and socialize in the ways they like have been limited by the new developments there. This is despite the construction of a 1.5-mile perimeter walkway along the water's edge and an expensive 16-acre waterfront park, both of them—officials admit—highly underutilized. While a few portions of Boston's Harborwalk, mainly those near Faneuil Hall Marketplace and the New England Aquarium, are heavily used by the public, most stretches—like that in the Navy Yard—are largely quiet, unpeopled, and physically inaccessible to a broadly diverse range of users. These are new waterfront places whose "emptiness" has been historically and socially constructed, as Gary McDonogh would say (McDonogh, this volume), reflecting space still under social contestation, space avoided, if not boycotted.

As in many other areas of the waterfront, these ostensibly public recreational areas are mainly used by mostly affluent waterfront residents of adjoining luxury housing and are perceived by most working-class people as private. Extensive informal working-class leisure, however, still takes place in the yet undeveloped, somewhat ramshackle areas of the Yard that are more comfortable to locals, even though developer leaseholders and the city have sought to discourage public use of these "dangerous" areas. The choices that local people make in their use of space reflect the lack of fit between the social and moral controls inherent in bourgeois leisure planning and potential working-class users.

THE CITY AND NATURE

If the class implications of these design practices are clear, the issue of vision still remains. Why is the stress on vision, and on viewing water, so salient in these designs? How is the stress on vision related to the more general bourgeois features of waterfront planning and use? The answers to these questions lie in the historically problematic relationship between the city and nature in Anglo-American culture.

Ostensibly, the desire to enhance the public's physical proximity to the sea, and their visual connection to it, is part of a general movement of returning waterfronts to a more "human" scale of design and use, where pedestrian networks, smaller-scale buildings, smaller specially retail shops, and communal celebration and festivity are present, along with the "mixed-use" functions that characterized preindustrial seaside villages or waterfronts, where homes, stores, and workshops, public and private, were combined in the same location. Advertisements and promotions, for example, promise that developments offer "living in a cozy Nantucket-style village," or display "small-town values" in their design (see Exhibit 12.13).

A basic ingredient of these new, more "authentic," "human" waterfront environments and life-styles is, of course, close, direct, unpolluting ties to nature. Indeed, environmental education and awareness, as well as pollution control, seem to accompany waterfront redevelopment everywhere. In the design arena, this explains why it is so important for people to be able to view the water without impediment: they are believed to become closer to nature by doing so. This preoccupation with achieving a close tie to nature has also long been recognized as a prominent trait of the upper and middle classes, particular in Anglo-America since the Industrial Revolution (Urry 1990: 94–95; Keith 1983).

The paradox is that this closeness to nature is achieved through vision—a process that ultimately leads to objectification of the water and its definition as something other, something opposed to the city, and ameliorative of its own fundamental qualities. The contrast between city and water—between culture and nature, in other words—becomes more sharply drawn, more highly charged, and more ritualized through these new spatial arrangements than ever before. As Donald Lowe has noted, an emphasis on vision in orientation to the environment, a hallmark of the Western bourgeois sensibility (Lowe 1982: 38–39), "always presupposes a distance between the viewer and the viewed" (Lowe 1982: 101).

Exhibit 12.13. Real estate advertisement promoting a smaller-scale, more human living community on the waterfront. Even though the property (pictured at the top of the ad) is a modern apartment building, the surrounding mixed-use development—all newly constructed on an abandoned airfield—is presented as a "cozy, Nantucket-style village."

In the bourgeois Anglo-American tradition, at least, the long-standing objectification and romanticizing of "natural" elements—such as wilderness, the countryside, or animals—has historically accompanied, if not signified, their increasing lack of utility, their containment, even their "marginalization" (Berger 1982), as a part of people's everyday life in modern, urban settings. This is reflected in the history of zoos (Berger 1980: 1–26), aquariums (Sieber 1991: 127), parks (Cranz 1982), "natural wonders" (Sears 1989), wilderness regions (Batteau 1982), the countryside (Marx 1973; Keith 1983), and suburbanization (Warner 1962; Fishman 1987). In each of these arenas, urban people's efforts to represent nature in their own midst, through including natural elements in their environmental designs, paradoxically sharpen the boundaries between city and nature. The latest example of this process is now occurring in postindustrial waterfronts where the sea has been appropriated as a natural symbol and made the object of gaze.

As middle- and upper-class residents and visitors have "returned" to postindustrial cities, their gentrification of many urban neighborhoods has been ideologically driven by this same search for more "natural," smaller-scale communities (Sieber 1987). What is new about this trend is that the striving for smaller-scale, more "natural" communities—which in the past has always led the middle and upper classes to *separate* themselves spatially from the perceived disorder and pollution of the industrial city—can now be accommodated *in the city* itself, or at least in postindustrial ones. Now the city, or at least the waterfront, offers a natural connection, and a vista, formerly available only in the suburbs, countryside, or wilderness. By the sea, in other words, it is possible to live a nonurban, perhaps even anti-urban, life while in the city. Thus, the historical "return" of the public to the waterfront that developers and planners say is now occurring is not the literal return so often imagined, but simply the extension to contemporary postindustrial waterfront settings of much older urban-based patterns of symbolizing nature from within culture.

Although their importance in Anglo-American history and culture has long been recognized (e.g., Rapoport 1977: 57, 61; Keith 1983; Marx 1973; Williams 1973), it could be that these patterns—placing a high premium on vision and displaying ambivalence toward both nature and urbanism—are panurban. In his studies of urban gardening and landscape design in continental Europe, Rotenberg (1989 and this volume) has uncovered what he terms a "two-thousand-year-old discourse" in the West, linking natural elements, frequently reinvented, to healthy urban living. John Mock's work on urban Japan (this volume), moreover, suggests that similar preoccupations have guided landscape design there. As centers of power and elite control, perhaps cities cross-culturally have always promoted objectification and romanticization of nature, of the sort that we see in new guise today in the emerging waterfront designs of port cities and in the visions of their users. Cities are places that have always borne the imprint of massive and never ceasing human efforts to build and reshape the environment. Since they are settings where culture is always so patent, so dominating a feature of the landscape, perhaps we should not be surprised that their residents are so fixated on symbolizing and representing nature, or that they do so in the multiple voices that reflect their varying historical exigencies, political economies, and cultural contexts.

NOTE

Earlier versions of this chapter were presented at the symposium Urban Space and Urban Policy, organized by Robert Rotenberg and Gary McDonogh, at the American Anthropological Association Annual Meeting, December 1990, New Orleans, and at the departmental seminar, Department of Landscape Architecture and Regional Planning, University of Massachusetts-Amherst in March 1991. The research was supported through sabbatical funding and faculty development grants from the University of Massachusetts at Boston. I thank Susan Reverby for comments on an earlier version of the chapter; Ellen Pader for her important early encouragement; John Tuma for invaluable assistance in the project's visual documentation; Christopher R. Eck for drafting the Inner Harbor map in Exhibit 12.4; and the following people for general research assistance on various phases of my Boston Harbor work: Mary Concannon, Marjorie O'Neill, Christine Buckley, James Lonergan, Dimitra Doukas, Christine Chaisson, Diane Caleskie, Prisca Killough, and Charlotte Gorman. I also offer special thanks for permissions to use copyrighted images of advertisements to Makram L. Awdeh of Awdeh & Co.; Rick Harmon of the Boston Harbor Hotel; Marc Goldstine of East Bay Condominiums; Hassan Haydar of the Boston Harbor Marina Co.; and Sanford Kaplan of the Dolphin Real Estate Corporation. Klein Post Card Service and photographer Jonathan Klein also kindly gave permission to use the photograph of the Boston waterfront in Exhibit 12.1.

Bibliography

Academy for Educational Development. 1988. *Belize: Education Sector Assessment*. Washington D.C.: Academy for Educational Development.

Adams, John. 1984. "The Meaning of Housing in America." *Annals of the Association of American Geographers* 74 (4): 515–526.

Agnew, John A. 1989. "The Devaluation of Place in Social Science." In *The Power of Place*, ed. John A. Agnew and James S. Duncan. Boston: Unwin Hyman. Pp. 9–29.

Ajuntament de Barcelona. 1983. *Plans i projectes per a Barcelona 1981/82*. Barcelona.

———. 1985. *Inicis de la urbanística municipal de Barcelona: Mostra dels fons municipal de plans i projectes d'urbanisme 1750–1930*. Barcelona.

———. 1987. *Urbanisme a Barcelona: Plans cap al 92*. Barcelona.

Alberti, Leon Battista. [1485] 1986. *The Ten Books of Architecture*. New York: Dover Publications.

Albrecht, Jörg. 1989. "Alles Glück Dieser Erde." *Zeit Magazin,* May 5, pp. 98–100.

Alexander, Christopher. 1979. *The Timeless Way of Building*. New York: Oxford University Press.

Allemang, John. 1990. "Quick Solution a Costly One for Harbourfront, Mills Charges." *The Toronto Globe and Mail* May 2, 1990. P. A13.

Allen, Gene and Margaret Polanyi. 1989. "Ontario Declares Indefinite Freeze on New Harbourfront Building." *The Toronto Globe and Mail* December 14, 1989. P. A15.

Allen, Glen. 1990. "Harbourfront Can No Longer Develop Land by Lakeshore." *The Toronto Globe and Mail* May 1, 1990, P. A1.

Allinson, Gary D. 1978. "Japanese Cities in the Industrial Era." *Journal of Urban History* 4 (4): 443–476.

———. 1985. "Japanese Urban Society and its Cultural Context." In *The City in Cultural Context,* ed. J. A. Agnew, J. Mercer, and D. E. Sopher. Boston: Allen and Unwin. Pp. 153–185.

Althusser, Louis. 1971. "Ideology and Ideological State Apparatuses." In *Lenin and Philosophy,* and other essays. New York: Monthly Review Press.

Altman, Irwin. 1974. "Privacy: A Conceptual Analysis." In *Man-Environment Interactions: Evaluations and Applications,* ed. D. H. Carson. Washington D.C.: Environmental Design Research Association.

———. 1975. *Environment and Social Behavior.* Monterey, Calif.: Brooks/Cole.

———. 1977. "Privacy Regulation: Culturally Universal or Culturally Specific?" *Journal of Social Issues* 33 (3): 66–84.

Alvarado, Pedro de. 1969. *An Account of the Conquest of Guatemala in 1524.* New York: Cortes Society.

Alzaldúa, Gloria. 1987. *Borderlands/La Frontera.* San Francisco: Spinsters.

Anonymous. 1990. "Judge Rules Airport on Island Can Expand." *The Toronto Globe and Mail* March 31, 1990. P. A1.

Aoyagi Kiyotaka. 1983. "Viable Traditions in Urban Japan: *Matsuri* and *Chônaikai.*" In *Town-Talk: The Dynamics of Urban Anthropology,* ed. G. Ansari and P. Nas. Leiden: E. J. Brill. Pp. 96–111.

Arciniegas, German. 1975. *America in Europe: A History of the New World in Reverse.* San Diego: Harcourt Brace Jovanovich.

Arensberg, Conrad, and Solon Kimball. 1940. *Family and Community in Ireland.* Cambridge, Mass.: Harvard University Press.

Aronowitz, S., and H. Giroux. 1985. *Education Under Seige.* South Hadley, Mass.: Bergin and Garvey.

Artigues Vidal, Jaume, Francesc Mas Palahi, and Xavier Suñol Ferrer. 1980. *El Raval: història d'un barri servidor d'una ciutat.* Barcelona: Col·lecció el Raval, Number 1.

Ashcraft, N. 1973. *Colonialism and Underdevelopment in British Honduras.* New York: Doubleday.

Ashmore, Wendy. 1981. *Lowland Maya Settlement Patterns.* Albuquerque: University of New Mexico Press.

Ashton, Patrick. 1978. "The Political Economy of Suburban Development." In *Marxism and the Metropolis,* ed. W. K. Tabb and L. Sawers. New York: Oxford University Press.

Baird/Sampson Architects. 1987. *Harbourfront 2000: A Report to the Futures Committee of Harbourfront.* Toronto: Harbourfront.

Baker, Hugh D. R. 1979. *Chinese Family and Kinship.* New York: Columbia University Press.

Basso, Keith. 1982. "To Give Up on Words: Silence in Western Apache Culture." In *Language and Social Context,* ed. Pier Paolo Giglioli. New York: Penguin. Pp. 67–86.

Batteau, Alan. 1982. "The Sacrifice of Nature: A Study in the Social Production of Consciousness." In *Cultural Adaptations to Mountain Environment,* ed. Patricia D. Beaver and Burton L. Parrington. Athens: University of Georgia Press. Pp. 94–106.

Bauman, Richard. 1983. *Let Your Words Be Few: Symbolism of Speaking and Silence Among Seventeenth-Century Quakers.* Cambridge: Cambridge University Press.

Becker, Marshall J. 1982. *Ancient Maya Houses and Their Identification. Revista española de antropología americana* 12: 110–129.

Benevolo, L. 1969. "Las nuevas ciudades fundadas en el siglo XVI in América Latina." *Boletín Centro de Investigaciones Historicas y Esteticas* 9: 117–136.

Berger, John. 1980. *About Looking.* New York: Pantheon.

Bernstein, Basil. 1971. *Class, Codes and Control. Vol. 1.* London: Routledge and Kegan Paul.

Bestor, Theodore C. 1985. "Tradition and Japanese Social Organization: Institutional Development in a Tokyo Neighborhood." *Ethnology* 24 (2): 121–135.

———. 1989. *Neighborhood Tokyo.* Stanford, Calif.: Stanford University Press.

Bian Lei. 1987. "Should a Teacher Inspect a Student's Book Bag?" *Qing Shao Nian Ri Ji,* September 6.

Bigges, Walter. 1588. *Expedito Francisci Draki.* London.

Birch, D. L. 1971. "Towards a Stage Theory of Urban Growth." *Journal of the American Institute of Planners* 37 (2): 78–87.

Bisceglia, Joseph G. 1973. " 'Block-busting': Judicial and Legislative Response to Real Estate Dealers' Excesses." *De Paul Law Review.* Summer, 818–838.

Blair, John P. 1973. "A Review of Filtering Down Theory." *Urban Affairs Quarterly* (March): 303–316.

Blaser, Werner. 1955. *Temples and Tea-Houses of Japan.* Bern: Urs-Graf.

———. 1958. *Classical Dwelling Houses in Japan.* Teuten, AR, Switzerland: Arthur Niggli.

Borah, W. 1972. "European Cultural Influences in the Formation of the First Plan for the Urban Centers That Has Lasted to Our Time." In *Urbanización Proceso Social América,* ed. J. E. Hardoy, N. S. Kinzer, and R. D. Schaedel. Lima: Instituto de Estudios Peruanos. Pp. 35–54.

Borah, W., J. Hardoy, and G. Stelter. 1980. *Urbanization in the Americas.* Ottawa: National Museum.

Boston Redevelopment Authority. 1984. *Harborpark: Interim Design Standards for the Inner Harbor.* Boston: Boston Redevelopment Authority.

———. 1987. *Harborpark Update.* Boston: Boston Redevelopment Authority.

———. 1990. *Harborpark Plan: City of Boston Municipal Harbor Plan.* Boston: Boston Redevelopment Authority.

Bourdieu, Pierre. 1970. "The Berber House, or the World Revisited." In *Echanges et communications: Mélanges offerts a Claude Lévi-Strauss a l'occasion de son 60eme anniversaire,* ed. Jean Pouillan and Pierre Maranda. Hague: Mouton. Pp. 151–169.

———. 1977. *Outline of a Theory of Practice.* Cambridge: Cambridge University Press.

———. 1984. *Distinction: A Social Critique of the Judgement of Taste.* Cambridge, Mass.: Harvard University Press.

Bourdieu, P., and J. P. Passeron. 1977. *Reproduction: Education, Culture, and Society.* London: Sage Publications.

Bowles, Samuel, and Herb Gintis. 1976. *Schooling in Capitalist America.* New York: Basic Books.

Boyer, Richard. 1980. "La ciudad de México en 1628." *Historia Mexicana* 115 (29): 447–471.

Bradbee, C. 1989. "Harbourfront: The Making of a Neighborhood." Paper submitted to the Royal Commission on the Future of the Toronto Waterfront.

Bradford, Calvin. 1979. "Financing Home Ownership: The Federal Role in Neighborhood Decline." *Urban Affairs Quarterly* 14 (3): 313–335.

Branigan, W. 1989. "Crack, L.A.-Style Gangs Trouble Torpid Belize." *Washington Post,* September 18.

Braudel, Fernand. 1949. *La Méditerranée et le monde méditerranéan à l'époque de Philippe II.* Paris: Librarie Armand Colin.

Broadbent, G., R. Bunt, and T. Llorens. 1980. *Meaning and Behavior in the Built Environment.* Chichester, England: John Wiley.

Bronner, Fred. 1986. "Urban Society in Colonial Spanish America." *Latin American Research Review* 21 (1): 7–72.

Brown, Keith. 1976. "Community and the Territorial Principle: Neighborhood Relations in a Japanese Town." Paper presented at the Workshop on the Japanese City, Mt. Kisco, NY, April 23–27.

Browne, Charlene Alyce. 1988. "Space, Time and Social social, A Multidimensional Approach to Design: Case Study in Mérida, Yucatán, Mexico." In *Proceedings of the Environmental Design Research Association 19,* ed. Denise Lawrence, Reiko Habe, Art Hacker, and Drury Sherrod. Pomona: California Polytechnic University.

Calmettes, Claude, Dode Cornu, Quitterie y Calmettes. 1986. *Le batie ancien en bastide.* Paris: Centre D'Etude des Bastides, Villefranche-de-Rouergue.

Calnek, Edward E. 1972. "The Internal Structure of Cities in America: Pre-Columbian Cities: The Case of Tenochtitlán." In *Urbanización y proceso social en América,* ed. R. Schaedel et al. Lima: Instituto de Estudios Peruanos. Pp. 347–358.

———. 1978. "The Internal Structure of Cities in America: Pre-Columbian Cities, the Case of Tenochtitlán." In *Urbanization in the Americas,* ed. R. Schaedel et al. The Hague: Mouton. Pp. 315—326.

Carnoy, M. 1974. *Education as Cultural Imperialism.* New York: McKay.

Carrasco, Davíd. 1990. "Myth, Cosmic Terror and the Templo Mayor." In *The Great Temple of Tenochtitlán,* ed. J. Broda, D. Carrasco, and E. Matos Moctezuma. Berkeley: University of California Press.

Castells, Manuel. 1977. *The Urban Question.* Cambridge, Mass.: MIT Press.

———. 1978. *City, Class and Power.* New York: St. Martin's Press.

Central Statistical Office. 1991. Preliminary 1990 Census Figures. Unpublished. Belmopan, Belize: Central Statistical Office.

Cerdà, Ildefons. [1867] 1968–1971. *Teoría de la urbanización y aplació n de sus principios y doctrinas a la reforma de Barcelona.* Barcelona: Instituto de Estudios Fiscales.

Cervantes de Salazar, Francisco. [1554] 1953. *Life in the Imperial and Loyal City of Mexico in New Spain.* Austin: University of Texas Press.

Chu, David S. K. 1985–86. "Introduction: One Hundred Court Cases on Marriage." *Chinese Sociology and Anthropology* 18, nos. 1–2: 3–9.

Cil, Joaquín, José de Letamendi, R. Domenech, and J. Arrau. 1858. *Informe dado a la instancia de la Illustre Junta Administrativa del cementerio general de Barcelona.* Barcelona: Tomas Gorchs.

Clark, Rodney. 1979. *The Japanese Company.* New Haven, Conn.: Yale University Press.

Clendinnen, Inga. 1987. *Ambivalent Conquests: Maya and Spaniard in Yucatán, 1517–1570*. New York: Cambridge University Press.

Clifford, James. 1988. *The Predicament of Culture*. Cambridge: Harvard University Press.

Coaldrake, William H. 1981. "Edo Architecture and Tokugawa Law." *Monumenta Nipponica* 36 (3): 235–284.

Coe, Michael. 1987. *The Maya*. London: Thames and Hudson.

Cole, Robert E. 1971. "The Theory of Institutionalization: Permanent Employment and Tradition in Japan." *Economic Development and Cultural Change* 20 (1): 47–70.

Columbus, Christopher. 1493. *De Insulis inventis*. Basle.

Cooper, Matthew. 1990. "On the Waterfront: Tranformations of Meaning on the Toronto Lakeshore." Paper delivered at the Annual Meeting of the American Anthropological Association, New Orleans.

Cooper, Matthew, and Margaret Rodman. 1990. "Conflicts over Use Values in an Urban Canadian Housing Cooperative." *City and Society* 4 (1): 44–57.

———. 1992. *New Neighbours: A Case Study of Cooperative Housing in Toronto*. Toronto: University of Toronto Press.

Cortés, Hernán. [1524] 1986. *Praeclara . . . de nova maris oceani*. Nuremburg.

Cosgrove, D. 1982. "The Myth and Stones of Venice: An Historical Geography of a Symbolic Landscape." *Journal of Historical Geography* 8: 145–169.

Coutts, Jane and Beverley Smith. 1989. "End Involvement in Development on Waterfront, Ottawa is Urged." *The Toronto Globe and Mail* August 31, 1989. P. A1.

Cranz, Galen. 1982. *The Politics of Park Design: A History of Urban Parks in America*. Cambridge, Mass: MIT Press.

Crouch, Dora P., Daniel J. Garr, and Axel I. Mundigo. 1982. *Spanish City Planning in North America*. Cambridge, Mass.: MIT Press.

Dale, S. 1990. "Pier Pressures." *Toronto Life* 24 (6): 46–49, 71–87.

Daniels, Gordon. 1975. "The Great Tokyo Air Raid, 9–10 March 1945." In *Modern Japan: Aspects of History, Literature, and Society*, ed. W. G. Beasley. Berkeley: University of California Press.

Darnton, Robert. 1990. *The Kiss of Lamourette: Reflections in Cultural History*. New York: W. W. Norton.

D'Auteroche, Chappe. 1778. *A Voyage to California to Observe the Transit of Venus with an Historical Description of the Author's Route through Mexico and the Natural History of That Province*. London: Edward and Charles Dilly.

Davis, S. 1986. *Parades and Power*. Philadelphia: Temple University Press.

DeJean, Joan. 1987. "No Man's Land: The Novel's First Geography." In *Everyday Life*, ed. A. Kaplan and K. Ross. *Yale French Studies* 73: 175–189.

Desfor, G., M. Goldrick, and R. Merrens. 1988. "Redevelopment on the North American Water-Frontier: The Case of Toronto." In *Revitalising the Waterfront: International Dimensions of Dockland Redevelopment*, ed. B. S. Hoyle, D. A. Pinder, and M. S. Husain. London and New York: Belhaven Press. Pp. 92–113.

———. 1989. "A Political Economy of the Water-Frontier: Planning and Development in Toronto." *Geoforum* 20: 487–501.

Díaz del Castillo, Bernal. 1963. *The Conquest of New Spain*. Harmondsworth: Penguin.

Dore. R. P. 1958. *City Life in Japan*. Berkeley: University of California Press.

————. 1973. *British Factory—Japanese Factory: The Origins of National Diversity in Industrial Relations*. Berkeley: University of California Press.

Dorst, John D. 1989. *The Written Suburb: An American Site, An Ethnographic Dilemma*. Philadelphia: University of Pennsylvania Press.

Downs, Anthony. 1981. *Neighborhoods and Urban Development*. Washington, D.C.: Brookings Institution.

Drexler, Arthur. 1966. *The Architecture of Japan*. New York: Museum of Modern Art, Arno Press.

Dundes, Alan. 1975. "Seeing Is Believing." In *The Nacirema: Readings on American Culture*, ed. James P. Spradley and Michael A. Rynkiewich. Boston: Little, Brown. Pp. 14–19.

Eickelman, Christine. 1984. *Women and Community in Oman*. New York: New York University Press.

Eksteins, Modris. 1989. *Rites of Spring: The Great War and the Birth of the Modern Age*. Boston: Houghton Mifflin.

Elliot, J. H. 1987. The Spanish Conquest. In *Colonial Spanish America*, ed. L. Bethell. New York: Cambridge University Press. Pp. 1–58.

Elvin, Mark. 1986. "Between the Earth and Heaven: Conceptions of the Self in China." In *The Category of the Person: Anthropology, Philosophy, History*, ed. M. Carrithers, S. Collins, S. Lukes. Cambridge: Cambridge University Press. Pp. 156–189.

Enbutsu Sumiko. 1984. *Discover Shitamachi*. Tokyo: Shitamachi Times.

Evans, Sara, and Harry C. Boyle. 1986. *Free Spaces: The Sources of Democratic Change in America*. New York: Harper & Row.

Everitt, J. C. 1986. "The Growth and Development of Belize City." *Belizean Studies* 14 (1): 2–45.

Ewens, D. 1990. "The Red and Blue Children." *Forum* 1: 17–30.

Farazali, C. 1987. "Belize City: Background Planning Study." Unpublished. School of Urban Planning, McGill University.

Farley, Reynolds, and Walter R. Allen. 1989. *The Color Line and the Quality of Life in America*. New York: Oxford University Press.

Fefferman, Hilbert. 1976. "The Redlining of Neighborhoods by Mortgage Lending Institutions and What Can Be Done About It." In *Redlining: A Special Report*. Washington, D.C.: Federal National Mortgage Association.

Ferid, Les. 1990. "Neighborhood Watch: Courting Controversy." *New York*, May 28.

Fernandez, James. 1977. *Fang Architectonics*. Philadelphia: Institute for the Study of Human Issues.

Fernández de Oviedo y Valdés, Gonzalo [1535–1547] 1959. *Historia general y natural de las Indias*. Madrid:

Fine, Sean. 1989. "Harbourfront, City Agree on Tentative Deal." *The Toronto Globe and Mail* June 2, 1989. P. A17.

Fischer, Friedrich. 1971. *Die Grünflächenpolitik Wiens bis zum Ende des Ersten Weltkrieges*. Vienna: Spring Verlag.

Fishman, Robert. 1987. *Bourgeois Utopias: The Rise and Fall of Suburbia.* New York: Basic Books.

Foster, Byron, 1987, *The Bayman's Legacy: A Portrait of Belize City.* Benque Viego del Carman, Belize: Cubola Publications.

Foster, George M. 1960. *Culture and Conquest: The American Spanish Heritage.* New York: Viking Fund Publications in Anthropology.

Foucault, Michel. 1975. *Discipline and Punish: The Birth of the Prison.* New York: Vintage Books.

Francé, Raoul Heinrich. 1908. "Das Gesetz des Waldes." *Der Wandervogel. Zeitschrift des Bundes für Jugendwanderungen "Alt-Wandervogel"* 3 (7/8): 100–105.

Francis, Cheryl. 1990. "Tourist Appeal of Harbourfront Evolved as Unexpected Bonus." *The Toronto Globe and Mail* April 17, 1990. P. B25.

Franck, Karen, and Ahrentzen, Shelley (eds.). 1989. *New Households, New Housing.* New York: Van Nostrand.

Fraser, Valerie. 1990. *The Architecture of Conquest: Building in the Viceroyalty of Peru.* Cambridge: Cambridge University Press.

Freedman, Adele. 1987. "This Time, There's Hope for the Harbourfront." *The Toronto Globe and Mail* October 31, 1987. P. C17.

Freedman, Mildred (ed.). 1986. *Tokyo: Form and Spirit.* Minneapolis: Walker Art Center; and New York: Harry N. Abrams.

Frew, Patricia. 1990. "The Homeless in Sarasota." Senior thesis, New College.

Frey, William. 1979. "Central City White Flight." *American Sociological Review* 44: 425–428.

Fridell, Wilbur M. 1973. *Japanese Shrine Mergers, 1906–1912: State Shintô Moves to the Grass Roots.* Tokyo: Sophia University Press.

Friedman, David. 1988. *Florentine New Towns: Urban Design in the Late Middle Ages.* Cambridge, Mass.: MIT Press.

Fruin, W. Mark. 1983. *Kikkoman: Company, Clan, and Community.* Cambridge, Mass.: Harvard University Press.

Fujioka Kenjiro. 1980. "The Changing Face of the Japanese *Jokamachi* (Castle Towns) Since the Meiji Period." In *Geography in Japan*, ed. Association of Japanese Geographers. Tokyo: Teikoku Shoin. Pp. 146–160.

Fussell, Paul. 1982. *The Great War and Modern Memory.* New York: Oxford University Press.

Gage, Thomas. 1655. *A New Survey of the West Indies.* London: E. Cates.

Galster, George C. 1988. "The Ecology of Racial Discrimination in Housing: An Exploratory Model." *Urban Affairs Quarterly* 24: 87–117.

———. 1990a. "White Flight from Racially Integrated Neighborhoods in the 1970s: The Cleveland Experience." *Urban Studies* 27 (3): 385–399.

———. 1990b. "Racial Steering by Real Estate Agents: Mechanisms and Motives." *Review of Black Political Economy* 19 (1): 39–63.

Gans, Herbert. 1962. *The Urban Villagers.* Glencoe, Ill.: Free Press.

Gasperini, G. 1978. "The Colonial City as the Center for the Spread of Architectural and Pictorial Schools." In *Urbanization in the Americas,* ed. R. Schaedel et al. The Hague: Mouton. Pp. 269–281.

Gibson, Charles. 1964. *The Aztecs Under Spanish Rule.* Stanford, Calif.: Stanford University Press.

Giddens, Anthony. 1979. *Central Problems in Social Theory*. Berkeley: University of California Press.

———. 1984. *The Constitution of Society*. Berkeley: University of California Press.

Gillespie, Susan. 1989. *The Aztec Kings*. Tucson: University of Arizona Press.

Gillette, T. L. 1957. "A Study of the Effects of Negro Invasion on Real Estate Values." *American Journal of Economics & Sociology* 16: 151–162.

Glassie, Henry. 1975. *Folk Housing in Middle Virginia: A Structural Analysis of Historic Artifacts*. Knoxville: University of Tennessee Press.

Goffman, Erving. 1961. *Asylums*. Garden City, N.Y.: Doubleday.

———. 1971. *Relations in Public*. New York: Basic Books.

Gordon, Andrew. 1985. *The Evolution of Labor Relations in Japan: Heavy Industry, 1853–1955*. Cambridge, Mass.: Council on East Asian Studies, Harvard University.

Gottdeiner, Mark. 1985. *The Social Production of Space*. Austin: University of Texas Press.

Greenbaum, Susan. 1980. *The Afro-American Community in Kansas City, Kansas*. Kansas City, Kansas: City Department of Community Development.

Greenbie, Barrie B. 1981. *Spaces: Dimensions of the Human Landscape*. New Haven: Yale University Press.

Grigsby, W., M. Baratz, G. Galster, and D. Maclennan. 1987. "The Dynamics of Neighborhood Change and Decline." *Progress in Planning* 28: 5–75.

Gutierrez, Ramón. 1983. *Arquitectura y Urbanismo in Iberoamerica*. Madrid: Ediciones Cáedra, S. A.

Hägerstrand, T. 1975. "Space, Time, and Human Conditions." In *Dynamic Allocation of Urban Space*, ed. A. Karlqvist. Farnborough: Saxon House.

Hall, Edward T. 1969. *The Hidden Dimension*. Garden City, N.J.: Doubleday.

Hall, John W. 1955. "The Castle Town and Japan's Modern Urbanization." *Far Eastern Quarterly* 15 (1): 37–56.

Hammond, Norman. 1982. *Ancient Maya Civilization*. New Brunswick, N.J.: Rutgers University Press.

Harbourfront. 1978. *Harbourfront, Site History*. Toronto: Harbourfront Corp.

Hardoy, Jorge. 1973. *Pre-Columbian Cities*. New York: Walker.

———. 1978. "European Urban Forms in the Fifteenth to Seventeenth Centuries and Their Utilization in Latin America." In *Urbanization in the Americas*, ed. R. Schaedel et al. The Hague: Mouton. Pp. 215–248.

Hardoy, Jorge, and Ana Maria Hardoy. 1978. "The Plaza in Latin America: From Teotihuacan to Recife." *Culturas* 5: 59–92.

Harris, Christopher. 1990a. "Ottawa Moves to Implement Harbourfront Restructuring Plan." *The Toronto Globe and Mail* November 28, 1990. P. A6.

———. 1990b. "Harbourfront to Cut 45 Jobs." *The Toronto Globe and Mail* November 29, 1990. P. A13.

———. 1991. "Harbourfront Unveils 3-Year Plan." *The Toronto Globe and Mail* February 26, 1991. P. C2.

Harvey, David. 1973. *Social Justice in the City*. Baltimore: Johns Hopkins University Press.

———. 1985. *Consciousness and the Urban Experience*. Baltimore: Johns Hopkins University Press.

Hastings, Sally Ann. 1980. "The Government, the Citizen, and the Creation of a

New Sense of Community Social Welfare, Local Organizations, and Dissent in Tokyo, 1905–1931." Ph.D. diss., University of Chicago.

Hawthorne, Nathaniel. 1860. *The Marble Faun; or The Romance of Monte*. Boston: Ticknor and Fields.

Hayden, Dolores. 1984. *Redesigning the American Dream*. New York: Norton.

Helper, Rose. 1969. *Racial Policies and Practices of Real Estate Brokers*. Minneapolis: University of Minnesota Press.

Heng Liang, and Judith Shapiro. 1983. *Son of the Revolution*. New York: Knopf.

Hennebo, Dieter. 1963. *Geschichte der deutschen Gartenkunst*. Vol. 1: Der Garten in Mittelalter. Hamburg: Brosclek.

Heritage Conservation and Recreation Service. 1980. *Urban Waterfront Revitalization: The Role of Recreation and Heritage*. Washington, D.C.: U.S. Department of the Interior.

Herzog, Thomas, and Gregory A. Smith. 1988. "Danger, Mystery and Environmental Preference." *Environment and Behavior* 20 (3): 320–344.

Hibbert, Christopher. 1985. *Rome: The Biography of a City*. New York: Penguin.

Hikone Castle Museum. 1989. *Historical Display Guide Book*. Hikone.

Hiss, Tony. 1990. *The Experience of Place*. New York: Knopf.

Hobsbawm, Eric. 1983. "Introduction: Inventing Traditions." In *The Invention of Tradition,* ed. Eric Hobsbawm and Terence Ranger. New York: Cambridge University Press. Pp. 1–14.

Hobsbawm, Eric, and Terence Ranger (ed). 1983. *The Invention of Tradition*. Cambridge: Cambridge University Press.

Honig, Emily, and Gail Hershatter. 1988. *Personal Voices: Chinese Women in the 1980s*. Stanford, Calif.: Stanford University Press.

Hough, Michael. 1990. *Out of Place: Restoring Identity to the Regional Landscape*. New Haven, Conn.: Yale University Press.

Howard, Ebenezer. 1902. *Garden Cities of Tomorrow*. London: S. Sonnenschein & Co.

Hoyle, Brian. S. 1991. "Development dynamics at the port-city interface." In *Revitalizing the Waterfront: International Dimensions of Dockland Redevelopment*. ed. B. S. Hoyle, D. A. Pinder and M. S. Husain. New York: Belhaven Press. Pp. 3–19.

Hsu, F. L. K. [1948] 1967. *Under the Ancestors' Shadow: Kinship, Personality and Social Mobility in China*. Stanford, Calif.: Stanford University Press.

———. 1971. "Psychosocial Homeostasis and Jen: Conceptual Tools for Advancing Psychological Anthropology." *American Anthropologist* 73: 23–44.

Hua Shan. 1987. "Rejoinder to the Critique." *Qing Shao Nian Ri Ji*, January: 26.

Hummon, David. M. 1990. *Commonplaces: Community Ideology and Identity in American Culture*. Albany: State University of New York Press.

Hyde, Evan, 1986, "Editorial" *Amandola,* 30. May 1986. No. 880:2.

Illich, I. 1971. *Deschooling Society*. New York: Harper and Row.

Inkeles, A., and D. Smith. 1974. *Becoming Modern*. Cambridge, Mass.: Harvard University Press.

Jackson, J. B. 1984. *Discovering the Vernacular Landscape*. New Haven, Conn.: Yale University Press.

Jacobs, Jane. 1961. *The Death and Life of Great American Cities*. New York: Random House.

Jesuit Mission. 1944. "British Honduras, Tropical Battleground." *Jesuit Bulletin* 12 (5): 1–14.

Jones, G. 1971. *The Politics of Agricultural Development in Northern British Honduras.* Winston-Salem, N.C.: Wake Forest University.

Kain, J., and J. Quigley. 1975. *Housing Markets and Racial Discrimination.* New York: National Bureau of Economic Research.

Kamm, H. 1990. "G.I.'s or Russians? Time to Show the Snapshots." *New York Times,* April 11, 1990.

Kampffmeyer, Hans. 1909. *Die Gartenstadtbewegung.* Leipzig: B. G. Teubner.

Kata Koji. 1972. *Edokko.* Kyoto: Tankosha.

———. 1980. *Shitamachi no Minzokugaku.* Kyoto: PHP Kenkyujo.

Kawamura Nozomu. 1983. "The Transition of the Household System in Modernizing Japan." *Jinbu Gakuho,* no. 159: 1–18.

Kawashima Chujii. 1986. *Minka: Traditional Houses of Japan.* Tokyo: Kodansha.

Keith, Thomas. 1983. *Man and the Natural World: A History of the Modern Sensibility.* New York: Pantheon.

Kellogg, Peter J. 1983. "Neighborhood Segregation by Race and Class: An American Tradition." In *Ethnicity, Law, and the Social Good.* Vol. 2, Ethnicity and Public Policy Series, ed. W. Van Horne and T. V. Tonnesen. Madison: University of Wisconsin.

Kelly, William W. 1986. "Rationalization and Nostalgia: Cultural Dynamics of New Middle-Class Japan." *American Ethnologist* 13 (4): 603–618.

Kern, Stephen. 1983. *The Culture of Time and Space, 1880–1913.* London: Weidenfield and Nicholson.

Kertzer, David. 1984. *Family Life in Central Italy.* New Brunswick, N.J.: Rutgers University Press.

King, Anthony. 1980. *Buildings and Society.* London: Routledge and Kegan Paul.

———. 1984. *The Bungalow: The Production of a Global Culture.* Boston: Routledge and Kegan Paul.

Kingston, Maxine Hong. 1976. *The Woman Warrior.* New York: Vintage.

Kong Zheqiang. 1989. "Sense of Community in Modern China." *Media Development,* Vol. 3.

Kornhauser, David. 1976. "The Japanese Landscape." In *Urban Japan: Its Foundations and Growth.* New York: Longman.

Kostof, S. 1991. *The City Shaped.* Boston: Little, Brown.

Kristof, Nicholas D. 1989. "China Erupts . . . The Reasons Why." *New York Times Magazine,* June 4. Pp. 28ff.

———. 1990. "Chinese Quietly Cripple Policies of Crackdown." *New York Times,* January 24.

Kubler, George. 1948. *Mexican Architecture in the Sixteenth Century.* New Haven, Conn.: Yale University Press.

———. 1975. *The Art and Architecture of Ancient America: The Mexican, Mayan and Andean Peoples.* Harmondsworth, England: Penguin.

———. 1978. "Open-Grid Town Plans in Europe and America." In *Urbanization in the Americas,* ed. R. Schaedel et al. The Hague: Mouton. Pp. 327–342.

Kuper, Hilda. 1972. "The Language of Sites in the Politics of Spaces." *American Anthropologist* 74: 411–424.

Lane, Mills. 1969. *Savannah Revisited: A Pictorial History.* Savannah: Bee Hive Press.

Las Casas, Fray Bartolomé de. 1957. *Historia de las Indias*. Mexico City: Fondo de Cultura Económica.

Lawrence, Denise L., and Setha M. Low. 1990. "The Built Environment and Spatial Form." *Annual Reviews in Anthropology* 19: 453–505.

Lawrence, Roderick J. 1982. "Domestic Space and Society: A Cross-cultural Study." *Comparative Studies in Society and History* 24 (1): 104–130.

———. 1987. *Housing, Dwellings and Homes: Design, Theory, Research and Practice*. Chichester, England: John Wiley.

Lefebvre, Henri. 1979. "Space: Social Product and Use Value." In *Critical Sociology: European Perspective*, ed. J. Freiberg, New York: Irvington Publishers.

Leo, John. 1986. "Some Stirrings on the Mainland." *Time*, February 10.

Leven, C., J. Little, H. Nourse, and R. Read. 1976. *Neighborhood Change: Lessons in the Dynamics of Urban Decay*. New York: Praeger.

Levi, Carlo. 1947. *Christ Stopped at Eboli: The Story of a Year*. New York: Farrar, Strauss.

Lévi-Strauss, Claude. 1968. *Structural Anthropology*. London: Allen Lane.

Ley, David, and K. Olds. 1988. "Landscape as Spectacle: World's Fairs and the Culture of Heroic Consumption." *Society and Space* 6: 191–212.

Leys, Simon. 1990. "The Art of Interpreting Nonexistent Inscriptions Written in Invisible Ink on a Blank Page." *New York Review of Books*, October 11, pp. 8–13.

Li, Nelson. [1988] n.d. "Influence of Politics and Economics on Housing Form in Shanghai." Unpublished. University of California at Berkeley.

Lieber, M. 1981. *Street Scenes: Afro-American Culture in Urban Trinidad*. Cambridge, Mass.: Schenkman.

Little, James T. 1976. "Residential Preferences, Neighborhood Filtering and Neighborhood Change." *Journal of Urban Economics* (January): 68–81.

Logan, J., and H. Molotch. 1987. *Urban Fortunes: The Political Economy of Place*. Berkeley: University of California Press.

López Cogolludo, Diego. 1688. *História de Yucathan Compuesta*. Madrid: Juan Gracia Infanzon.

Lotz, Wolfgang. 1981. *Studies in Italian Renaissance Architecture*. Cambridge, Mass.: MIT Press.

Loven, Sven. 1935. *Origins of the Tainan Culture, West Indies*. Göteborg: Elanders Bokfryckeri Akfiebolag.

Low, Setha. In press. The Plaza as a Reflection of Urban Culture. In *The Urban Condition II*, ed. L. Duhl. London: Grey Seal.

Lowe, Donald M. 1982. *History of Bourgeois Perception*. Chicago: University of Chicago Press.

Lynch, Kevin. 1960. *The Image of the City*. Cambridge, Mass.: MIT.

———. 1981. *A Theory of Good City Form*. Cambridge, Mass.: MIT.

Lynch, Kevin, and Gary Hack. 1984. *Site Planning*. Cambridge, Mass.: MIT Press.

Lynd, Robert. 1929. *Middletown: A Study of Contemporary American Culture*. New York: Harcourt, Brace.

Lyon, Larry. 1987. *The Community in Urban Society*. Philadelphia: Temple University Press.

Madsen, Richard P. 1981. "The Maoist Ethic and the Moral Basis of Political

Activism in Rural China." In *Moral Behavior in Chinese Society,* ed. R. Wilson, S. Greenblatt, and A. Wilson. New York: Praeger. Pp. 152–75.

Marchetti, Gianluigi. 1985. *Il Castello di Sermoneta.* Sermonte.

Margulis, Stephen T. 1977. "Conceptions of Privacy: Current Status and Next Steps." *Journal of Social Issues* 33 (3): 5–21.

Marin, Peter. 1987. "Helping and Hating the Homeless: The Struggle at the Margins of America." *Harper's* 274 (January): 39–44, 49.

Markham, S. D. 1978. "The Gridiron Town Plan and the Caste System of Colonial Central America." In *Urbanization in the Americas,* ed R. D. Schaedel et al. The Hague: Mouton. Pp. 471–490.

Markus, Andrew L. 1985. "The Carnival of Edo: *Misemono* Spectacles from Contemporary Accounts." *Harvard Journal of Asiatic Studies* 45 (2): 499–541.

Marshall, Douglas. 1973. *The City in the New World.* Ann Arbor: William L. Clements Library, University of Michigan.

Martorell Portas, V., A. Florensa Ferrer, and V. Martorell Otzet. 1970. *Historia del urbanismo en Barcelona: Del Pla Cerda al Area Metropolitano.* Barcelona: Labor.

Marty, Peter. 1511. *Opera Legatio Babylonica.* Seville.

Marx, Leo. 1973. "Pastoral Ideals and City Troubles." In *Western Man and Environmental Ethics: Attitudes Toward Nature and Technology,* ed. Ian Barbour. Reading, Mass.: Addison-Wesley. Pp. 93–115.

Massey, Douglas S. 1990. "American Apartheid: Segregation and the Making of the Underclass." *American Journal of Sociology* 96 (2): 329–357.

Massey, Douglas S., and Mitchell Eggers. 1990. "The Ecology of Inequality: Minorities and the Concentration of Poverty." *American Journal of Sociology* 95: 1153–1188.

Matos Moctezuma, Eduardo. 1987. "The Templo Mayor of Tenochtitlán: History and Interpretation." In *The Great Temple of Tenochtitlán,* ed. J. Broda, D. Carrasco, and E. Matos Moctezuma. Berkeley: University of California Press.

———. 1990. *The Great Temple.* Mexico City: National Institute of Anthropology and History.

McCamant, Kathryn, and Charles Durrett. 1988. *Cohousing: A Contemporary Approach to Housing Ourselves.* Berkeley, Calif.: Ten Speed Press.

McClain, James L. 1980. "Castle Towns and Daimyô Authority." *Journal of Japanese Studies* 6 (2): 267–299.

———. 1982. *Kanazawa: A Seventeenth-Century Japanese Castle Town.* New Haven, Conn.: Yale University Press.

McClellan, Edwin. 1985. *Woman in the Crested Kimono.* New Haven, Conn.: Yale University Press.

McDonogh, Gary. 1986. *Good Families of Barcelona: A Social History of Power in the Industrial Era.* Princeton, N.J.: Princeton University Press.

———. 1987. "The Social Construction of Evil: Barcelona's Barrio Chino." *Anthropological Quarterly* 60 (4): 174–185.

———. 1990. "Curing the City: Organic Metaphors and City Planning in Industrial Barcelona." Paper delivered at the meetings of the Southern Anthropological Society/American Ethnological Society, Atlanta, Ga.

———. 1991. "Discourses of the City: Planning in Post-Transitional Barcelona." *City & Society* 5 (1): 40–63.

McDonogh, Gary, and Gaspar Maza. Forthcoming. "Chaval del Barrio, Hijo de la Ciudad." *Revista de Ciencies Socials.*

McLaren, P. 1986. *Schooling as a Ritual Performance.* London: Routledge and Kegan Paul.

McRobbie, A. 1980. "Settling Accounts with Subcultures." *Screen Education* 34: 37–49.

Mendelson, R. E., and M. A. Quinn. 1976. *The Politics of Housing in Older Urban Areas.* New York: Praeger.

Meredith, H. 1985. "An Architectural History of Belize." *Belizean Studies* 13 (2): 1–7.

Merrens, R. 1988. "Port Authorities as Urban Land Developers: The Case of the Toronto Harbour Commissioners and Their Outer Harbour Project, 1912–1968. *Urban History Review*/Revue d'histoire urbaine 17 (2): 92–105.

Methodist Church. 1975. "A Review of the Educational Work in the Belize/Honduras District over the Past One Hundred and Fifty Years. *Methodist Sesquicentennial Brochure.* Belize City: Methodist Church Belize/Honduras District.

Miner, Horace A. 1939. *St. Denis: A French-Canadian Parish.* Chicago: University of Chicago Press.

Mitchell, Timothy. 1988. *Colonising Egypt.* Cambridge: Cambridge University Press.

Mock, John A. 1980. "Social Change in an Urban Neighborhood: A Case Study of Sapporo, Japan." Ph.D. diss. Michigan State University.

———. 1988. "Social Impact of Changing Domestic Architecture in a Neighborhood in Sapporo, Japan." *City & Society* 2 (1): 41–49.

———. 1989. "Private Uses of Public Spaces: Neighborhoods in Two Japanese Cities." Paper presented at the American Anthropological Association meetings, Washington, D.C.

Moeran, Brian. 1984. *Lost Innocence: Folk Craft Potters of Onta, Japan.* Berkeley: University of California Press.

Molotch, Harvey. 1969. "Racial Change in a Stable Community." *American Journal of Sociology* 75: 226–238.

Monlau, Pere Felip. 1841. *Abajo las murallas!!!* Barcelona.

Moore, Barrington. 1984. *Privacy: Studies in Social and Cultural History.* Armonk, N.Y.: M.E. Sharpe.

Morris, A. E. J. 1974. *History of Urban Form, Prehistory to the Renaissance.* London: George Godwin.

Morse, Richard. 1987. "Urban Development." In *Colonial Spanish America,* ed. L. Bethell. Cambridge: Cambridge University Press.

Mullen, Robert. 1975. *Dominican Architecture in Sixteenth-Century Oaxaca.* Tempe: Arizona State University Press.

Mumford, Lewis. 1961. *The City in History.* New York: Harcourt Brace and World.

Murakami, Yasusuke. 1982. "The Age of New Middle Mass Politics." *Journal of Japanese Studies* 8 (1): 29–72.

Newman, Oscar. 1972. *Defensible Space.* New York: Macmillan.

Nishiyama, Matsunosuke, et al. (comp). 1984. *Edogaku Jiten.* Tokyo: Kobundo.

Novy, Klaus, and Wolfgang Förster. 1985. *Einfach Bauen: Genossenschaftsliche Selbsthilfe nach der Jahrhundertwende.* Vienna: Verein für moderne Kommunalpolitik.

Odaffer, D. 1969. "The Three Capitals of British Honduras." Ph.D. diss., San Francisco State University.

Ogi Shinzô. 1980. *Tôkei Jidai: Edo to Tôkyô no Aida de*. Tokyo: Nippon Hôsô Shuppan Kyôkai.

Oliver, Paul (ed.). 1969. *Shelter and Society*. London: Barrie & Rockiff.

———. 1971. *Shelter in Africa*. New York: Praeger.

Olmsted, Frederick Law. [1871] 1973. "Public Parks and the Enlargement of Towns." In *American Environmentalism: The Formative Period, 1860–1915*, ed. Donald Worster. New York: John Wiley & Sons. Pp. 111–132.

Olschki, Leonard. 1949. *The Genius of Italy*. New York: Oxford University Press.

Oxford English Dictionary (Compact Edition). 1971. Oxford University Press.

Pader, Ellen. 1988. "Inside Spatial Relations." *Architecture and Behavior* 4: 251–268.

Painter, Nell I. 1976. *The Exodusters*. New York: Norton.

Palm, Erwin Walter. 1955. *Los Monumentos arquitectónicos de la Española*. Ciudad Trujillo: República Dominicana.

———. 1968. "La ville espagnole au nouveau monde dans la première moitié du XVI siècle." In *La decouverte de l'Amerique*. Paris: 10 eme Stage International d'Etudes Humanistes.

Park, R. E., E. W. Burgess, and R. D. MacKenzie. 1925. *The City*. Chicago: University of Chicago Press.

Parry, J. M., and R. G. Keith. 1984. *New Iberian World*, vol. 3. New York: Hector and Rose.

Pellow, Deborah. n.d. "No Place to Live, No Place to Love: Coping in Shanghai." In *Urban Anthropology in China: Proceedings of the First International Urban Anthropology Conference*, ed. A. Southall and G. E. Guldin, Leiden.

Perin, Constance. 1977. *Everything in Its Place*. Princeton, N.J.: Princeton University Press.

Petrunko, Oksana. 1990. "History Does Not Tolerate Empty Spaces: Report from a History Lesson." *History and Social Science Teacher* 35, (2): 80–81.

Pirenne, Henri. 1925. *Medieval Cities*. Garden City, N.Y.: Doubleday.

Pitkin, Donald S. 1959. "The Intermediate Society: A Study in Articulation." In *Intermediate Society: Social Mobility and Communication*, ed. Vernon F. Ray. Seattle: University of Washington Press.

———. 1963. "Mediterranean Europe." *Anthropological Quarterly* 36 (6): 120–129.

———. 1990. *Mamma Casa Posto Fisso: Sermoneta Revisitata, 1951–1986*. Naples: Edizione Scientifiche Ittaliane.

Platiel, Ruby. 1989. "Hearings Open with Attacks on Harbourfront." *The Toronoto Globe and Mail* April 11, 1989. P. A15.

Plotnicov, Leonard. 1987. "The Political Economy of Skyscrapers: An Anthropological Introduction to Advanced Industrial Cities." *City & Society* 1 (1): 35–51.

Polanyi, Margaret and Robert MacLeod. 1989. "Toronto Seeks Cap on Island Airport Flights." *The Toronto Globe and Mail* November 17, 1989. P. A13.

Posch, Wilfried. 1981. *Die Wiener Gartenstadtbewegung: Reform Versuch zwischen ersten und zweiten Gründerzeit*. Vienna: Tusch-Urbanistica.

Pulgram, Ernst. 1958. *The Tongues of Italy*. Cambridge, Mass.: Harvard University Press.

Quantrill, Malcolm. 1987. *The Environmental Memory*. New York: Schocken Books.

Rabinow, Paul. 1989. *French Modern*. Cambridge, Mass.: MIT Press.

Rapoport, Amos. 1969. *House Form and Culture*. Englewood Cliffs, N.J.: Prentice-Hall.

———. 1977. *Human Aspects of Urban Form: Towards a Man-Environment Approach to Urban Form and Design*. New York: Pergamon.

———. 1982. *The Meaning of the Built Environment*. Beverly Hills: Sage Publications.

Relaciones Geográficas. 1890–1900. "Relaciones de Yucatán." In *Colección de documentos inéditos relativo de descubrimiento, conquista y organización de la antiquas posesiones españolas de Ultramir*. 2d series. Vols. 11, 13.

Relph, Edward. 1990. *The Toronto Guide*. Prepared for the Annual Meetings of the Association of American Geographers, Toronto. Toronto: The Association.

Rent, G. S., and J. D. Lord. 1978. "Neighborhood Racial Transition and Property Value Trends in a Southern Community." *Social Science Quarterly* 59 (1): 51–59.

Reps, John W. 1965. *The Making of Urban America*. Princeton, N.J.: Princeton University Press.

———. 1969. *Town Planning in Frontier America*. Princeton, N.J.: Princeton University Press.

Ricard, Robert. 1947. "La Plaza Mayor en Espagne et en Amérique espagnole." *Annales, Economic-Sociétes-Civilisations* 2 (4): 433–438.

———. 1950. "La Plaza Major en España y en América española." *Estudios Geográficos* 11: 321–327.

Richardson, Miles. 1980. "Culture and the Urban Stage: The Nexus of Setting, Behavior, and Image in Urban Places." In *Environment and Culture*, ed. I. Altman and M. Chemers. New York: Plenum. Pp. 209–241.

———. 1982. "Being-in-the-Market Versus Being-in-the-Plaza: Material Culture and the Construction of Social Reality in South America." *American Ethnologist* 9 (2): 421–436.

———. 1989. "Place and Culture: Two Disciplines, Two Concepts, Two Images of Christ, and a Single Goal." In *The Power of Place*, ed. John A. Agnew and James S. Duncan. Boston: Unwin Hyman. Pp. 140–156.

Roberts, John M., and Thomas Gregor. 1971. "Privacy: A Cultural View." In *Privacy*, ed. J. R. Pennock and J. W. Chapman. New York: Atherton. Pp. 199–225.

Robertson, Jennifer. 1986. "Revolutionary Nostalgia: Concepts of Furusato." Paper presented to the Annual Meeting of the Association of Asian Studies.

Rodman, Margaret C. 1990. "Cooperative as Home." Paper presented at the Society for Applied Anthropology Annual Meeting, York, England.

Rodman, Margaret C., and Matthew Cooper. 1989. "The Sociocultural Production of Urban Space: Building a Fully Accessible Toronto Housing Cooperative." *City and Society* 3 (1): 9–22.

Rosaldo, Renato. 1980. *Ilongot Headhunting, 1883–1974: A Study in Society and History*. Stanford, Calif.: Stanford University Press.

Rose, Harold M. 1971. *The Black Ghetto: A Spatial Behavioral Perspective*. New York: McGraw Books.

Ross, Michael Franklin. 1973. "Modern Technology Changes the Built Environment: Japanese Cultural Values and Architechnology." *Japan Interpreter* 8 (3): (Autumn): 334–352.

Rotenberg, Robert. 1989. "The Reinvention of Nature in the Landscape Garden: The Viennese Experience." Paper delivered at the 5th Biennial Meeting of the International Society for the Study of Human Ideas on Ultimate Reality and Meaning, Toronto.

———. 1992. Recruitment and the Reproduction of Community in Cooperative Garden Estates in Vienna, Austria. Special Issue on Cooperative Housing. *Open House International* 17 (2): 17–29.

Royal Commission on the Future of the Toronto Waterfront. 1990. *Watershed.* Interim Report. Toronto: The Commission.

———. 1989a. *Persistence and Change: Waterfront Issues and the Board of Toronto Harbour Commissioners.* Report no. 6. Toronto: The Commission.

———. 1989b. *Parks, Pleasures, and Public Amenities.* Report no. 4. Toronto: The Commission.

———. 1989c. *The Future of the Toronto Island Airport: The Issues.* Report no. 7. Toronto: The Commission.

———. 1989d. *Housing and Neighbourhoods.* Report no. 2. Toronto: The Commission.

Rust, Franz. 1924. "R. Francé, Die Entdeckung der Heimat." *Der Wanderer* 19 (5/6): 165.

Rutheiser, Charles. 1991. "Culture, Schooling, and Neocolonialism in Belize." Ph.D. diss., Johns Hopkins University.

Ryan, William. 1972. *Blaming the Victim.* New York: Vintage Books.

Sadler, A. L. 1962. *A Short History of Japanese Architecture.* Tokyo: Charles E. Tuttle.

Sahlins, Marshall. 1982. *Historical Metaphors and Mythical Realities.* Ann Arbor: University of Michigan Press.

Saotome Katsumoto. 1971. *Tôkyô Daikûshû.* Tokyo: Iwanami Shoten.

Saville, M. H. 1917. *Narrative of Some Things of New Spain . . . by the Anonymous Conquerer, A Companion of Hernán Cortés.* New York: The Cortes Society.

Schaedel, Richard P. 1978. "The City and the Origin of the State in America." In *Urbanization in the Americas,* ed. R. Schaedel et al. The Hague: Mouton. Pp. 31–50.

Schaedel, R. P., J. E. Hardoy, and N. S. Kinzer. 1978. *Urbanization in the Americas from Its Beginning to the Present.* The Hague: Mouton.

Schell, Orville. 1984. *To Get Rich Is Glorious: China in the 80s.* New York: Pantheon Books.

———. 1988. *Discos and Democracy: China in the Throes of Reform.* New York: Doubleday.

Schell, William J. 1986. *Medieval Iberian Tradition and the Development of the Mexican Hacienda.* Latin American Series, no. 8. Syracuse, N.Y.: Foreign and Comparative Studies.

Schivelbusch, Wolfgang. 1986. *The Railway Journey.* Berkeley: University of California Press.

Schmidt, Peter. 1969. *Back to Nature: The Arcadian Myth in America.* New York: Oxford University Press.

Schuyler, David. 1986. *The New Urban Landscape: The Redefinition of City Form in Nineteenth-Century America.* Baltimore: Johns Hopkins University Press.

Schwab, William A. 1987. "The Predictive Value of Three Ecological Models: A

Test of the Life-Cycle, Arbitrage, and Composition Models of Neighborhood Change." *Urban Affairs Quarterly* 23 (2): 295–308.

Sears, John F. 1989. *Sacred Places: American Tourist Attractions in the Nineteenth Century.* New York: Oxford University Press.

Seidensticker, Edward. 1983. *Low City, High City: Tokyo from Edo to the Earthquake.* New York: Knopf.

Sieber, R. Timothy. 1987. "Urban Gentrification: Ideology and Practice in Middle-Class Civic Activity. *City & Society* 1 (1): 52–63.

———. 1989. "Revitalization and Gentrification on the Urban Waterfront: From Workplace to Playland in Boston Harbor." Paper delivered at the Annual Meeting of the Society for Applied Anthropology, Santa Fe.

———. 1990. "Selecting a New Past: Emerging Definitions of Heritage in Boston Harbor." *Journal of Urban & Cultural Studies* 1 (2): 101–122.

———. 1991. "Waterfront Revitalization in Postindustrial Port Cities of North America." *City & Society* 5(2): 120–136.

Siller, Franz, and Camillo Schneider. 1920. *Wiens Schrebergärten, Kleingärten, und Siedlungswesen.* Vol. 1. Vienna: Verlag der Österreichischen Gartenbaugesellschaft.

Sjoberg, Gideon. 1960. *The Preindustrial City.* Glencoe, Ill.: Free Press.

Slotnick, Lorne. 1989. "Toronto City Council Supports End to Waterfront Freeze." *The Toronto Globe and Mail* July 15. P. A1.

Smith, Henry D., II. 1978. "Tokyo as an Idea: An Exploration of Japanese Urban Thought Until 1945." *Journal of Japanese Studies* 4(1): 45–80.

———. 1979. "Tokyo and London: Comparative Conceptions of the City." In *Japan: A Comparative View,* ed. Albert M. Craig. Princeton: Princeton University Press. Pp. 49–99.

———. 1986. "The Edo-Tokyo Transition: In Search of Common Ground." In *Japan in Transition: From Tokugawa to Meiji,* ed. Marius B. Jansen and Gilbert Rozman. Princeton, N.J.: Princeton University Press. Pp. 347–374.

Smith, Robert J. 1960. "Preindustrial Urbanism in Japan: A Consideration of Multiple Traditions in a Feudal Society." *Economic Development and Cultural Change* 9: 1 Pt. 2: 241–254.

———. 1973. "Town and City in Premodern Japan: Small Families, Small Households and Residential Instability." In *Urban Anthropology: Cross-cultural Studies of Urbanization,* ed. A. Southall. New York: Oxford University Press.

———. 1983. *Japanese Society: Tradition, Self, and the Social Order.* Cambridge: Cambridge University Press.

Soustelle, Jacques. 1961. *The Daily Life of the Aztecs on the Eve of the Spanish Conquest.* London: Weidenfeld and Nicolson.

SPEAR. 1989. "Belize City Youth Survey: August 1989." Unpublished. Society for the Promotion of Education and Research.

Stanislawski, Dan. 1946. "The Origin and Spread of the Grid-Pattern Town." *Geographical Review* 36: 105–120.

———. 1947. "Early Spanish Town Planning in the New World." *Geographical Review* 37: 94–105.

Sternlieb, George, and Robert Burchell. 1973. *Residential Abandonment.* New Brunswick, N.J.: Rutgers University Center for Urban Policy Research.

Strathern, Marilyn. 1991. *Partial Connections*. ASAO Special Publication no. 3. Lanham, Md.: University Press of America.

Stull, W. 1978. "The Landlord's Dilemma." *Journal of Urban Economics* 7: 119–140.

Sun Longji. 1989. "The Deep Structure of Chinese Culture." In, *Seeds of Fire: Chinese Voices of Conscience,* ed. G. Barme and J. Minford. New York: Farrar, Straus and Giroux. Pp. 30–35, 136, 163–65, 226–231, 250, 311.

Suttles, Gerald. 1968. *The Social Order of the Slum*. Chicago: University of Chicago Press.

Taeuber, Karl, and Alma Taeuber. 1965. *Negroes in Cities*. Chicago: Aldine.

Tanabe Hiroshi. 1978. "Problems of the New Towns in Japan." *GeoJournal* 2 (1): 39–46.

Tannen, Deborah, and Muriel Saville-Troike, eds. 1985. *Perspectives on Silence*. Norwood, N.J.: Ablex.

Taub, Richard, D. G. Taylor, and Jan Dunham. 1984. *Paths of Neighborhood Change*. Chicago: University of Chicago Press.

Taylor, Paul. 1987. "Harbourfront's History Marked by Controversies and Bickering." *The Toronto Globe and Mail* April 21, 1987. P. A14.

Thompson, E. P. 1967. "Time, Work-Discipline, and Industrial Capitalism." *Past and Present* 38: 56–97.

Tianjing Daily. 1989. "Gay Couple Held Wedding Ceremony Openly in Fujian." February 12.

Torre Villar, Ernest de la. 1978. *Guia bibliográfica para la historia y desarrollo de la arquitectura y el urbanismo en México*. México: Coordinación de Humanidades e Instituto de Investigaciones Bibliográficas.

Toussaint, M. F., Gomez de Orozco, and J. Fernandez. 1938. *Planos de la ciudad de México. Siglos XVI y XVII. Estudio Histórico, Urbanistico y bibliográfico*. México: XVI Congreso Internacional de Planificación y de la Habitación.

Tschumi, Bernard. 1990. *Questions of Space: Lectures on Architecture*. London: Bernard Tschumi and the Architectural Association.

Tuan Yi-Fu. 1979. *Landscapes of Fear*. Minneapolis: University of Minnesota Press.

Tunbridge, John. 1988. "Policy Convergence on the Waterfront? A Comparative Assessment of North American revitalization strategies." In *Revitalizing the Waterfront: International Dimensions of Dockland Development,* ed. B. S. Hoyle, M. S. Husain, and D. Pinder. New York: Belhaven. Pp. 67–91.

UNICEF. 1990. *A Summary of the Analysis of the Situation of Women and Children in Belize*. Belize City: UNICEF/Belize.

Urban Development Corporation. 1989. *Belize City: Comprehensive Development Plan*. Belize City: Urban Development Corporation/University of the West Indies.

Urry, John. 1990. *The Tourist Gaze*. Newbury Park, California: Sage.

U.S. Department of Housing and Urban Developmnent. 1975. *The Dynamics of Neighborhood Change*. San Francisco: U.S. Department of Housing & Urban Development, Office of Policy Development and Research.

Vaughan, Colin. 1987. "Shoring Up Harbourfront. What Went Wrong? Can It Be Fixed?" *Toronto Life* 21 (8): 54–61.

Vincent, Isabel. 1990. "Which Two Will Be Axed." *The Toronto Globe and Mail* December 12, 1990, p. C1.

Virilio, Paul. 1981. *L'esthétique de la disparition*. Paris: Ballard.

————. 1991. *The Lost Dimension.* New York: Semiotexte.

Virilio, Paul, and Sylvère Lotringer. 1983. *Pure War.* New York: Semiotexte.

Vitruvius Pollio, Marcus. 1931. *On Architecture.* Trans. Frank S. Granger. New York: Putnam.

Vogel, Ezra F. 1971. *Japan's New Middle Class.* 2d ed. Berkeley: University of California Press.

Wagner, Henry Raup. 1942. *The Discovery of Yucatan by Francisco Hernández de Córdoba.* Berkeley: Cortés Society.

————. 1944. *The Rise of Fernando Cortés.* Los Angeles: Cortés Society.

Waley, Paul. 1984. *Tokyo Now and Then: An Explorer's Guide.* New York and Tokyo: Weatherhill.

Wallace, David, ed. 1970. *Metropolitan Open Spaces and Natural Process.* Philadelphia: University of Pennsylvania Press.

Walter, Eugene V. 1988. *Placeways: A Theory of the Human Environment.* Chapel Hill: University of North Carolina Press.

Ward-Perkins, J. B. 1974. *Cities of Ancient Greece and Italy.* New York: George Braziller.

Warner, Sam Bass, Jr. 1962. *Streetcar Suburbs: The Process of Growth in Boston, 1870–1900.* Cambridge, Mass.: Harvard University Press.

Waterson, Roxana. 1990. *The Living House: An Anthropology of Architecture in South-East Asia.* Oxford: Oxford University Press.

Watson, K. 1982. "Educational Neocolonialism—The Continuing Legacy." In *Education in the Third World,* ed. K. Watson. London: Croon Helm. Pp. 181–197.

Webb, Ansel. 1989. "Citizen Policing in Urban Space: Function and Identity." Unpublished paper. New College, University of South Florida.

Weeks, John M. 1988. "Residential and Local Group Organization in the Mata Lowland of Southwestern Campeche, Mexico." In *Household and Community in the Mesoamerican Past,* ed. R. R. Wilk and W. Ashmore. Albuquerque: University of New Mexico Press. Pp. 73–96.

White, Harrison. 1971. "Multipliers, Vacancy Chains, and Filtering in Housing." *Journal of the American Institute of Planners* 37: 88–94.

White, James W. 1982. *Migration in Metropolitan Japan.* Berkeley: University of California, Institute of East Asian Studies.

Whorf, Benjamin L. 1956. "The Relation of Habitual Thought and Language to Behavior." In *Language, Thought and Reality: Selected Writings of Benjamin Lee Whorf,* ed. J. B. Carroll. Cambridge, Mass.: MIT. Pp. 134–159.

Whyte, Martin King, and William L. Parish. 1984. *Urban Life in Contemporary China.* Chicago: University of Chicago Press.

Whyte, William H. 1980. *The Social Life of Small Urban Spaces.* Washington, D.C.: Conservation Foundation.

————. 1988. *City: Rediscovering the Center.* New York: Doubleday.

Wilk, Richard, and Michael B. Schiffer. 1979. "The Archaeology of Vacant Lots in Tucson, Arizona." *American Antiquity* 34 (3): 530–536.

Wilk, Richard R., and Wendy Ashmore. 1988. *Household and Community in the Mesoamerican Past.* Albuquerque: University of New Mexico Press.

Williams, Raymond. 1973. *The Country and the City.* New York: Oxford University Press.

———. 1989. "The Importance of Community." In *Resources of Hope: Culture, Democracy, Socialism.* New York: Verso. Pp. 111–119.

Willis, P. 1977. *Learning to Labour: How Working Class Kids Get Working Class Jobs.* Farnborough, England: Saxon House.

Wilson, Richard W. 1981. "Moral Behavior in Chinese Society: A Theoretical Perspective." In *Moral Behavior in Chinese Society,* ed. R. Wilson et al. New York: Praeger. Pp. 1–20.

Wilson, P. 1973. *Crab Antics.* New Haven, Conn.: Yale University Press.

Wilson, Samuel M. 1990. *Hispaniola: Caribbean Chiefdoms in the Age of Columbus.* Tuscaloosa: University of Alabama Press.

Xiu Jun. 1990. "A Bad Insect in a Rural Office." *Beijing Nongcun Qing Ye* June: 16..

Yamazaki Masakazu. 1984. *Yawarakai Kojinshugi no Tanjo.* Tokyo: Chuo Koronsha.

Yang Yi. 1989. *The China Daily.* May 11.

Zawiska, L. M. 1972. "Fundación de las ciudades Hispano-americanas." *Boletin Centro de Investigaciones Históricas y Estéticas* 13: 88–128.

Zerubavel, E. 1984. *Hidden Rhythms: Schedules and Calendars in Social Life.* Chicago: University of Chicago Press.

Zhang Jing Ai. 1990. "Father is God." *Si Dai Qing Nian* 3: 34–35.

Zhang Wan Hua. 1987. "A Critique of the Practice of Inspecting Students' Diaries." *Qing Shao Nian Ri Ji* January: 26.

Zhou Xiao. 1989. "Virginity and Premarital Sex in Contemporary China." *Feminist Studies* 15(2): 279–289.

Zhou Yu Chang. 1985. "Psychological and Social Factors and Obstacles to Sex." *Shehui* 2: 45–47.

Zucker, Paul. 1959. *Town and Square.* Cambridge, Mass.: MIT Press.

Index

About the Editors and Contributors

ROBERT ROTENBERG is Associate Professor of Anthropology and Director of the International Studies Program at DePaul University.

GARY W. MCDONOGH is Professor of Anthropology and Director of the Growth and Structure of Cities Program at Bryn Mawr College.

THEODORE C. BESTOR is Associate Professor of Anthropology at Columbia University.

MATTHEW COOPER is Associate Professor of Anthropology at McMaster University.

SUSAN D. GREENBAUM is Associate Professor and Chair of the Department of Anthropology at the University of South Florida.

SETHA M. LOW is Professor of Environmental Psychology and Anthropology at the City University of New York Graduate Center.

JOHN MOCK is Assistant Professor of Social Science at Rose-Hulman Institute of Technology.

DEBORAH PELLOW is Associate Professor of Anthropology at Syracuse University.

DONALD S. PITKIN is Professor of Anthropology at Amherst College.

MARGARET RODMAN is Associate Professor of Anthropology at York University.

CHARLES RUTHEISER is Assistant Professor of Anthropology at Western Michigan University.

R. TIMOTHY SIEBER is Associate Professor of Anthropology at the University of Massachusetts–Boston.